Knock-Out Marketing

Powerful Strategies to Punch Up Your Sales

Current titles from Entrepreneur Media Inc.:

Business Plans Made Easy:
It's Not as Hard as You Think!

Start Your Own Business:
The Only Start-up Book You'll Ever Need

303 Marketing Tips Guaranteed
to Boost Your Business

Where's the Money? Sure-Fire Financial
Solutions to Your Small Business

Young Millionaires: Inspiring Stories to
Ignite Your Entrepreneurial Dreams

Forthcoming titles from Entrepreneur Media Inc.:

Success for Less: 100 Low-Cost Businesses
You Can Start Today

Gen E: Generation Entrepreneur Is Rewriting
The Rules of Business—And You Can, Too

Get Smart: 365 Tips to Boost
Your Entrepreneurial IQ

Entrepreneur
MAGAZINE'S

Knock-Out Marketing

Powerful Strategies to Punch Up Your Sales

By Jack Ferreri

Entrepreneur Media Inc.
2392 Morse Ave., Irvine, CA 92614

Managing Editor: Marla Markman
Copy Editor: Jeff Campbell
Interior Book Design: Sylvia H. Lee
Proofreader: Mandy Erickson
Production Company: Coghill Composition Co.
Cover Design: Olson Kotowski & Co.
Indexer: Alta Indexing

This publication is designed to provide accurate and authoritative information in regard to the subject matter covered. It is sold with the understanding that the publisher is not engaged in rendering legal, accounting or other professional services. If legal advice or other expert assistance is required, the services of a competent professional person should be sought.

ISBN 1-891984-04-7

Library of Congress Cataloging-in-Publication Data
Ferreri, Jack.
    Knock-out marketing: powerful strategies to punch up your sales/by Jack Ferreri.
        p.   cm.
    Includes index.
    ISBN 1-891984-04-7
    1. Marketing—United States.   I. Title: Knock-Out Marketing
HF5415.1.F47   1999
658.8—dc21   98–52837
                                                            CIP

Printed in the United States of America

09 08 07 06 05 04 03 02 01 00 10 9 8 7 6 5 4 3 2 1

Acknowledgements

A book is a team project. I've had the help of several people with this book, and the quality of the final product attests to their contributions.

First of all, I'd like to express my appreciation to Sarah White, herself a successful author, for linking me up with this project. I also want to thank John Woods of CWL Publishing Enterprises, the packager of this book for Entrepreneur, who worked with me on the overall concept and project development. Thanks to Marla Markman at Entrepreneur, who provided me with detailed feedback on each chapter that sharpened my thinking and led to many refinements. Finally, thanks to copy editor Jeff Campbell, who edited the final manuscript.

On a personal level, I'd like to thank two people: my wife, Judy, the light of my life; and my dear late friend Don Itkin, with whom I enjoyed many years swapping insights and experiences about marketing and about life.

Table Of Contents

Chapter 1

Think Like A Marketing Guru 1

Chapter 2

On A Clear Day . . .
You Can See The Market 21

Chapter 3

Define Yourself And Your Customers ..39

Chapter 4

How To Write (Yes, Write) Your Marketing Plan 57

Chapter 5

The Basics Of Selling 77

Table Of Contents

Chapter 6

Selling: Your Next Steps 99

Chapter 7

Target Your Advertising
To Your Business 121

Chapter 8

Sales Promotions:
The Turbocharger 159

Chapter 9

Public Relations: The Softest Sell . . .175

Chapter 10

Be A Good Corporate Citizen 193

Table Of Contents

Chapter 14

Database Marketing
Expands Your Horizons 247

Chapter 15

Keeping On Top 277

Introduction

So you've decided it's time to get some marketing under your belt. That's good. Let's face it, most entrepreneurial spirits are much more comfortable playing with their product or service than doing the hard work of marketing it. There's no doubt that the typical marketing terrain can be an unfamiliar landscape, populated with alien concepts (like demographics and segmentation) and exotic languages (like CUME and push-pull). But the reality is, you don't have any choice about marketing. Your market will form an opinion about your product or service one way or another. And it will act on that opinion. Do you want to leave to chance the public's perception of your product . . . or do you want to play a role in its creation?

Knock-Out Marketing is based on almost two decades of experience in marketing on behalf of small businesses, not to mention hundreds of interactions with colleagues and lots of research. This book will show you marketing as you're most likely to need it and use it . . . practical, understandable and affordable. Too many of today's marketing texts speak in intellectual constructs that can prove very useful for a billion-dollar multinational corporation but that deliver precious little benefit to the small-business entrepreneur like yourself, eager for some tips on how to make your business more successful.

Many small-business owners consider marketing "soft knowledge," which they can pick up along the way by trial and error. That is true. But marketing can be a breathtakingly inexact field, and trial and error gets very discouraging and very expensive—and it has sunk a lot of small businesses before they ever ventured out of port. However, don't think marketing is something you just *can't* learn or, in fact, get darned good at. Marketing certainly isn't a hard science, but some three generations of practice have given marketing an immense track record we can study. And we can draw some good conclusions about what's worked, what hasn't and why.

Knock-Out Marketing

The time you spend educating yourself about marketing will deliver a splendid return on investment. While it's true that you make money from your equipment and employees, putting some marketing power behind your sales and promotional efforts will multiply your success many times over.

Knock-Out Marketing will give you a solid grounding in what you need to know to grow a small business. No single book can make you an expert, but this one will show you the full range of marketing and advertising tools you can put to work in building your business, regardless of whether you sell a product or a service, market locally or regionally, employ a cast of hundreds or can fit your entire organization on a single chair.

You'll learn how to look at your potential market—who's going to buy your product and why. You'll understand how to position your product or service in the marketplace: how you describe it in terms that will trigger your customers' buying response (hint: think benefit, not feature).

Think you can treat all your customers the same way? If you said yes, think again. You can't market to all your customers in the same fashion because they buy your product or service for different reasons. In this book, you'll learn how to customize your marketing to different customer segments.

You'll also write a marketing plan for your business that gives you direction, motivation, tactical guidance and a way to measure results. You'll hone your selling techniques, both personal and in the advertisements you create to market your product or service. You'll pick up insights into selecting the right media to carry your message. With the increased availability of highly accurate mailing lists and demographic information, you'll learn how to use direct marketing to bring new customers in and keep existing customers happy. And you'll find out how to use market promotion as a short-term tool to boost your sales volume.

With *Knock-Out Marketing*, you'll learn some of the subtler aspects of marketing your business: how to use public relations to raise your profile in the community and your trade marketplace, and how to promote yourself as (and actually *be*) a good corporate citizen. You'll grasp the importance of using the Internet, and you'll learn how to judge whether it's a good fit for your business. Finally, you'll appreciate the value of a training program to enhance your own skills and those of your staff.

Introduction

When you're done with this book, you'll understand the way you need to look at your product or service, your sales force and your marketing from the most important viewpoint—your customer's.

Knock-Out Marketing will give you a set of tools that will work for any business, an approach that focuses on the customer in terms of defining your product or service, targeting your advertising, and thinking about often-unconsidered issues such as product distribution and the selection of a sales force.

To make this book even more useful, I've included four types of tip boxes, short asides designed to help you by focusing on ideas and practices that I want to highlight or that deserve a little more explanation. Here's a description of each type:

Insight

This box is designed to give you another perspective on the principles and practices I've covered. By giving an example or an analogy, these boxes can help you get to that "ah ha" point where a particular idea comes into better focus.

Jargon Alert

Every discipline has its special terms. Those that are unique or of special importance are highlighted and explained in this box.

Danger

Mistakes and miscues are always a possibility in creating and executing your marketing plan. This box alerts you to what might go wrong and how to minimize that possibility.

How To

Every field has tricks of the trade that those in the know take advantage of. Use the ideas in this box to simplify the tasks involved in effectively marketing your product or service.

Finally, at the end of the book, you'll find an appendix filled with marketing resources to help you in your business, from books and publications to associations and Web sites.

At its heart, marketing is a high-energy *mental* game. Since you're likely smaller than a lot of your competitors (and your financial pockets may not be as deep), you've got to outthink 'em.

Pull up a chair, then, because here's where you'll learn how.

Chapter 1

Think Like A Marketing Guru

If you can develop true marketing vision, you'll transform your business. You'll establish a tight bond with your customers that will be impossible for your competitors to break.

Look around us in turn-of-the-millennium America. The marketing concept is the dynamo of our consumer culture: It's the realization that pleasing the customer is central to business success. The success of marketing is a large part of why we and the rest of the developed world enjoy the abundance that we do.

We tend not to realize the enormous impact marketing has made on us, and it's easy to forget that marketing, the careful union of the consumer's needs and the products and services that satisfy those needs, has not always existed as it does today. We are very fortunate. We enjoy high-quality and affordable foods and exotic taste treats from around the world. For a modest expenditure, we can buy electronics unimaginable a generation ago. Through books, magazines, television and the Internet, we browse in an evening more information than Horatio ever dreamed of in his philosophy. Marketing is one of the key catalysts of this abundance.

A Brief History Of Marketing

It's helpful to take a quick look back to see how this has all come about. In the earliest times, people made only what they would use. The countryside was largely self-sufficient, with families and small communities generally making everything they needed. The customer had not yet been invented. As time passed, people began to barter and trade among themselves. It was a simple exchange: You give me some of what you make or grow, and I'll give you some of what I have. Eventually, community marketplaces sprouted up where this bartering could take place, and as bartering became complicated and unwieldy, money was used as a substitute for the direct exchange of goods. Middlepersons emerged (as they always do): They would buy from lots of different growers and makers and then distribute a range of those products to everyone. People now became customers as well as producers, and as societies grew and the process continued, people began to specialize: They would produce one thing to sell, or they would sell their services to a company, and with the money they made they would purchase everything they might need or want.

Fast forward to the Industrial Revolution in the mid-19th century. Technological advances made production easier; trade increased among a growing number of nations. Machinery spit out goods quickly—much more quickly than people could do

Insight

I once hosted a visiting professor from Magadan, a small city in the Russian Far East. She had made very limited trips to the West before and wanted to visit an American grocery store. We've all heard stories of visitors seeing our stores for the first time, but it's stunning to see the impact. She was mute and breathless as we wandered the produce aisles and freezer cases. It's seductively easy to forget the immensity of our prosperity. And marketing—the effort to satisfy customers' wants and needs—is a driving factor behind that prosperity.

manually. Despite the well-chron-icled problems of this time, peo-ple welcomed the wide range of new and improved products and inventions that came on the mar-ket. You couldn't make enough. In this rapidly changing era, the truism that "a good product sells itself" was born. It was industrial-ists' heaven!

Direct marketing was born at this time, as manufacturers mailed lists of their products to customers at home and had them order through the mail. Toward the end of this period, mail order catalogs invaded the living rooms (and other rooms) of rural American homes.

Over the next century or so, as more and more factories kept

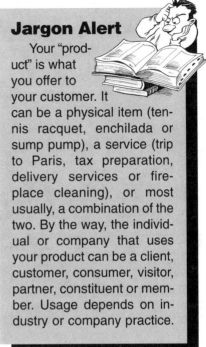

Jargon Alert

Your "prod-uct" is what you offer to your customer. It can be a physical item (ten-nis racquet, enchilada or sump pump), a service (trip to Paris, tax preparation, delivery services or fire-place cleaning), or most usually, a combination of the two. By the way, the individ-ual or company that uses your product can be a client, customer, consumer, visitor, partner, constituent or mem-ber. Usage depends on in-dustry or company practice.

cranking out goods, the market became flooded with many different types of similar items. Businesses found they had to "push" goods harder to get them bought. This process ushered in the era of the salesperson, along with advertising and advertising baubles (most advertising memorabilia come from this era). It wasn't enough any-more just to make something; you had to differentiate it from all the other products around. Roles became more defined: It was manufac-turing's job to make stuff, and it was the sales force's job to sell it. No one bothered much about the customer at this point. Demand was still great enough that real customer satisfaction wasn't a vital issue.

Selling proved to be very successful, but at first it was one-sided: It was all about the product. And eventually overexuberant manufac-turers made too many products that didn't really meet people's needs. Customers became wiser, more discerning, more demanding. A new approach was needed.

Marketing, as we know it today, came of age in the late 1950s. Customers may tire of a product, but they never tire of themselves. Salespeople realized they needed to build their offerings around cus-tomers' needs and desires. The marketing era was born when manu-

Insight

Marketing is getting frighteningly personal. Computer databases allow marketers to create mailings with our names and addresses printed throughout the sales material. "Hey, Fred Garnes, won't your neighbors on Magnolia Lane be surprised when you tell them you've won $10,000,000!" Some wags predict that we'll soon each have our own *personal* magazine delivered each month . . . with every article hand-picked to please us.

facturers began to consult the customer first, tailoring what they made and how they delivered it to meet customer demand and expectation. Retailers converted to a marketing orientation first, and the industrial and service sectors followed.

Today we have a new revolution: computers. They have affected the selling environment in two major ways:

- **We can gather and manipulate enormous amounts of data for direct-marketing efforts, market research, product testing and so on.** Historically, selling has gone from personal, through mass marketing, and now increasingly back to personal again. Computers let marketers focus their efforts with stunning precision.

- **The Internet has emerged and grown more quickly than anyone could have imagined.** No one knows how this will change the marketplace, but almost everyone's convinced the decades to come will be computer-exciting.

Marketing Your Business In Today's World

You're in a small business. You're the top person or one of the key players. Or maybe you're the entire company. With the marketing revolution, with computers and with simple and powerful communications, this is *your* time. Just as the mammals took over the world from the dinosaurs, so small businesses have the nimbleness, the resources and the energy to make great advances, no matter how intimidating the large companies may appear.

It's important for you to think of your business from a marketing standpoint: You're not a company making a product and looking for customers to buy it. You're a company with an understanding of a particular class of customers—their needs and problems—and you're developing products and services that fill those needs and solve those problems. This is the key marketing insight.

The ramifications of this idea are many, but in itself it is very simple: Your focus is the customer, not the product. You're a people-pleasing company (as all companies are today) and your main goal is, well, pleasing people. Get beyond the product you're manufacturing or the service you're providing, no matter how excellent or essential it may seem, and instead figure out what the needs of your customers are and how to best fulfill them. Successful companies forget about their products as products; their products are only the means by which they satisfy customers.

As a small business, you are in the best position to do this. Marketing a small business is fun and exciting stuff because it requires you to stretch your creativity and to test your resourcefulness and flexibility. Being small, you can adjust more quickly and be more responsive. The communication between you and the customer can be very direct and immediate. Put together the right mix of product and market, and your profits will increase and your company will grow. It's puzzle-solving that will net you a lot more return than the Sunday crossword. And the challenge of marketing a small busi-

Spread The Word

You've got to market internally as well as externally. The marketing concept for your business must be believed by your employees as well as confirmed by your customers. Everyone in your company should share the same market insight. Talk to your team about how marketing works, how to turn sales into marketing-driven operations, and how to use the customer to teach you more about the market. Conduct some training lunches—you provide the lunch, they provide the ears and eyes. Photocopy good articles and circulate them. Use the company bulletin board to disseminate marketing messages. Announce your marketing activities internally before they take place. Build understanding and enthusiasm for marketing throughout your company.

ness is more than compensated for by the satisfaction you'll feel as you succeed.

In fact, you've been marketing all your life. It's part of being human; every day, every one of us is creating messages that address the specific needs of particular audiences. Remember when you brought home a bleak report card from school? Recall when you met your partner's parents for the first time? Or your early job interviews? What product were you marketing then? That's right, your favorite product: *you*. You were tailoring your product, yourself, to meet the expectations of the customer—your parents, your in-laws or your future boss. That's the short-form answer to "What's marketing?"

Is it really that simple? Well, yes and no. It really *is* that simple. But here's how the American Marketing Association defines marketing more formally:

> "Marketing is the process of planning the conception, pricing, promotion, and distribution of goods and services to create exchanges that satisfy individual and organizational objectives."

The key thing to notice here is how inclusive marketing is. It's not just sales. It's not just promotion. And if you remember anything from this book, it's not just advertising.

Let's define marketing as the planned exchange between buyer and seller, in which both the customer and the product maker are satisfied. Think of it as a pure exchange of stuff, almost like a barter. The manufacturer or retailer or service provider has the product or service, while the customer (whether another business or the final consumer) has the money.

You should also take to heart a few other truisms about marketing and small businesses:

Danger

Don't wait to market. Fight the tendency to pay too little attention to your customers and to resist marketing until you're in trouble. Too much small-business marketing takes place when the steely aroma of flop sweat fills the air. Market when times are good, and you're more likely to keep the good times rolling. So make marketing hay while the sun shines!

- The customer is both judge and jury, and you're the one he or she is deciding about.
- It's just you, the customer and the "exchange."
- Even a little marketing is a good thing.
- You're never finished marketing.

Learning and applying the fundamental tools of marketing will change the way you do business. If you can take the concept of marketing into your business personality—if you become a real marketer—good things will happen with your company and the products and services you offer. You may even have some fun along the way.

> ## Jargon Alert
>
> In an "exchange," your customers give you some of their money (at least usually) for your [fill in the blank]. When it's done, both you and the customer must leave feeling the exchange provided fair value. The customer has to get his or her "money's worth"; you have to get a "fair price." If both sides of the exchange come out satisfied, chances are good for *another* exchange. And so business happens.

Of one thing you can be sure: The marketing approach is the central engine that runs and maintains so much prosperity in the United States, and it can lead you to prosperity in your business, no matter what you do for a living. If you develop marketing vision, if you're able to look at the selling terrain with the eye of your customer, you'll avoid 90 percent of the mistakes made by small businesses.

The Logic Of Marketing: Lots Of Simple Thoughts

Let's start with a basic proposition: On the scale of human knowledge, marketing lies precisely midway between science and art.

On the one hand, top marketers can target and define an unexplored or underexplored market segment, develop a product to fit an unfulfilled need, and move the goods. We have lots of data on consumer behavior in the market, and we can often use that information to deliver predictable results. This is the science part.

On the other hand, marketing can be unpredictable and unscientific, subject to the whimsy of human desire. Some of the smartest marketers in the world have shaken the marketplace with their flops: New Coke, Edsel, IBM Home PCs, Sony's BetaMax and many others. All the resources in the world can't keep marketers from making inept decisions, nor will marketers ever turn into mind readers. Marketing deals with human psychology on a very fundamental level. And despite all the years of serious study, the human mind and how it works remain a mystery. This is the art part.

Let's start our lengthy journey together by defining some terms.

The Components Of Marketing

Marketing includes market research, advertising, sales, public relations, direct marketing, product promotion, pricing and distribution—as well as lots of other things. Some say it includes the seeds of the decline and fall of Western civilization. But you're busy, so we won't take time to discuss that here.

Here are marketing's key elements:

- **Market research** helps you form and refine your understanding of your audience. How does the market feel about you and your competitors? What are the market trends? Market research doesn't have to be complex and expensive. But it should be systematic.

- **Advertising** helps most businesses get their message to their customers. Once you have your message, you embody it in an advertisement, align your media with your target audience, and cross your fingers.

- **Sales** is the intimate "closing" part of marketing. It's where the exchange actually takes place. You make the sale. You satisfy the customer. You scratch the itch. And you take the steps to make sure that customer stays happy. Think of sales as the endgame of the marketing process. You've selected the market, you've established the price, you've settled on a mode of business (mail order, international sales, retail and so on), you've developed the product or service, you've picked an advertising message, and you've decided how to send that message out to your audience. It worked. Your audience has responded. There they are in front of you, fingering their wallets. Now, it's sales time.

- **Public relations** helps make the story of your success a news story. And this works to make you even more successful. People like to see a positive tale, and the more you can spread the upbeat story of your business, the greater the results. Purchasers like to buy from successful companies—they feel validated in their buying decision.

- **Direct marketing or database marketing** are other elements of the marketing puzzle. Some businesses, especially those that sell to other businesses, lend themselves very well to building (or buying) a database of prospects and "working" it with scheduled contacts.

- **Product promotion** gives you options for pushing your product into the marketplace, generally over a short period of time. Coupons, special offers, event tie-ins and celebrity endorsements are all types of promotions. You can even send a van around with a team of people to give out $10 million checks. Product promotion can boost a new product, announce a new location, fight off a competitor or take advantage of a special purchasing opportunity.

- **Pricing** pulls together all the costs that go into delivering your product and then determining how much your customers will be willing to pay. Many small-business people don't see this as a part of marketing. But doesn't price impact the "buyability" of your product? It sure does. It's part of the marketing mix. Incidentally, high price doesn't equal bad, nor does low price equal good. A coffeehouse owner in Greenwich Village in the '70s offered a range of elaborate coffee drinks at high prices. His top coffee was $6.25 a cup; the second most expensive was $4. A friend once asked him why he offered such an expensive coffee since no one was going to spend $6.25 on a single drink. "You're right," he replied with a smirk, "but it sure helps me sell a lot more of my $4 cup."

Danger Watch out for "dangerous pricing." Building a business on low price is a time-honored custom. But it has a built-in danger. Price breeds disloyalty. If you succeed by low price, you can also fail by low price. Every new gunslinger drifting into town will want to take you down by shaving a few cents off the price. What customers long for is value, which includes not only a good product but accompanying services as well. Pay attention to price . . . but pay even more attention to value when building a loyal customer base.

How To

Bankers are impressed by marketing plans. While your banker knows little about your business beyond operational ratios, he or she will recognize a serious-minded marketing plan. The next time you're planning to visit your local bank for a financing chat, take along your marketing plan. It may help you get the dough.

- **Distribution** covers how you get your product into the customer's hands. Do you deliver? Does the customer come to you? Is there a middleperson? It's not uncommon for businesses to use many different distribution systems. Lands' End clothing, for example, built its business on catalog sales. But they've lately opened several varieties of retail outlets: overstock stores and some special "come in, try the clothes on, and then order over the phone" stores. They've done this because their research revealed that a significant portion of their target market remains skeptical of ordering clothing over the phone.

Marketing includes a mix of complicated variables, not to mention the obscurities of the consumer mind. Harnessing all these elements to work together demands a sure hand and quick feet. But not to worry—you'll need no more skill and courage than, say, the average lion tamer.

If you find yourself continually putting off your marketing duties, look at them as necessary homework. If you have kids, you know what it's like trying to convince them that they should get started on their sociology paper before the day it's due. You present them with your logical arguments—if they wait, they'll only make life harder on themselves and increase the risk of getting a bad grade—but still they resist. We all do. When faced with dull or unattractive chores, we procrastinate. But fail on enough papers, and we begin to become believers in homework. Once you get started and keep at it, you'll develop your marketing skills more rapidly, and they'll become more intuitive. Soon, you'll find yourself naturally adopting a marketing perspective.

Most people start their businesses because it's something they love. They don't necessarily like the selling part of the business, and they often don't know much about marketing. On the other hand, most marketers don't have much detailed knowledge of their products . . . especially technical ones like infrared spectrometers, electrical distribution or protein analysis.

If you're in the position to hire professionals to do your marketing, great. If you're not (and most small-business owners aren't)—then you'll just have to wade into battle and master marketing yourself.

Your Business And The Four P's

The Four P's provide a lens through which you can look deeply into your business and see how to improve it. They're a cornerstone of marketing-oriented thinking, and they apply to every business in the solar system. They are:

- product
- place
- price
- promotion

Wash your hands and tie on an apron for a moment. Let's put you in the pizza business and demonstrate how you can use these ingredients to create what's called a "marketing mix."

Each of the Four P's is a variable that you manipulate until you get the right balance for a profitable business. It's much like taking pictures with a 35mm camera—you adjust the shutter speed, exposure and focus every time you take a picture, and every time the light or your location changes, you have to adjust them again. The Four P's aren't static, either, and you will have to continually adjust them to keep your business at its most profitable.

If you're in the pizza business, just think of the things that can compel you to change the way you operate:

- Growth on the edge of your prime market

Jargon Alert

"Marketing mix" is the blending of the Four P's (product, place, price and promotion) to deliver the highest value to customers at the lowest cost to you. Think of it as the recipe for success, although the recipe always changes in response to customer demand and competitive pressure.

- New competitors
- The passing of old competitors
- External factors: the cost of gas, tight labor pool, property tax increase
- Cost of ingredients
- New product introductions

  Now let's consider your options based on the Four P's:

- **Vary the Product:** Offer thick-crust pizza, asparagus and tuna fish pizza, sauerkraut and boysenberry pizza or maybe some hero sandwiches? And how about salads and soups?
- **Vary the Place:** Offer sit-down meals, a drive-thru window, free lunch delivery to offices, a fax line, catering for office parties, a pizza wagon outside factories and so on.
- **Vary the Price:** Cut the price, raise the price.
- **Vary the Promotion:** Buy a pizza and get concert tickets, two for the price of one, special child discount, newspaper coupons and so on.

We'll talk a lot more about the Four P's in the chapters to come (they're absolutely key to your marketing plan). But at this stage, just be aware of them. They control the details of your business, and every time your business picture starts to look fuzzy or underexposed, you adjust them till it looks right again.

Every marketing writer talks about Ralph Waldo Emerson's famous dictum that if you create a better mousetrap, the world will beat a path to your door. Emerson's remark makes several assumptions that we should reflect on: The world has to know about your mousetrap (promotion), it has to know where you live (place), it has to have enough money to buy your mousetrap (price), and it has to have a mouse problem (to which your product is the solution). If all this doesn't come together, you won't make your fortune and go down in marketing history for solving the vexing Mousetrap Enigma.

When Henry Ford was conquering the automotive world with his Model T, would-be drivers asked whether they could order vehicles in special colors. "You can order a Model T in any color," sniffed Henry, "as long as it's black." It's so easy to assume your product can dictate to the market. In the '20s, General Motors decided customers could have lots of different colors along with cars that were more mechanically sound, and it nearly killed the Ford Motor Co. Later, all of Detroit learned a similar lesson when the Japanese started delivering high-quality cars at reasonable prices. Only recently have American cars caught up in quality with those of their international competitors.

The market delights in teaching expensive lessons to arrogant manufacturers and service providers. Eventually someone will figure out a way to meet an unmet need. And then those black cars get harder and harder to sell. Only the companies that learn to evolve and change survive.

Your Business And The Four Utilities

There's another way to look at your relationship with your customers. It's kind of a parallel universe: the customer side of the Four P's. The Four Utilities remind us that what customers value and what they buy are not products or services themselves but the utility they expect to derive from their purchase. Consider what you are selling in terms of the Four Utilities to decide whether what you're offering will actually appeal to your customers.

The Four Utilities are form/ function, place, time and ease of possession.

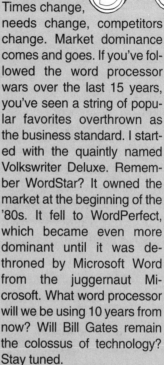

Insight

Dominance doesn't last. Times change, needs change, competitors change. Market dominance comes and goes. If you've followed the word processor wars over the last 15 years, you've seen a string of popular favorites overthrown as the business standard. I started with the quaintly named Volkswriter Deluxe. Remember WordStar? It owned the market at the beginning of the '80s. It fell to WordPerfect, which became even more dominant until it was dethroned by Microsoft Word from the juggernaut Microsoft. What word processor will we be using 10 years from now? Will Bill Gates remain the colossus of technology? Stay tuned.

- **Form/function** corresponds to the product of the Four P's, but it's from the customer's perspective. Is the product easy to use? Is it attractive? Is it durable? Does it solve my problems? In terms of services, how do I receive them? Is getting the service a pleasant experience in an attractive atmosphere? Is receiving the service convenient and memorable?

- **Place** means where or how the product is received. Do customers come to you? Do you go to them? Do you mail it to them? Do they download it? Do they pick it up at a retail store? Making your offering available in a convenient place has value to customers.

- **Time** means customer convenience in terms of hours of operation, quick shipping, large inventory (so no back ordering) and so on. This has grown increasingly important: Today's customers, retail and commercial, are short on patience. If a product is available when customers want it, this has value to them. If it's not, they'll likely go elsewhere.

- **Ease of possession** is connected with price, which includes the initial cost and two other issues as well: 1) financing terms, interest rates, lines of credit and/or acceptance of credit cards, and 2) warranties—will the customer's VCR break down six months from now or can he or she expect it to operate trouble-free for several years? If it does break down, do you stand behind it? The assurance this utility provides also has value to customers.

The point of outlining the Four Utilities is to focus on what it is that customers value about what you offer. If your offering is easy to use, attractive and durable, if it's available at a convenient location, if it's available when customers want it, and if it's reasonably priced and you stand behind it, customers are more likely to want to do business with you. And they will be willing to pay you a reasonable price for offering these different utilities.

The Four P's and the Four Utilities present slightly different but complementary ways of looking at the exchange between you and your customers. They represent the perspectives of the company and the customer on what the company offers. There is a famous line attributed to Charles Revson, the founder of Revlon cosmetics. He is reputed to have said, "In the factory we make cosmetics; in the store we sell hope." His customers weren't buying cosmetics, but a more attractive self. That idea is true in a million different contexts. The Four P's are the means by which you can announce and deliver the Four Utilities.

The Customer Is Always Right, Right?

Now that you're thinking like a marketer and paying attention to the customer's wants and needs, does that mean that, as they say, the customer is always right?

Talking About Your Business (Stage 1)

Here's a work sheet for you to fill out about your business. After reading this chapter, you should have basic answers to these questions, but don't worry if you don't have answers to all of them. As you go through the book, I'll present the same work sheet a few more times with slightly different questions. You'll be able to refine your answers, becoming ever more sophisticated in your understanding of how you can use marketing to increase your sales and profitability. You'll also understand how to improve your customers' satisfaction and grow your business.

1. What's your product?

2. Who do you sell your product to?

3. Why do customers want to buy your product? (What problem does it solve for them?)

4. Why do some people decide not to buy your product?

5. Are you satisfied with the sales of your product?

6. What other markets might exist for your product?

As I said earlier, the customer is "usually" right. But if you have a customer who simply wants to take advantage of you or pay you less than your costs, or who makes unreasonable demands, then that's a customer you don't need. The goal in any exchange is win-win. Both the customer and the company should feel good about the transaction. In this case, politely explain that you're unable to meet this customer's demands and that the customer should, unfortunately, look elsewhere. Always assume good faith on the part of your customer, but if it proves to be otherwise, show him or her the door.

In fact, they usually are. You're in business to deliver products and services that customers believe they need and want. If they don't believe you're doing that, they're not going to do business with you, no matter how great you think your offerings are. If you go out of your way to satisfy a customer, you're more likely to retain that customer and to sell him or her more stuff tomorrow. In other words, you're building a base of satisfied customers on which to grow your business.

Another way to look at it is this: It costs a lot less to retain customers than it does to attract new ones. And if you lose customers who are dissatisfied, they're likely to tell all their friends, so who's to say how many additional customers you may have lost as well? When firms talk about "satisfaction guaranteed," they're marketing their willingness to go all out to please the customer. Of course, they have to live up to this promise, or else they're going to suffer the consequences.

The Illogic Of Marketing: Making Sense Of Madness

In battle, they call it the fog of war. Trying to read the market is rarely a simple thing. You never have enough information. The market's always packed with contradictions. You constantly have more options than you can deal with. Your competitors aren't acting fair. Your employees could be more helpful. And your customers are just so unpredictable!

After all the talk in this chapter about the Four P's and the Four Utilities, I don't want to leave you with the impression that marketing is always logical. It certainly isn't. It can be satisfying to chart out all the aspects of your business, but there will always be an element of art in the mix that can make a folly of all your plans. Many seemingly good products and services have failed. And many troublingly stupid products have made their inventors millions. Odds are, you and I are certainly smarter than at least a few of those millionaires—so what gives?

Insight

Science or art? Young people pay up to $10 extra for a simple T-shirt with the Nike swoosh on it. Let's not even talk about sneakers. Or about Beanie Babies. Not logical, but very successful. Many people pay $2 for a liter of water shipped from Evian, France. Science or art? For years, purchasers bought IBM-brand personal computers long after their technological inferiority was evident. Science or art?

If your best thinking doesn't appear to pay off, don't despair. Learn from the experience. For whatever reason, you didn't connect with your customers in that instance. Think about what they're telling you. Go back to the drawing board, and use the experience to refine your marketing expertise.

Becoming A Marketing Guru

If you're new to business or to marketing, the whole endeavor can seem very intimidating. Who are these "marketing gurus" who come in and wave their wands of business success? Back in the '50s and '60s, they used to be called "marketeers." And new terms creep in every day to deepen the mystery: database marketer, Web marketer, affinity marketer, nonprofit marketer, public information marketer. Does the term "marketer" have any meaning left? How does any of it apply to the small-business person who just wants to give his or her company a boost in sales, a change in product direction or a shift in market focus?

You'll be glad to know that, despite all the trendiness of names and definitions, marketing at its core is simple and easy to understand. Large corporations have marketing departments full of "mar-

Pop Quiz

How would you market the products and services listed below? Who would you talk to and how would you reach this audience? How might you combine the Four P's? What combination of the Four Utilities might be most relevant and generate the most success? As you think about your answers, consider what they have in common and what's different about how you approach each of these challenges.

- Casinos/lotteries
- Weight-loss programs
- Body-piercing services
- Personal trainer
- Soft drinks with extra caffeine
- Wearing seat belts while driving
- A new type of tennis racket
- Building signs for large corporations
- Pipe coating to reduce rusting and leakage
- A Victorian bed and breakfast on the south Jersey shore
- Cemetery plots
- Getting companies to site new facilities in South Dakota
- PC system maintenance
- Nuns for the Catholic Church
- Chemicals for flavoring processed food

keting gurus" who sit around every day thinking about how to advertise, promote and move their products. But the typical reader of this book probably has a marketing department of one: himself or herself. You may be the owner, manager, clerk and chief floor sweeper as well. Whether you're ready or not, you now have a new title to add to your stationery: Marketing Guru.

This book will help you earn that title—and even enjoy it. You are the expert in your business, at least the technicalities of it, and this book can help you approach your business with a marketing frame of mind. This is essential for your ultimate success (unless you are one of the extremely lucky ones). In fact, most small-business people know their companies pretty well, but they run into trouble in one of three ways: either with money (undercapitalization has many notches on its six-shooter), with people or with marketing.

Basically, to think like a marketer, you need to talk to your customers. If you don't have regular contact with them, you're working by hunch. And a hunch is a dangerous basis for a business and for risking the financial future of yourself and your family. Pick half a dozen of your main customers and take them to lunch over the next couple of months. Tell them you're doing a market check. You want to know what's going on in their businesses. You want to know their problems. You want to know how you can help them do whatever it is that they do. You're not just looking for larger orders but to gain an understanding of the challenges they face in their businesses or their lives. If you're sincere, this is how you build relationships, and it's how you learn how to deliver what customers want. Replace hunches with lunches.

Now let's begin building your marketing knowledge to support your business.

Chapter 2

On A Clear Day . . . You Can See The Market

L et's start by talking about one of the entrepreneur's greatest dangers: "marketing myopia." Theodore Levitt coined this term back in 1960 in a well-known article in the *Harvard Business Review*. He pointed out that exactly the same personality traits that create a strong entrepreneur also make someone vulnerable to a large dose of self-deception. Like the gap between madness and genius, the distance between hard-charging entrepreneur and self-deceiving businessperson is a narrow one.

Self-Deception: The Entrepreneur's Most Dangerous Trap

How would you describe your basic entrepreneur? Strong-willed, full of perseverance and certainty of vision, hard-working, a born leader, and never a follower. These are great qualities for business leadership, but they can make for a lack of objectivity that can strip a business of the perspective it needs.

Sometimes it's easy to understand. You've got a product or service you think is terrific. It's better than the competition's, despite their ridiculously high prices. You've got an armful of testimonials and a track record of pleasing certain clients who are well-known terrors. Your company is moving ahead of projections. Maybe you've garnered a few awards. And you're driving a brand-new Mercedes, which doesn't exactly foster self-doubt.

In a scenario like that, is it any wonder that entrepreneurs begin to feel infallible—to feel they have a special and unique understanding of the market that renders them competitively unbeatable? It's only natural, given the self-affirming personality of most business leaders. These strengths predispose entrepreneurs to feel they know the market. If they were strong doubters, they never would have even tried to climb to the top of the hill.

You must protect yourself against self-deception. Without sowing the seeds of self-doubt, be skeptical of what you know and don't know. Test your assumptions. Avoid stumbling into the trap of believing there's nothing to be learned about the marketplace, and that all you need to do is keep pumping out the message and your customers will eventually respond.

In business and in life, things are not always what they seem, so it's healthy to have a little doubt about almost everything you know. Long-running, established businesses that know their markets very well are surprised all the time, even though they're supposed to be run with consummate professionalism and layers

Insight

In 1974, *Rolling Stone* magazine did an interview with legendary rock guitarist Eric Clapton. At one point the interviewer asked him why, given his tremendous talent and success, he'd lost so many years to drug problems. Clapton replied that both the heroin and the music were different ways to take away his pain. "And I enjoy the pain in a way because I can make use of it. And I knew that it was something I had to go through." The point for the entrepreneur: Sometimes our strengths are also our weaknesses.

of safeguards. Ask Roberto Goizueta, the highly paid CEO and introducer of New Coke. Ask the producers of any number of big-name, big-budget Hollywood flops. The largest, most sophisticated businesses in the world—with thousands of very smart people and hundreds of millions of dollars to spend—still sometimes make catastrophic marketing mistakes. Both comforting and scary, isn't it?

After all, you may be right. You may know your market exactly and intuitively. But if you don't, if your seemingly clear sense of what the market is actually looking for is wrong, even slightly, you may be in for a very difficult time. You will put your company's message into the market (and battle against the messages of the competition) based on false assumptions, and there's a good chance you'll be disappointed with your results. The only way to find out before you put your money on the line is to talk to your customers.

Insight

They say that one good definition of self-delusion is doing the same thing over and over again and expecting different results. Unless you're dealing with a random-number generator, life doesn't work that way. If something's not working in your marketing efforts, reexamine your thinking and try something different. Recall that marketing is only half science.

That was the point of Levitt's article. He wrote about the railroads and their management. They thought they were in the railroad business. They thought their competition was other railroads. They didn't recognize that they were in the *transportation* business and that trucks and other forms of transport could take business away from them. Entrepreneurs often make the same mistake. They focus on the product or service they're offering rather than the benefit that customers are buying. Remember, customers don't buy products and services; they buy the benefits or the value they expect to derive from those items. Entrepreneurs with marketing myopia forget this.

You have to stay in touch with your market and your customers, and you must continue to do so. Avoid thinking that the market will remain the same indefinitely. Restaurateurs will tell you that—with rare exception—they have to change their menus every two years and change the look or concept of the place every five years. And this

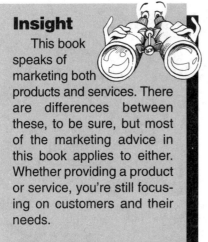

Insight

This book speaks of marketing both products and services. There are differences between these, to be sure, but most of the marketing advice in this book applies to either. Whether providing a product or service, you're still focusing on customers and their needs.

is just the *successful* restaurants. The unsuccessful restaurant owners change careers.

Of course, you want to be humble about what you do and don't know without being completely insecure or lacking in confidence. In fact, by admitting your lack of omniscience, accepting your limitations, and going to school on understanding your customers, you'll emerge with more genuine knowledge of your marketplace than you *ever* had—and your entrepreneurial ego will get a boost in the bargain. If you know your customers, if you know the benefits your products or services offer, and if you've got access to your market, then you're primed for success.

Look Through Your Customers' Eyes

How do you know what your customers think—and how can you learn to think like them? Every businessperson has to ask this question. It's key to the marketing process.

While Chapter 5 talks about how to frame the description of your product's capabilities in terms that address your customers' needs (which is pretty easy to do), what you need to do here is harder and more subtle. You need to examine the way you think about customers, and this may entail changing your attitude.

You may have gone into business to make a lot of money. Nothing wrong with that. But the way you're going to achieve that—at least the most certain path—is to give people what they want. If you make an excellent product that no one wants, you're not going to get rich. The same happens if you make a great product that everyone might want but doesn't know about. The adjustment that some businesspeople have to make is realizing that caring about your customers, putting them first, is the most important way to improve and protect your company's bottom line.

This is not just some exercise in positive thinking. When a business really cares about you and what you think, you know it. It's real.

It's an attitude that affects nearly every aspect of the business exchange, in big and little ways. We've all had hotel experiences, both good and bad, that tell us more about the quality of the hotel than any brochure, travel agent or Web site. Perhaps it was the concierge who was able to get your dry cleaning back a day before schedule. The courteous waiter who took a personal interest in getting the steak returned to the kitchen and prepared correctly. The front desk person who took extra time to sort out an error in phone charges. These are the times when you're treated not like a customer but a person.

You've got to capture that same personal warmth in the way you conduct your business and relate to your customers. Because if you don't, customers will know it immediately. You know it when the dry cleaning is late, your dinner is burnt and the desk person could care less that you didn't understand the phone charges before you made all those calls.

Every marketing book ever written relates the insight that the customer looking for a drill is not really looking for a particular piece of equipment. He or she needs a hole in something. Your customers are looking for the end result. And there may be many ways to achieve it. In the business-to-business marketplace, this end result is most often very specific and concrete; in the consumer marketplace, it can sometimes be just the desire to possess something beautiful, cute or impressive. It may be an emotional end result that doesn't depend on a specific product.

Keep In Touch

The key systemic advantage a small company has over a larger competitor is its lack of a corporate infrastructure. For a customer trying to get something done, a corporation with rules, gatekeepers and protocols can seem like nothing more than a set of hurdles blocking the way to the finish line. Use this entrepreneurial advantage to its fullest by keying in on your customers' needs:

- Read your customers' trade publications.
- Become an associate or supplier member of your customers' trade organizations.
- Share your marketing plan in draft form with major customers for their insights.

Your customers, everybody's customers, want to think their money is well spent. They want value. The Four Utilities (form/function, place, time and ease of possession) are what feed into the customer's decision on value. A thirsty customer at a hot farmer's market will pay a premium price for a tall glass of lemonade. It has more value when the weather is hot and the customer is parched. Change that lemonade to a hot coffee (alter the form/function), and its value plummets.

It is also often the case that after a while businesses forget about the customer. They begin strongly enough, paying attention to each customer's needs, but then they get caught up in their own operations, dealing with their own suppliers and employees, waxing paranoid over the competition, fretting about insurance and legislation and so on. Left behind in all this lies the customer, the ultimate guiding star of the business.

It's not unlike what happens to many parents who get involved in their children's athletic activities. You encourage little Jimmy or Jane to get into his or her sport because you know from your own life that it will be a character-building experience. You probably remember how much fun it was for you and how sports helped your development. But once the league or competitions begin, the child's desires and development can slip into the back seat, while you get caught up in the amount of playing time, won-loss records and inept referees. Before too long—and with the best of intentions—your focus is entirely on the game, not the child, and no one is having much fun anymore. Certainly your child isn't.

Especially with small businesses, the involvement is so emotionally intense that you have to make a conscious effort to constantly refocus yourself and your company on the customer. If you've chosen your market and your product wisely, focusing on your customer will always serve you best in the long run.

What Do Customers Want?

No matter what business you are in or what you are selling, your customers always want the same thing: value. This is the quality you want your business to project. Value is extremely subjective, but it can still be calculated with some exactness. Value is a balance between a fair price, a quality product and a convenient, service-oriented environment. The right combination of those factors triggers the mutually beneficial exchange between buyer and seller.

Another way to look at it is the old business quip that you can get our product fast, good and cheap—pick any two. If you want your product quickly and of good quality, it won't be cheap. And if you want it good and cheap, you won't get it fast. On some level, almost all of us make our calculations of value based on this formula.

Where I live, the local all-night convenience store sells a 2-pound chunk of cheddar cheese for $1.10 more than the exact same product at a Sam's discount superstore. Why, then, would anyone buy the product at the convenience store and throw that money away? Because the convenience store is convenient. It's four minutes from my home (vs. 20 minutes to Sam's). It's open whenever I feel like going. And it's designed for quick in and out (parking space to cheese to register to parking space is probably a total of 20 yards). I buy cheese at both places at different times depending on what seems like a better value: Can I afford the extra time and effort to get it cheaper, or is it worth it to spend more and get it faster?

People don't spend their money foolishly. They calculate an equation every time they open up their wallets. And the equation is almost always the same: If something costs more, is the extra price worth the savings in time or hassle? Or is the quality that much better than a cheaper, inferior product?

Federal Express has built its business on the calculation that you'll think it's worth spending $10 or more to send a package overnight—guaranteed. Fancy mail order catalogs charge premium prices, wagering that people will pay a premium for the convenience of shopping at home—calling in an order and having it arrive in a matter of days. Stores on Rodeo Drive in Los Angeles and the Magnificent Mile in Chicago know that low price isn't what brings in cus-

Jargon Alert

Marketers and economists use the paired terms "elastic" and "inelastic" prices to talk about the sensitivity of a market to pricing changes. An inelastic price is one that, when raised or lowered moderately, doesn't have much impact on sales. An elastic price impacts demand significantly when it changes—the demand snaps along with the price, like an elastic band.

tomers. Customers pay more for the excitement of shopping in a glamorous place, for the pleasure of saying "I got this at Gucci," and for the perceived (if not always actual) superior quality. Prices at these stores are very inelastic; they can charge far more for items without losing customers than can stores in small towns 50 miles away.

All companies, self-consciously or not, place themselves in the minds of their customers at a spot in the following "value triangle":

Let's go back to my cheddar cheese. The convenience store sits firmly in the service/convenience apex of the triangle. Quality and price are satisfactory, but the primary appeal is convenience. Sam's primary appeal is price, with satisfactory quality and service/convenience. Some 10 miles away, there's a Whole Foods store that makes (in my judgment) credible claims for the superior wholesomeness and nutritional value of its dairy and produce products. It's in the quality apex of the triangle, with satisfactory price (it's a bit more expensive) and service/convenience (it's not 50 miles away, after all).

In terms of the value triangle, where is your company in the minds of your customers? Are you more expensive than most of your competition . . . or cheaper? Do you provide higher product quality than your competition . . . or lesser quality? Do you provide more service with your product . . . or less? Remember, you decide this. You're not a slave to your product. You shape your product to the market you target.

However, an even more important question is this: Do you *like* your current position in the minds of your customers? Is your current position the *best* position for the long-term success of your company? Again, talking to your customers is one of the best ways to find out.

Shifting Gears

Every product of every company occupies a position in the value triangle. Changing your position within the triangle can present a challenge. Every movement alters your position relative to all three points. So changing your position in the minds of your customers gets complicated.

If you want to move further into the price apex—making your pricing more attractive—chances are you're going to have to yield on quality or service/convenience. The trick is to try to maintain the impression of sustained quality and service/convenience. Several of the major cereal manufacturers recently cut their prices significantly. Their challenge is to keep you from thinking that they've also dropped their quality—or that they've been overcharging you for years.

If you look to increase quality, you'll probably need to raise your prices, since markets generally equate quality with price. But if you've been low-priced for some time, the market will need some convincing that you're worth the extra money. A restaurant that moves upscale will lose some business initially . . . at least until public perception reacts to the restaurant's promotion of its new menu and ambiance.

Moving further into the service/convenience apex means you can probably raise your prices, since the public is comfortable paying for better service. But they'll expect you to deliver.

Let The Customer Teach You: Getting Feedback

If you learn nothing else from this book, remember this: Talk to your customers. Most customers are only too happy to talk to vendors who ask for their opinions. They're flattered, they're not "responsible" for their opinions, and they figure they may get better deals in the future by speaking frankly with you.

You can have your customers train you in a number of ways:

1. **Informal interview:** Whenever you're dealing with customers yourself, ask them what they're thinking about your product and the competition. Make it casual and not inquisitorial—just a

friendly conversation in which you're asking their opinion. This works for both retail and commercial customers.

2. **Formal market research:** You can contract with a company that specializes in getting information from current and prospective customers. These firms have used computers to grow very sophisticated in recent years. Chapter 14 will tell you more about how they can help you market and sell smarter.

3. **Focus groups and informational dinners:** These events fall between an informal interview and formal market research. Host a dinner or group interview to get more structured information from your customers. Explain that you're soliciting their insights into the market, reactions to a new product, feedback on existing products and so on. You'll have the best luck with evening events, away from your workplace. Marketing and research firms also have trained "facilitators" who specialize in running such events, developing event programs and formalizing results.

4. **Annual customer meeting:** You should be meeting with your key customers at least once a year to discuss how you're treating them. Use this opportunity to learn how to serve them (and others like them) better.

5. **Independent researcher:** Call a local college or university with an advertising or marketing department and ask if some of their students will take on your business as a class project. For the experience, they'll generally work without pay and under the supervision of a faculty member. If you give them the right guidance and familiarize them with your particular marketplace, you can get valuable insights into marketing your products. And your cost will be minimal.

6. **Your national trade organization:** Every profession has a trade association, and they're generally eager to justify their existence. In addition to the normal legislative lobbying, they often produce reports on the state of the industry, coming trends and market demographics. Scour these reports for market information you can use.

7. **The trade press:** This country has a large and vigorous business press, with thousands of publications from *Forbes* and *Fortune* to the most microtargeted journals you can imagine . . . and some you can't. Review every trade publication you can get your hands on. Some you'll drop because they don't repay the time to read them. But the good ones are absolutely invaluable. Learning

about your customers from a national perspective makes you smarter and more strategic in your thinking. For a comprehensive list of magazines in every field, go to the largest library in your area and look for Standard Rate and Data Service's red-covered volumes on trade media. Also see the "Appendix" in this book to learn about more sources for market information.

Avoid Four Common—And Fatal— Marketing Assumptions

Let's eliminate four false ideas that are poison to intelligent marketing. This quartet of fatal marketing assumptions can doom even the most ambitious marketing effort. The hard-driving entrepreneur is especially prone to these errors of judgment. Swept up in the kind of enthusiasm that's essential to starting or running a small business, the entrepreneur loses perspective, misplaces a sense of irony, and falls victim to ungrounded prophecies of success. Guard against these four cancers of the small business. You're *especially* vulnerable to them when you're doing well.

1. **"My competitors are stupid!"** You can learn from your competitors, both their successes and failures. Let them waste their time dismissing you. You're more insightful than that. Two heads are better than one: Study your competitors and try to dissect their strategy.

   Study the printed literature of your competitors. What can you learn?

   - Customer benefits you've overlooked

   - A new technology or service being introduced

   - A new market being explored or a new office opened

How To

Increase what you know about your markets and your customers by spending an evening with your industry's best trade publication. Read every article. Review every advertisement. Study the schedule of upcoming trade events. Check out the publication's masthead and see who's running things. Send away for free reports. Major trade journals are a gold mine of information, yet busy entrepreneurs don't often find time to get to all the good stuff.

- Revised terms of sale
- Strategic alliances with other companies
- New ways of handling service and/or reorders
- Who's on their client list and how it compares with previous ones
- New personnel who are on board or established stars who are no longer there
- Market expectation for literature—do you need to upgrade your materials?

Think of yourself and your competitors as fellow explorers searching for the same pot of gold. No matter how sure you may be of your own path to the treasure, it doesn't hurt to keep one eye on the direction the other people are taking.

2. **"My customers won't know the difference!"** Your customers are specialized at one thing: being customers. They use your product or service in running their own lives or businesses. You can't know everything about how they use your product. Nor—in most situations—can you know how they view your company and your product in their heart of hearts. It pays to be a little insecure about this. They may be talking to other suppliers. They may not understand the actual value of your product. They may be looking to close out the inventory line for which you supply key components. They may be the target of a major account development pitch by a competitor.

As for the quality of your product or service, you have to remember that *your* focus on your product is typically production- and cost-related. You'll naturally tend to focus on the aspects of your product related to its manufacture and delivery. These are the aspects of your product you control most easily. Unfortunately, your client looks at your product from precisely the opposite direction.

Once they're satisfied your production expertise is up to snuff, they turn their attention to what's most important to them: How they can use the product to make more money or lead a more comfortable life.

3. **"My product is vastly superior!"** Every entrepreneur, especially every entrepreneurial manufacturer, considers his or her product to be truly astounding.

   Some marketers feel the engineering mind and the marketing mind are antithetical, that they can never occur in the same person. It's true that engineering and technical types tend to get more wrapped up in the mechanical specifications of their products. This can take place even at the top of an organization. People can get trapped in the details of the product's technical superiority, completely losing the customer in the process. In some businesses, every competing company may make a claim of superiority, and these claims can tend to cancel each other out in the mind of the customer, who sometimes doesn't have the knowledge or experience to truly understand the shades of difference. Even if your product *is* superior, don't become complacent: The customer has a wider range of concerns than simply quality.

4. **"My people are special!"** Few companies in the country don't feel this way. Unless you can quantify their specialness, this claim will hold no water with most clients. How are they special . . . more awards, more degrees, more training, more experience, more patents? This is the service company's version of "My product is vastly superior."

   I once sat in a meeting between a large financial services provider and an advertising agency to talk about beginning a marketing and advertising campaign. This meeting took place some years ago, before financial services did any advertising. The campaign was going to be revolutionary in the local market, and they all knew that

How To

If your product is truly superior, can you come up with a head-to-head demonstration that makes you No. 1? Someone's product has to be the best. How can you prove to an objective observer that yours is the one? If you can develop such a demonstration, your sales force will be eternally grateful.

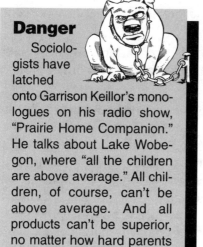

Danger

Sociologists have latched onto Garrison Keillor's monologues on his radio show, "Prairie Home Companion." He talks about Lake Wobegon, where "all the children are above average." All children, of course, can't be above average. And all products can't be superior, no matter how hard parents or entrepreneurs wish them so.

they had to come up with something super while at the same time not looking "too retail."

The head marketing person for the client said they'd done a lot of thinking internally about the issues involved, and he thought they'd zeroed in on their unique appeal to the market: "It's our people. They're just the best."

When he was asked what he meant, it soon became clear that there was nothing objectively special or unique about the set of skills they possessed. They were bright, personable, darned good-looking people— just the sort of folks prospective clients would like to work with. Hardly a marketing focus, and not something that would stupefy clients with your marketing acumen. The major competitors had comparable people who were probably even more good looking.

Don't overestimate the impact of your people. There are millions of bright and adept people in this country, no matter where you do business. If you're going to claim your staff as a key selling benefit, you'd better have something genuinely special to talk about, or something specific that quantifies their expertise, such as more training, more degrees or more experience.

How Does Your Product Fit The Market?

To figure out how your product fits the market, let's go back to the Four P's in Chapter 1: product, place, price and promotion. You can combine those four aspects in different ways to position your product in the market. That is, you can manipulate the Four P's so that when your customers evaluate your product using the value triangle, they will see it the way you want them to. This is the end result of thinking like your customers: adjusting your product or service to appeal to their desires and expectations.

Product Appeal: Highest Quality

Quality is the loftiest appeal, and the one to which most companies aspire. This is, after all, where the money is concentrated. But in the real world, not everyone can make a product of the highest quality. Not every product in a category can be tops.

If you create this perception in the mind of your customer, the rules of the capitalist game say you're allowed to charge a premium for your product. There are many ways to define quality:

- Most technologically advanced (Intel)
- Supported by the best service (Sears)
- Dominant in the market (Microsoft)
- "Produced by artisans" (Wisconsin cheese, Amish furniture, pottery)
- Most expensive—yes, in a circular sort of logic, most expensive leads to a perception of quality (Rolls-Royce, Jaguar, Rolex)
- Simply promoted as quality, yes, the vigor of the message can overwhelm the reality (Häagen-Dazs, Godiva chocolates)
- Connected with other quality items through endorsements, celebrities, awards and so on
- Independently tested as superior in quality (*Consumer Reports* tests and so on)

Each of these definitions of quality—the more objectively supported, the better—can be used as the basis for crafting a marketing message of quality for your product.

Place Appeal: Most Easily Available

When you're selling to consumers, the lower the price of the product, the greater should be its distribution. Since each individual piece of merchandise contributes minimally to your profit, you must sell a large quantity. Consider the newspaper. It's cheap, so it has to be accessible at every corner: The more newsstands and kiosks at which it's available, the more copies will be sold. The Internet gives newspapers both a great challenge and a wonderful alternative distribution possibility. Time will tell how skillfully they handle it.

Making your product "most easily available" doesn't mean it has to be everywhere. It just has to be able to get everywhere . . . and fast. Mail order clothiers like Lands' End, J. Crew and L.L. Bean make a living on the convenience of at-your-door service provided by reliable shippers.

In industrial markets, place appeal can mean carefully planned deliveries to meet production deadlines: "just in time" inventory. It can also mean drop-shipping from the supplier's factory to multiple client assembly sites across the country. In the auto industry, suppliers frequently put up large plants right next to their clients' auto plants.

Place appeal also applies to service businesses. Look how many tax preparers open mall offices when tax time looms. The phone sex industry (it is a "service," after all) has become successful because it has made sex (or a version of it) more easily available: simply dial a number from home. The medical profession has come to understand the competitive importance of place: Consider the growing number of urgent care and nonemergency clinics spreading across our cities. Colleges, universities and trade schools are also making their classes more accessible through satellite campuses and Internet study programs.

Do you want to give your product maximum exposure in your region? In the country? Do you want to deal only with cities, or is the rural marketplace worth the distribution efforts? How about overseas—will other nations be interested in your product? How can you be every place your customers want you to be?

You decide the relative availability of your product. Chapter 6 will give you some ideas on how to work with distributors.

Price Appeal: Cheapest

If you're selling household nails or soda in the consumer market, cheap is probably a good place to be. There's rarely an upside to taking the high-price, high-quality route with many commodities. People don't particularly care about quality here. They're only looking to get the most nails or sugar water for their dollar. It's no different for many commodity-type products in the industrial marketplace. With some exceptions, copper wire is copper wire.

The trick is figuring out which products have the possibility of an upside pricing strategy. Automobiles, for example, have a great opportunity to charge high prices for luxury, for perceived sophistications, for legendary engineering. Not so with nails. They're a commodity. People will tend to pay the lowest prices for those items that they perceive offer no difference from brand to brand. When was the last time you paid attention to the brand name of the spices in the supermarket, of toilet paper or of gasoline at the convenience store?

Manufacturers often try to instill brand loyalty (and the ability to charge higher prices) in products that don't actually deserve it. You'll occasionally see advertisements for branded gasolines, for example, but these companies are hard-pressed to point out any real difference. And unless they can attach a "style" cachet to the product (like bottled water), their advertising dollars are wasted.

If you're in a market that lives or dies by pricing, you have two choices:

- Cut your prices to the bone and compete on value. Find a way to instill greater perceived value in your brand—with a special ingredient, a fashionable allure, a "used by the big guys" claim and so on.

- Develop personal relationships that transcend to some degree the dollars-and-cents basis of buying decisions.

Part of the magic of marketing is the ability of some talented marketers to instill quality in products simply by charging high prices. This is one area where the perception of value can be strange indeed. Many upscale shopping districts are filled with top name-brand merchandise that's grossly overpriced related to its actual "value." But the fact that it's high priced makes it seem desirable and a good buy. Try and figure that out! The fact is, people with too much money have to spend it on something.

Promotional Appeal: Most Highly Visible

In the late '80s and early '90s, if you had a child between 8 and 16, you were probably besieged with gift requests for Swatch watches. These bright and cheery little timepieces, favored mostly by young females, served as both timekeepers and fashion statements. Developed and manufactured in Switzerland (a wry comment on how far the Swiss have come in timepiece marketing), they came in scores of styles, and the high-profile advertising made it clear that you didn't simply buy one and wear it all the time—no, you simply had to have a range of different styles to go with what you were wearing (or your mood) at the moment. They made a killing.

Heavily promoted products in the consumer marketplace benefit from spur-of-the-moment purchases, based on general brand familiarity and remembered advertising. In the commercial marketplace, most highly visible products develop a reputation for solidity and re- liability, which enables purchasers to select them without anxiety.

You develop high visibility as part of your marketing effort. The more money you have to market your business, the sooner it gains visibility. To a large extent (fortunately), you can replace money with knowledge and tenacity. A small business starts out invisible—no one knows it. You grow in visibility by a combination of advertising, promotion, public relations and the praise of satisfied customers.

Chapter 3

Define Yourself
And Your Customers

I t's a proven fact: Using the tools of marketing, you can spur customers to action. But you can't be successful unless you are specific. You must first define the *need* that your product satisfies as well as the customers who have the *ability* to acquire it. Only then can you point your advertising and promotional machinery at the market with any success.

Some 150 years ago, mass production and improved communication led to mass marketing. If you had the capital to set up a factory and the knowledge to manufacture a product, you could turn out a vast quantity of bells, books or candles and sell them throughout a region. This kind of mass marketing, where manufacturers make a whole bunch of the same thing and sell it to everyone in the same way, is called *undifferentiated marketing*. Common examples are toilet paper, gasoline, canned tuna, rice, pencils, extension cords and so on.

The opposite of undifferentiated marketing is *differentiated marketing*. In differentiated marketing, you focus on a variety of sub-markets and sell different products to those different markets. Consider the automobile market. If all we wanted was transportation, we wouldn't need all those car models, would we? Nor would we need station wagons, vans, recreational vehicles, sport utility vehicles, Jeeps or pickups. We have the different car companies and their different car models because different people want different things. By using differentiated marketing, small manufacturers and retailers can successfully compete with the big boys.

Mix 'N' Match

The following chart illustrates the different approaches your company might take in marketing its product or service.

- In an *undifferentiated* market, you sell almost the same product to every customer (such as paper towels).
- In a *differentiated* market, you can:
  1. focus all your energies on a particular submarket (Porsche), in an all-for-one strategy, or
  2. sell several different products to different markets (GM cars), selling segment by segment.

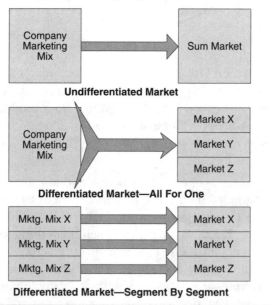

Undifferentiated Market

Differentiated Market—All For One

Differentiated Market—Segment By Segment

Define Yourself And Your Customers

To work in a differentiated market, you scout out an audience segment that will be interested in a slightly different product, and you sell to that market. Sometimes those new markets won't be large enough to merit the attention of the big guys. Then you and some other little businesses have the smaller market (a "niche" market) all to yourself.

Of course, if that niche market grows too big, you'll hear and feel the Jurassic footsteps of the approaching corporations. But if you've built solid customer relationships that rely on service as much as they depend on the product itself, the big guys will have a hard time eating your lunch. Small companies also frequently prove smarter than the big guys. They often possess more marketing agility and can adjust to changing conditions quickly.

Large companies have their own way to win in differentiated markets. They do this all the time, using line or brand extension. Remember when there was just one "Coca-Cola"? No? That was several marketing generations ago. Coke has since differentiated its own market to embrace more customers (not to mention capture more shelf space in the supermarket). Now they make regular Coca-Cola, Coke Classic, Diet Coke, Cherry Coke, and caffeine-free Diet Coke, each targeted in its advertising toward a slightly different market segment. When you have the manufacturing capacity to make a

Undercover Products

Look out for the wolf in sheep's clothing. Since product differentiation is hot these days, big companies like their share of it, too. But they can't always do it under their own names. Many small companies have successfully positioned their products by saying, "We're not big guys. We're little guys just like you, and we take a personal interest in our product." We all like underdogs, and there's a marketing undercurrent at play today that smaller is better. This kind of market approach can't be taken by the large companies directly. But they can assume it by buying small, feisty companies and staying behind the scenes. And that's just what they're doing. In fact, many of the most visible and successful microbreweries are owned by the largest brewers. Think you're quaffing a crafted-by-artisans small-company brew? Probably not.

lot of something, why not vary it a bit and make a lot of several similar things? After all, Baskin-Robbins doesn't make all those flavors just for fun, do they? Look at all the different plastic bags in which you can store food. They began as a simple item, but now you can purchase them in different thicknesses and sizes, with places to write, with holes so produce can breathe, with special plastic for freezers, with locking zippers, pinch-locks and fold-overs. It's all brand extension.

Segmentation: Select Your Best Markets

Segmentation means analyzing the different submarkets within your overall market—and then giving selected segments the right level of marketing attention. The segmentation process is a refinement of the general marketing approach:

1. Define your overall market to include all segments.
2. Pick the segments that offer the greatest opportunity.
3. Research those segments in detail.
4. Describe the target customers within those segments.
5. Start your market planning to address those segments.

Insight

Think of segmentation as a four-lane highway, with all the lanes heading in the same direction: to your consumers. You can't set your own pace if you go in the lane with the big rigs. They call the shots. But not all lanes are in use all the time. Look for an empty lane. That's where you want to put your company . . . where the fewest cars are driving. If necessary, drive on the shoulder for a few miles until you find the best lane to cut in to.

You can sell your product line to several different segments within the same overall market, but your marketing plan should address each of these segments separately. And one segment shouldn't see the materials speaking to the other segments. Kodak sells high-end film to photo professionals, and it also markets low-end print film to Joe and Jan consumer. It's a rare company that sells to only one market; those that do generally sell to superlarge customers. For example, some suppliers sell only to the government. Some provide specific products almost exclusively to a handful of particular customers (such as computer screen manufacturers or makers of automobile headlights). Such a situation is inherently very risky. One car crash, as they say, can decimate your customer base.

However, the more individual segments to which you market, the more campaigns you'll need, which, of course, increases production and media costs. This may tempt you to use the same campaigns for several different markets. Don't do it—it's a false economy. If your campaign looks like it speaks to two different markets equally well, it probably doesn't address either market effectively. You can't be all things to all people. Heck, you can't even be all things to two people. Remember, one campaign per market.

To be worth addressing, a market segment has to have certain characteristics. It must be:

- **Identifiable:** Can you describe the customers in this segment with several characteristics in common? If not, you don't have a segment.

- **Reachable at an affordable price:** How much will you need to spend in media advertising to generate the buying impulse? You must be able to fund your necessary advertising and promotional expenses.

- **Large enough to merit the effort:** Thinking about opening a Greek-language art film theater in Iceland? Think again.

- **Self-sustaining:** Your product has to 1) be desired by many people, 2) be cyclical or wear out quickly, or 3) have new customers arriving regularly. You don't want to pick a market that will become saturated immediately. That's why satellite dish and cable providers sell you programs monthly for an indefinite period; if they just sold you the equipment and let you watch what you wanted, they'd be out of business.

How To Identify A Market Segment

You can identify a market segment in two major ways: either survey the marketplace or survey your customers.

Your marketplace is your selling area, both current customers and potential customers who may buy from you in the future. Generally, it's easier to have a market research firm study your marketplace rather than undertaking the task yourself. It's time-consuming and complicated, and there's just no sense in reinventing the wheel. Good research firms have lots of useful data right on hand.

To learn more about your customers (and to identify market segments among your customers), the only road is research. You've got to get your customers to tell you about themselves. A survey is the easiest way to garner information for most small businesses. You can have your customers fill out such a questionnaire, or you can call them at home and fill it out yourself with their answers.

Consider, for a minute, that you're the director of marketing of Market Hills Country Club. Your main job—since the restaurant under Chef Raoul seems to be taking care if itself—is to promote activity on the golf course. So you take on the task of identifying your market segments: You read the vast golf trade press, you hand out customer surveys, and you simply watch what kinds of people are hitting the links on yours and other golf courses. You assess all this information and discover that your golf market consists of several segments:

- **Business golfers:** largely males 25 to 60, not afraid of playing during the week. Price is no object. High-volume golfers.

- **Retirees:** older golfers who'll continue to golf at Market Hills as long as the prices stay reasonable.

- **Female golfers:** some overlap with both the previous markets but also a segment by itself.

- **Golf tourists:** avid golfers who like to combine travel with their sport. Many states have active plans promoting tour packages with a golf and sightseeing orientation.

- **Youth market:** Tomorrow's golfers must come from somewhere. This market can use your links at unusual times, but they don't have much money.

- **Event market:** Many organizations like to use golf events as fund-raisers and for publicity drives. You need to have your marketing finger on the pulse of this market.

- **Professional market:** Market Hills is large enough to host an occasional professional event. You have to bird-dog this market years ahead to get yourself on the short list for selection.

Each of these markets, of course, is looking for slightly different things in a golf course. By segmenting your market, you can very specifically address the needs of each of these groups. Your marketing to the professional market, for example, will be very different from your approach to the business golfer.

Segmenting For The General Consumer Market

To segment a market for the consumer market, you have to do some research. First, look no further than your own business:

- What do you know about your current customers and how do you know it?

- Which of your current customers do you want more of?

- Where can you find more of them . . . these nice customers?

You can analyze your market segment in a variety of ways, trying to create the most specific picture possible of who these customers are:

Danger
Don't just open the bomb bay doors: Use the bombsight. It's important to define your target market as accurately as possible. All your marketing will be based on your conception of your market, so you've got to get it right. Be specific: What's their income? What's their gender and age? Where do they live? How much education do they have? How much does the average customer buy from you in a year?

1. Geography
2. Urban, suburban, rural
3. Demographic
   - gender
   - age
   - income
   - occupation
   - education
   - household size
   - family life cycle—empty nesters, DINK (dual-income, no kids) and so on

Segmenting For Business Customers

You can break down business markets into two main subsets:

- **Industrial:** companies that buy products (frequently raw materials) and then use them as part of other products. For instance, a

Current Customer Marketing Survey

This is an example of a customer marketing survey, which you can adjust to accurately reflect the needs of your business. When you conduct the survey (either written or over the phone), begin with your rationale for doing it. For example, say "We're looking for ways to serve our customers better. We value your business and want to do an even better job in the future. Could you give me just a few minutes of your time to answer some questions?"

1. Name _____

2. Address _____

3. Phone _____

4. Age _____

5. Who else is in your family? _____

6. What is your educational level? _____

7. Can you place your family income in a category?

   - $20-35,000 _____

   - $35-50,000 _____

   - $50-75,000 _____

   - $75,000 or more _____

8. Why do you use our product/service? _____

9. Did you consider any other options? _____

10. How often do you purchase our product/service? _____

11. Would you make any changes to our product/service? _____

Current Customer Marketing Survey, cont'd.

12. Any other comments that would help us?_____

_____

13. What is your job? _____

14. Which local magazines or newspapers do you read?

_____

15. Which local television or radio stations do you listen to?

_____

This short survey provides information on how your clients fall into the following segments:

- *Why your customers are choosing you over the competition*
- *The type of work they do for a living*
- *The frequency of repeat purchase*
- *How best to reach them through advertising*
- *How old they are*

You can gather all the responses and distribute them into categories or submarkets by occupation, frequency of purchase, age and media.

---

company that buys plastic to make automobile bumpers or pigments to make watercolor paints.

- **Commercial consumers:** companies that buy products or services as end-users. These are usually companies that either make capital purchases from you—big-ticket items that aren't factored into the cost of producing their product—or standard operational buys for ongoing production supplies or services.

For business markets, the government (for a change) has actually made your job a little easier. The government's Standard Industrial

Classification (SIC) breaks down American business as a whole into a system of categories and subcategories. Most business-to-business marketers and marketing suppliers (mailing lists, research companies) use this system as a basis for organizing their activities.

First, the SIC system breaks everything into 10 large categories, each of which carries a series of two-digit numbers (except for numbers 68 and 69, which are not used):

Survey Says . . .

You don't want to survey only your current customers. That's too restricted and doesn't tell you anything about the world at large. You also want to develop an understanding of the demand for your product or service in the broader marketplace.

A survey of the general public will tell you how many people have heard of you and your competitors, whether they've ever used your type of product or service, and whether they are ever likely to. This is valuable information to have.

This type of survey is probably best conducted through a random phone survey. You can do this yourself (using the services of a temporary agency), hire a marketing consultant to do it for you or hire a marketing firm. Those choices are in order of increasing cost.

Here are some sample questions you can ask of the general public, which can guide you in selecting market segments for your attention:

- The standard demographic data (as in listed in the current customer survey)
- Have you ever used [product category]?
- Which brand of product in this category are you personally familiar with?
- On a scale of 1 to 5 (from low to high), how personally satisfied are you with the different brands?
- How often do you use this product or service in a given year?
- How much do you spend on this product or service in a given year?

Major SIC Classifications	
01-09	Agriculture, forestry, fishing
10-14	Mining
15-19	Contract construction
20-39	Manufacturing
40-49	Transportation, communications, electric, gas
50-59	Whole and retail trade
60-67	Finance, insurance and real estate
70-89	Services
90-98	Government and nonprofit
99	Other

To refine a company description, you add more numbers. The standard SIC (pronounced "sick") classification code includes four digits. The third and fourth numerals tighten the focus of the description. This brief selection from Household Appliances Manufacturing shows you how it works.

Household Appliances Manufacturing	
99	Other
36	Electronic & Other Electric Equipment
363	Household Appliances
3631	Household cooking equipment
3632	Household refrigerators and freezers
3633	Household laundry equipment
3634	Electric housewares and fans
3635	Household vacuum cleaners
3639	Household appliances, nec*
*nec = not elsewhere covered	

Of course, once you identify your customers—whether consumer or business—the question becomes, How can you reach them? And once you know how to reach them, How can you convince them to be your customer? From here we go back to the marketing basics outlined in the first two chapters. We'll apply your marketing vision to a subset of your market and increase the accuracy of your message.

The Positioning Statement: You In A Nutshell

Positioning: staking a claim in the mind of the consumer. You plot the positioning of your competitors, and then you look for an open spot for your own product to assume (or a spot currently taken by a weak competitor). You're going to position your product there. The grounds for positioning are legion: You can claim to be the technological leader, to have the lowest price, to be tops in convenience, to be the classic choice, the luxury choice, the choice of the big guys, the alternative product and so on.

Your positioning statement doesn't have to be absolutely, verifiably accurate, but it does have to be believable. You shouldn't position yourself as the finest bake shop in the universe; it's more believable and convincing to say you've got the freshest doughnuts in town. It's more credible to say you offer the biggest selection of tools in the county, not that you carry every tool ever made. Don't go overboard with your positioning statement, lest you be seen as overreaching and boastful, without the goods to back it up.

Tagline	Positioning Statement
External focus	Internal focus: directed toward your own marketing people as a target perception to "plant" in the customers' minds
Very short . . . like all good advertising copy	Can be a long sentence or two
Changes occasionally enough to keep it fresh	Changes rarely. Think of it as your company's core definition
Speaks to end-user	Speaks to marketing orientation of company
Can speak to competition	Must speak to competition

Don't confuse your positioning statement with an advertising tagline. They have to be consistent, but they shouldn't be identical. They differ in several important aspects (see the chart on page 50).

Once you decide how best to position yourself, develop a positioning statement—a brief description of how you want your customers to see you. The goal of your advertising and marketing is to drive that positioning deep into the mind of the consumer. When someone asks a consumer, "What do you think of XYZ Corporation and its products?" you want that consumer's response to mirror your positioning statement.

> ## Jargon Alert
>
> A "tagline" is a short phrase or sentence that's typically connected with your company name. It's a positioning "nugget" that describes the way you want customers to see your company. Some examples:
> - "Just leave the driving to us."
> - "When it absolutely, positively has to be there overnight."
> - "It's the real thing."
> - "It does a body good."

Here's a sample positioning statement for a small catering firm:

> "Kaycee Catering provides value-priced, full-featured catering services for wedding receptions, business meetings and other social events throughout Lane County. We prepare hearty home-cooked Midwestern fare (without borrowing from fancy, exotic cuisines) designed to appeal to the broadest possible audience."

A portion of Kaycee's business focuses exclusively on the wedding marketplace. So this area has its own positioning statement:

> "Kaycee Catering provides personal, full-service catering for wedding receptions throughout Lane County. We work closely with the bridal party to select from our popular menu of reasonably priced Midwestern favorites, all designed to make the reception a worry-free success."

As you do your research and develop your positioning statement, you may well find a new category in which to position your product. A new product category is like the western Oklahoma territory on April 22, 1889, when settlers lined up at the borders of the state. The western part of the state held no settlements at that

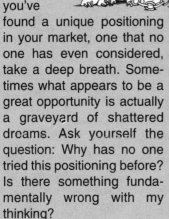

Danger

If you think you've found a unique positioning in your market, one that no one has even considered, take a deep breath. Sometimes what appears to be a great opportunity is actually a graveyard of shattered dreams. Ask yourself the question: Why has no one tried this positioning before? Is there something fundamentally wrong with my thinking?

time. It was unowned land, open for the taking by the first person to put a stake in the ground. The guns went off at high noon, and they all rushed into the open territory together to claim the best land.

But there aren't too many new product categories around. The terrain of the American marketplace is a very crowded place indeed. Almost everywhere you want to settle down and establish a business homestead, you'll find someone already there putting in crops and raising chickens.

You can fight with the existing landholders, or you can choose another method. Work the same land in a different way. Or leave behind the homesteading metaphor—instead, consider the marketplace as an array of choices, and you must offer a different, more compelling benefit to the same market to draw consumers from the competitor.

Your Company's Market Personality

Positioning is a sophisticated way to portray yourself to the marketplace. But there's an even more subtle aspect of that, which works right along with your positioning statement and its reflection in your advertising and marketing efforts. It's your company's *market personality*.

Leaving aside the benefits your company offers to its customers, what personality do you want your company to project in the marketplace?

- Cool, professional and unflappable, no matter what's happening
- Folksy, small-town, trustworthy
- The biggest and the best—very confident
- Always on the edge, a fountainhead of innovation: If there's something new, we've got it
- We have *everything*, from the sublime to the ridiculous

Talking About Your Business (Stage 2)

Here's a second work sheet for you to fill out on your business. Now that you've done some thinking about markets and submarkets, about segmentation and market niches, you should have some fresh ideas about your business.

1. What is your product and are there different categories of products?

2. Do you sell your product in differentiated or undifferentiated markets?

3. Which different markets do you sell your products to?

4. What is your positioning statement for each of these different markets?

These types of comments are similar to positioning, but they're really establishing a psychographic profile for your company, a "personality" that goes beyond its positioning. Think of Martha Stewart, Ben & Jerry's, Smith & Hawken, Lands' End, Disney, and Allstate Insurance. Each of these companies (yes, Martha is a company) uses their established personality to influence a customer's buying decision. Even though these companies are large and successful, they perceive the need to be recognized as a "character"—they want to portray themselves as more than just a corporation. You need to do this, too.

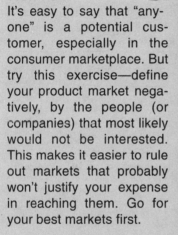

Danger

Who's *not* your customer? It's easy to say that "anyone" is a potential customer, especially in the consumer marketplace. But try this exercise—define your product market negatively, by the people (or companies) that most likely would not be interested. This makes it easier to rule out markets that probably won't justify your expense in reaching them. Go for your best markets first.

Overlooked Markets

Not all markets are obvious. It's easy to fall into the rut of selling to your traditional customers. Then one day you get a request from someone who's come up with an entirely different application for your product or service. Pay attention to such odd requests—with some fast-footed exploration you may discover niche markets in the most unlikely of places.

Niche Marketing

A niche is a small—sometimes very small—market segment. By nature, large companies are prone to overlook niche markets or to judge them not worth their attention. You can beat the big guys with clear-thinking nichemanship.

Little shipping companies like Mail Boxes Etc. are a good example. These quick-ship firms realized that going to the post office was an unpleasant experience for most people, especially when it involved shipping something more than an envelope. They also noticed that there were no convenient places for people to buy small amounts of packing materials. If you needed only 10 or 12 of a particular box, you couldn't go to a cardboard box manufacturer—because they wouldn't sell you anything less than their minimum order of X number of boxes for $1,200. They weren't set up for sales to the general public. So, following the growing trend of service businesses in the '90s, these companies created a place where you could simply show up with your stuff and leave it there for prompt dispatch. They would provide a wide range of boxes and packing materials, quick computation of shipping costs, and reliable delivery through U.S. Post Office, UPS or the express delivery companies. It became a desirable service for the busy American consumer with disposable income—and a very nice niche for Mail Box Etc. franchise owners and stockholders.

We talked earlier about going with your best market first. That's still good advice. But niches lend themselves to quick exploitation without damaging your main markets.

What niches might exist for your product or service? There are four ways to discover niches:

1. **Stay in touch with your business colleagues across the country, and if they have new ideas that have proved successful where they are, be bold enough to use their brain power.** You don't have to invent something to benefit from it. Just take an idea that's worked elsewhere and apply it to your own geographic market. This is a tried-and-true route to success, and it's perfectly honorable, too.

2. **Talk to your customers.** They are the experts and probably have far more time and energy to experiment with your product than you do. How do they use your product? Do they all use it in ways you'd expect?

3. **Use sheer human inventiveness.** Think long and hard about your core product attributes and how they might work in totally different situations. Who would have ever thought of biodegradable packing peanuts? Who was the first person who put together the concepts of "car" and "radio"? What about low-power lasers as pointing devices and staples for closing surgical incisions? None of these are obvious applications that spring first to mind!

4. **Look for bigger niches based on shifting demographics.**

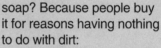

Insight

Why are there so many brands of soap? Because people buy it for reasons having nothing to do with dirt:

- On sale
- Most expensive soap
- Smells best
- Has different scents
- Largest/smallest bars
- Neat color or variegation
- Deodorizes
- Contains skin cream
- Packaging
- Comes from Europe
- On end display
- Environmentally safe
- Used by celebrity

That's why there are so many brands of soaps. Because there are so many brands of people. What's important to one is insignificant to another.

What about specialized markets for seniors and for ethnic populations? The Latino sector will be the largest minority in the country by 2020. Baby boomers continue their graying, and services for the seniors will doubtless be a boom industry in the next two or three decades. Is there something about your product with a special appeal to these markets?

Use your marketing nose to find out-of-the-mainstream niches that provide opportunities you can't get from your main audience. Niche marketing offers a way to boost your sales volume, meet new customers, maintain production and billing levels, and make some unanticipated money.

Chapter 4

How To Write (Yes, Write) Your Marketing Plan

You should now be at a point where you can put your marketing vision for your company down on paper. Firms that are successful in marketing invariably start with a marketing plan. Large companies have plans with hundreds of pages; small companies can get by with a half-dozen sheets. Put your marketing plan in a three-ring binder. Refer to it at least quarterly, but better yet monthly. Leave a tab for putting in monthly reports on sales/manufacturing; this will allow you to track performance as you follow the plan.

The plan should cover one year. For small companies, this is often the best way to think about marketing. Things change, people leave, markets evolve, customers come and go. Later on I suggest creating a section of your plan that addresses the medium-term future—two to four years down the road. But the bulk of your plan should focus on the coming year.

You should allow yourself a couple of months to write the plan, even if it's only a few pages long. Developing the plan is the "heavy lifting" of marketing. While executing the plan has its challenges, deciding what to do and how to do it is marketing's greatest challenge. Most marketing plans kick off with the first of the year, or with the opening of your fiscal year if it's different. So if you are going to unveil your plan by the new year, you should be well into putting it together by Thanksgiving.

Who should see your plan? All the players in the company. Firms typically keep their marketing plans very, very private for one of two very different reasons: Either they're too skimpy and management would be embarrassed to have them see the light of day, or they're solid and packed with information . . . which would make them extremely valuable to the competition.

You can't create a marketing plan without getting many people involved. You want to draw on the best thinking of all your people. No matter what your size, get feedback from all parts of your company: finance, manufacturing, personnel, supply and so on—in addition to marketing itself. This is especially important because it will take all aspects of your company to make your marketing plan work. Your key people can provide realistic input on what's achievable and how your goals can be reached, and they can share any insights they have on any potential, as-yet-unrealized marketing opportunities, adding another dimension to your plan. If you're essentially a one-person management operation, you'll have to wear all your hats at one time—but at least the meetings will be short!

What's the relationship between your marketing plan and your business plan or vision statement? Your business plan spells out what your business is about—what you do and don't do, and what your ultimate goals are. It encompasses more than marketing;

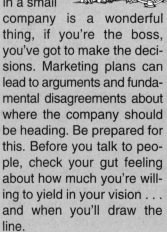

Danger

While democracy in a small company is a wonderful thing, if you're the boss, you've got to make the decisions. Marketing plans can lead to arguments and fundamental disagreements about where the company should be heading. Be prepared for this. Before you talk to people, check your gut feeling about how much you're willing to yield in your vision . . . and when you'll draw the line.

it can include discussions of locations, staffing, financing, strategic alliances and so on. It includes "the vision thing," the resounding words that spell out the glorious purpose of your company in stirring language. Your business plan is the U.S. Constitution of your business: If you want to do something that's outside the business plan, you need to either change your mind or change the plan.

Your company's business plan provides the environment in which your marketing plan must flourish. The two documents must be consistent.

> ## Insight
> While your business plan and your marketing plan have a lot in common, make sure to keep them separate. Your business plan should show how you plan to support the operation of your marketing. At the same time, your marketing plan should be a concrete working out of the ideas implicit in your business plan.

Marketing Plan Trumps Financial Plan

Don't misunderstand the title of this section. Financial plans are critically important for every business, big or small. Especially to bankers. But a financial plan is a house of cards. What makes the house stable is marketing. Without successful marketing, down come the cards.

We all know the seductions of spreadsheet games. Hmm, let's see . . . if I can increase my margin to 11 percent, then, wow!, look at

A Little Help From Your Friends . . .

Ask some of your business colleagues and professional friends if they have marketing plans and whether you can see them. While their businesses will be different from yours, you'll benefit from getting a close look at the marketing mind of a local company. What suppositions are they making about local conditions? How comprehensive is the plan? Is the plan good enough that you'd ask the plan writer to consider reviewing your marketing plan in draft form for comments? As much as people talk about marketing plans, most entrepreneurs have seen very few of them.

the impact on the bottom line! What if I add 20 percent to my sales in Cincinnati? Holy cow, we'll have plenty of money to expand that Stoughton Road store! The gods of business laugh at mortals and their spreadsheets. Root your plans in reality, not in the wonders of formulaic calculations. Every time you make a change from what *is* to what *might be,* ask yourself three questions:

1. Can this really happen?
2. How can I make this happen?
3. Where will this change (more sales or whatever) come from on the ground?

Your financial plan depends on the effectiveness of the marketing effort to render it meaningful and realistic. Without successful marketing, the financial plan is just a what-if spreadsheet—interesting historically, but with no practical application.

A marketing plan, on the other hand, is plump with meaning. It provides you with several major benefits. Let's review them.

- **Rallying point:** Your marketing plan gives your troops something to rally behind. You want them to feel confident that the captain of the vessel has the charts in order, knows how to run the ship, and has a port of destination clearly in mind. Companies often undervalue the impact of a "marketing plan" on their own people, who want to feel part of a team engaged in an exciting and complicated joint endeavor. If you want your employees to be committed members of your company, it's important to share with them your vision of where the company is headed in the years to come. People don't always understand financial projections, but they can get excited about a well-written and well-thought-out marketing plan. You should consider releasing your marketing plan—perhaps in an abridged version—companywide. Do it with some fanfare and generate some excitement for the adventures to come. Your workers will appreciate being involved.

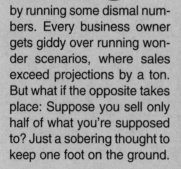

Insight

Cure yourself of spreadsheet narcosis by running some dismal numbers. Every business owner gets giddy over running wonder scenarios, where sales exceed projections by a ton. But what if the opposite takes place: Suppose you sell only half of what you're supposed to? Just a sobering thought to keep one foot on the ground.

How To Write (Yes, Write) Your Marketing Plan

- **Chart to success:** We all know that plans are imperfect things. How can you possibly know what's going to happen 12 months or five years from now? Isn't putting together a marketing plan an exercise in futility . . . a waste of time better spent meeting with customers or fine-tuning production? Yes, possibly, but only in the narrowest sense. If you don't plan, you're doomed, and an inaccurate plan is far better than no plan at all. To stay with our sea captain analogy, it's better to be 5 or even 10 degrees off your destination port than to have no destination in mind at all. The point of sailing, after all, is to get somewhere, and without a marketing plan, you will wander the seas aimlessly, sometimes finding dry land but more often than not floundering in a vast ocean. Sea captains without a chart are rarely remembered for discovering anything but the ocean floor.

- **Company operational instructions:** Your child's first bike and your new VCR came with a set of instructions, and your company is far more complicated to put together and run than either of them. Your marketing plan is a step-by-step, concrete guide for what your company needs to do to be successful during the year. It's more important than a vision statement. To put together a genuine marketing plan, you have to assess your company from top to bottom and make sure all the pieces are working together in the best way. What do you want to do with this enterprise you call the company in the coming year? Consider it a to-do list on a grand scale. It assigns specific tasks for the year.

- **Captured thinking:** You don't allow your financial people to keep their numbers in their heads. Financial reports are the lifeblood of the numbers side of any business, no matter what size. It should be no different with marketing. Your written document lays out your game plan. If people leave, if new people arrive, if memories falter, if events bring pressure to alter the givens, the information in the written marketing plan stays intact to remind you of what you'd agreed on.

- **Top-level reflection:** In the daily hurly-burly of competitive business, it's hard to turn your attention to the big picture, especially those parts that aren't directly related to the daily operations. You need to take time periodically to really *think* about your business—whether it's providing you and your employees with what you want, whether there aren't some innovative wrinkles you can add, whether you're getting all you can out of your products, your

Danger

You can't put together a marketing plan without getting the input of those whose compensation depends on its outcome. Salespeople are especially given to loud grumbling unless they're in the marketing planning loop early. They don't always have good ideas (sometimes salespeople focus too much on sales over marketing), but they can add a real-world grittiness to the plan.

sales staff and your markets. Writing your marketing plan is the best time to do this high-level thinking. Don't get so caught up in the beauty of individual trees that you forget to look at how the entire forest is growing. Some companies send their top marketing people away to a retreat. Others go to the home of a principal. Some do marketing plan development at a local motel, away from the phones and the faxes, so they can devote themselves solely to thinking hard and drawing the most accurate sketches they can of the immediate future of the business.

Ideally, after writing marketing plans for a few years, you can sit back and review a series of them, year after year, and check the progress of your company. Of course, sometimes this is hard to make time for (there is that annoying real world to deal with), but it can provide an unparalleled objective view of what you've been doing with your business life over a number of years.

Preparing To Write

Before you begin to write, pull together some information you'll need to have handy. Get it first, so you don't have to interrupt the thinking and writing process:

- Your company's latest financial reports (profit and loss, operating budgets and so on) for the current and the last three years

- The latest sales figures for the current year and the previous three years, by product and by region

- A listing of each product or service in the current line, along with target markets

- An organization table (if you can count your employees on one hand, you can probably omit this)

- Your understanding of your marketplace: your competitors, geographical boundaries, types of customers you sell to, existing distribution channels, latest and most useful demographic data, any information on trends in your markets (both demographic and product-related)

- Ask each of your salespeople and/or customer-relations people to list the six (no more) most crucial points, in their opinion, that need to be included in the coming year's marketing plan. Give them two weeks to come up with their best thoughts. You don't have to include all these, but you do have to take them into account.

The Ingredients For A Tasty Marketing Plan

Every how-to book on the market has a different take on the essential elements of a marketing plan. Those geared toward the big corporate crowd talk in a language few human beings understand. However, the words you use are much less important than how seriously you approach the task.

This section outlines the key elements you need to include in your marketing plan. However it's ultimately organized, your marketing plan should be a straightforward, easily understood company document. It will provide you with a clear direction for your marketing ef-

Lingo Lesson

First, some terminology, so we all know what we're talking about:

- **Marketing objective:** This is a marketing task you want to accomplish. It should be relatively independent, clearly graspable and measurable.

- **Marketing goals:** You set goals to enable you to reach the objective. They're the rungs on the ladder. Achieve the goals and you've reached your objective.

- **Marketing tactics:** You develop these basic action steps to enable you to reach your marketing goals.

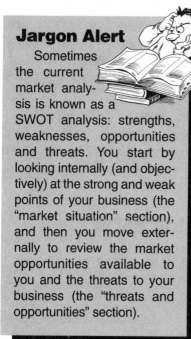

Jargon Alert

Sometimes the current market analysis is known as a SWOT analysis: strengths, weaknesses, opportunities and threats. You start by looking internally (and objectively) at the strong and weak points of your business (the "market situation" section), and then you move externally to review the market opportunities available to you and the threats to your business (the "threats and opportunities" section).

forts for the coming year, and it will give an incisive look into your company for all readers.

Market Situation

The "market situation" section should contain your best and most clear-headed description of the current state of the marketplace (this is no place for hunches).

- What are your products/services or product/service lines?
- What is the dollar size of your markets?
- What is your sales and distribution setup?
- What geographic area do you sell to?
- Describe your audience in terms of population, demographics, income levels and so on.
- What competitors exist in this marketplace?
- Historically, how well have your products sold?

Your market situation section might read like this:

> Sumners and Associates is a bookkeeping and accounting firm started in 1981. We provide tax services to individuals and to businesses under $500,000 in annual sales. We provide bookkeeping and payroll support to those same businesses. Our market area is Boulder, Colorado, and its northern suburbs.
>
> For the personal market, our clients typically are in the $75,000 and higher income range, or they are retired with assets of $200,000 or more. For the business market, most of our work is for restaurants, service stations, independent convenience stores and a large courier service.
>
> With the exception of a slump from 1988 through 1991, Sumners and Associates has grown steadily from its inception. Gross sales in 1997 were $145,000.

Our competition for our immediate market is a group of eight firms roughly comparable to ourselves. Only one of these firms, Acme Bookkeeping, has an interest in marketing itself. We believe we rank second in the group of competitors behind Acme.

We have a strong position in the restaurant portion of our business.

Much of this information exists in the heads of the management team, but in many companies it's never written down. Now is when you write it down. For example, how much information do you have in your office—right now—on your competition? The marketing plan gives you a chance to pull all this relevant information together in one place, to spur ideas and justify actions.

Consider each of your products or services up against the matching products or services of your competitors. How well do you stack up? Is there any significant market opportunity for you that neither you nor your competitors are currently exploiting?

You'll also find that the best thinkers in your company may well have different ideas about elements of the current situation. The marketing plan provides a good arena to test different snapshots of the market against each other.

Threats And Opportunities

The second section on "threats and opportunities" is an extension of the "market situation" section, and it should focus on the bad and good implications of the current market:

- What trends in the marketplace are against you?

- Are there competitive trends that are ominous?

How To

Get involved in the back-channel business communications that take place in your community. Tip groups serve as informal gatherings of businesspeople to help one another get ahead. Service clubs, like the Key Club or the Jaycees, exist to perform charitable work in the community, but they're typically made up of businesspeople and they're an excellent networking tool. With both, you'll make friends, expand your business contacts and better understand your market.

- Are your current products poised to succeed in the market as it now exists?
- What trends in the marketplace favor you?
- Are there competitive trends working to your benefit?
- Are the demographics of your market in your favor? Against you?

There are lots of places to go to get information on the trends in your market. City and state business publications frequently publish overview issues (talk to local business reporters) and local chambers of commerce publish projections, as do associations of manufacturers (the names are different in various parts of the country). Talk to your professional association and read your trade journals.

Here's an example of what a threats and opportunities section would look like for the Sumners and Associates firm:

Threats:

The company faces four identifiable threats in the coming year:

1. Our computer system needs upgrading to the latest version of our accounting and tax software. To do this with all of our machines will be too costly. We'll need to work with the existing version of our software for another 10 months. This may put us at a service disadvantage with some clients.

2. Two of our clients, Porkie's Carryout and the Magnus Group, are facing difficult business prospects in the short term. We will likely need to replace this business before the end of the year.

3. Acme Bookkeeping, our major competitor, has hired one of our staff members. We have to assume they now have a current client list of ours and will make solicitations based on their greater size and service capabilities.

4. Growth on the south side of town is outstripping growth on our north side. We'll need to consider opening a south-side office or look into ways to use couriers or electronic communications to make ourselves fully competitive in providing our services.

Opportunities:

1. Morrissey's Inc., a longtime client, has purchased three significant restaurants in the adjoining county and has expressed an interest in having us take over the accounting work for these operations. This should provide us a great chance to hire one and perhaps two additional people.

Goal For It

If you're new to the marketing plan racket, how do you set a quantifiable goal? Start with your past. Review your past sales numbers, your growth over the years in different markets, the size of typical new customers, and how new product introductions have fared. If over the last five years you've grown a cumulative 80 percent in gross revenues, projecting a 20 percent to 25 percent increase in the next year is reasonable; 45 percent is not. Make a low but reasonable projection for what you'll be able to accomplish with marketing support toward your new marketing objectives. Set modest goals to start, until you get a feel for the terrain.

2. Changes in the tax laws have made many small businesses uneasy with handling the bookkeeping by themselves or through a one-person bookkeeping service. As the details of these revisions become more public, we anticipate increasing calls for help.

3. We have been asked to participate in several educational venues in the coming year, which include three presentations at a small-business forum, an evening class at the university on starting a small business, and a role in the Boulder Entrepreneur Club. These will provide us good exposure and strong business prospects.

4. The local economy continues to be strong, and we believe our typical clients will continue to flourish in this growth cycle.

Marketing Objectives

In the "marketing objectives" section, you paint your picture of the future: What marketing objectives do you want to achieve over the course of the plan? Each of your marketing objectives should include both a narrative description of what you intend to accomplish along with numbers to give you something concrete to aim for. Just to say you want to make a first entry into the Swiss screw machine marketplace isn't providing much guidance. Saying you want to go from 0 percent to 8 percent of the local market in two years is easier to understand—and verifiable. If you're not sure of the size of the local market, then aim at a dollar figure in sales. Your accountant will

How To

You can get other people excited about and involved in your plan by giving them a marketing objective to tackle. Choose some employees you can delegate to, assign them an objective and have them develop the detailed goals and tactics. You'll probably get some fresh ideas, and you'll certainly get enthusiasm.

let you know whether you've succeeded or not.

You should make it a point to limit the number of marketing objectives you take on in a given year. Let's face it, change can bring stress, disorient staff and sometimes even confuse your target market. Keep your objectives challenging but achievable. Better to motivate yourself with ambitious but worthy targets than to depress yourself by failing at too many overenthusiastic goals.

Here are some typical marketing objective categories:

- Introduce new products
- Extend or regain market for existing product
- Enter new territories for the company
- Boost sales in a particular product, market or price range. Where will this business come from? Be specific.
- Cross-sell (or bundle) one product with another
- Enter into long-term contracts with desirable clients
- Raise prices without cutting into sales figures
- Refine a product
- Enhance manufacturing/product delivery

This third section of your plan should include perhaps a half dozen such objectives, spelled out with specific goals. Some examples:

- **Objective:** Introduce our accounting and audit services to Blankville. By the end of the first year, we want to have six clients of significance and billed time of $75,000.

- **Objective:** Reverse the decline in our package Caribbean winter tour sales in Chicago, Detroit and Minneapolis. Sales over the last three years have declined 11 percent. We intend to increase sales 4 percent this year and 8 percent next year.

- **Objective:** Introduce lunch fax business at the west side restaurant and deliver 420 lunches per week by June 1.
- **Objective:** Demo updated X-ray crystallography at selected trade exhibitions in the summer of 1999. Capture 250 leads per show and secure 75 on-site demos.

To repeat, make your objectives simple, concrete, countable, ambitious and achievable.

Marketing Goals: Where The Details Start

Here's where you come down out of the clouds and spell out how you're going to make things happen. While your spreadsheet has shown increasingly stunning profits each time you bump up the market gains, now you're in the real world, partner. Gains must be earned by marketing brains and brawn.

Each marketing objective should have several goals (subsets of objectives) and tactics for achieving those goals. In the objectives section of your marketing plan, you focus on the "what" and the "why" of the marketing tasks for the year ahead. In the implementation section, you focus on the practical, sweat-and-calluses areas of who, where, when and how. This is life in the marketing trenches.

When Eisenhower and the Allies decided to invade Normandy in 1944 to open up a mainland Europe offensive against the Axis powers, they developed detailed plans for victory. While successfully landing in Normandy and holding it were the overall objectives, many intermediate goals were set to make this possible: lining up the needed boats, air cover, behind-the-lines paratrooper drops to cut off communications, feints at a Calais landing to fool the enemy and so on. And, of course, each of those steps had its own list of details.

The key task is to take each objective and lay out the steps you intend to take to reach it. As an example, let's take the first marketing objective mentioned.

> **Objective:** Introduce our accounting and audit services to Blankville. By the end of the first year, we want to have six clients of significance and billed time of $75,000.

How can you make this happen?

Let's suppose you've assigned this objective to a group of people, and they've worked up some plans on moving into Blankville. Here are what some of their goals might look like:

1. Since accounting and auditing services don't work well at a remote site (except for the very largest companies), we'll probably need a local office in Blankville. We should schedule for this new office to open by July 2001. (Always include target dates when possible.)

2. If we're going to talk about our expertise, we have to have some of our professional staff there. We'll probably want to detail two or three of our experienced people in that new office, as well as hire local support staff.

3. We may want to do some direct-mail advertising to companies in Blankville. Our message might talk about special expertise in certain areas of business. We'll target those types of businesses in Blankville.

4. We'll talk to the business editor of the local paper and let him or her know we're coming to town. We might contribute a "tax tips" article or two for the exposure.

5. We'll approach several business associations in town and offer to give a talk on some specialized topic in which we can offer some expertise.

6. We'll ask our clients in other cities if they'd be willing to give us some referrals in Blankville.

7. We may run some modest advertising in the *Blankville Bugle* (a fine and respected newspaper) announcing our arrival and explaining our special expertise.

8. We'll have an open house to which we'll invite a number of the local business celebs, political people, potential clients and media.

9. We might look early on to get our Blankville office involved in some high-profile charity or public service work.

You get the idea. If your objective is to build a business in Blankville, you have to put together concrete goals to make it happen. Each of these actions makes sense. You might come up with others (there's no limit to human creativity, after all—especially in marketing). The point is that each goal should consist of concrete actions.

Each of these goals needs to have its own series of steps formalized. Who's going to check on the advertising rates for the *Blankville Bugle?* And when should those ads run? Which professionals are moving to Blankville and how do they feel about it? How do we get a list of companies in Blankville? Lots of work to do.

One of the best ways to handle such details is through an activity matrix. A matrix is a grid table that lets you plot actions across time. When you're developing a marketing plan, you'll soon reach the point where you have to turn to your calendar and see when things should happen. A matrix provides you with a clear and very usable framework for such time-line plotting.

Here's a sample marketing matrix covering some of the activities we just discussed:

Projected Date	Blankville Office Space	Blankville Staffing	Direct Marketing And Advertising	Business Editorial Contact	Association Contact
Jan 2001	AL: Work with broker to match need with availabilities	BF: Advertise for staff; interview and hire			
Feb 2001		BF, ER: Interview and hire			
Mar 2001	AL: Commit to space by end of month	MT: Train staff here			
Apr 2001	CF: Finalize furniture and decor procurement	MT: Train staff here		JY: Make contact	
May 2001	RT: Computers in		KL: *Bugle* notice of 7/1 opening		ER: Make contact
Jun 2001		MT: Orient staff there	KL: Invitations to opening event	JY: Recontact about opening	

You can make the matrix as detailed or as big-picture as you want. It should, however, include everything that's scheduled, when it's scheduled and who the responsible party is. And don't forget to delegate responsibility as you go.

One of the best things about working with a matrix is its adaptability. Each block on the matrix above lends itself to another chart, providing more detail. For example, in March 2001, Marge Turner (MT) will train staff at the home office. Marge, dutiful planner that she is, constructs her own matrix to help her stay on track. However, her itemized matrix wouldn't appear in the marketing plan. That level of operational detail would gum up the "big picture" overview the marketing plan is meant to provide.

Budgets

Business activity costs money. If done well, it also makes money. But whether done well or poorly, it always costs money. Your marketing plan needs to have a section in which you allocate budgets for each activity planned. This information shouldn't appear on the activity matrix since there's enough detail there already. But it should be in writing with the individual carrying overall program responsibility. People responsible for portions of the marketing activity should know exactly what funds are available to them. In fact, you would be wise to involve them in planning those budgets.

Be as objective as you can about those costs you can anticipate. For things with which you have no budget experience, add 25 percent to your best estimate. Your budget should allocate separate accounting for internal hours (staff time) and external costs (out-of-pocket expenses). Make sure to enter the budget on a Lotus or Excel spreadsheet so you can manipulate it during construction to see which variant works best.

How To

Blow up the current activity matrix at a local copy shop and use it as an easy-to-follow wall chart of your marketing activities. Use different color highlighters to draw attention to key elements of the campaign.

For help devising your budget, get a copy of *The Almanac of Business and Financial Ratios* (Prentice Hall) by Leo Troy. This useful volume gives you representative ratios for marketing and advertising spending (along with many other general business categories) for hundreds of industries. This will give you a benchmark to factor into your budget planning.

Your budget section might look like this:

Sample Budget		
Gross Sales		$142,000
Budget for Annual Marketing Efforts		$7,045
Yellow Pages	$2,600	
Sales letter mailing to prospects	$625	
Clerical help on mailing list	$125	
Advertising in local business magazine	$500	
Advertising in newspaper biz section	$1,200	
Brochure design and copywriting	$380	
Brochure printing	$315	
Registration for business exhibitions	$145	
Attend training session in Chicago	$930	
Purchase new mailing label software	$225	

Controls: Tracking Effectiveness

To track progress on your marketing plan throughout the year, establish a regular schedule of meetings, and spell this out in writing. How will you make adjustments to your plan midstream? How will you monitor progress in sales/costs to make changes during the year? You can't leave yourself without this capability.

The reason you pick measurable marketing objectives is to have the ability to track your progress toward reaching them. Too many marketing efforts aren't quantifiable, with the result that the achievements of your marketing campaigns aren't satisfactory, or they're just plain illusory.

All your marketing efforts will benefit from the classic feedback loop: act, observe, adjust, act again. Scheduling quarterly meetings is best. At these meetings, responsible individuals should report on what they've accomplished in the last quarter, including how much of the budget has been spent. Reports should be spoken, with a printed summary for the record.

As your activities move forward over time, you'll doubtless find the need to adjust the timing, the budget or the tasks themselves. At these points you must decide whether to intensify your efforts, add more tactical steps to pick up the pace, or scale back your objectives. Make your changes in an organized manner, adjusting all the dependent tasks so that the plan shifts as a whole. Whatever your decision, *make sure to update your marketing plan document*. Put in writing your understanding of why you didn't reach your goals. Keep the original, and date and number all changes. Your plan must be dynamic, but it shouldn't lose its sense of history. All this information will be extremely useful when you create next year's marketing plan.

Marketing isn't a science, but it is a skill in which you can make steady incremental improvement.

Your progress plan might look like this:

1.	Annual gross sales from the previous year	$865,000
2.	Marketing expenditures planned during the current year	$40,000
3.	Anticipated impact of marketing expenditures on gross sales	$110,000
4.	Actual marketing expenses during the current year	$32,500
5.	Annual gross sales at the end of the current year	$971,000
6.	Percentage of the actual difference between this year's sales and last year's sales that can be fairly attributed to the marketing effort	60%

Executive Summary

Put a brief summary at the front of your marketing plan binder. On a single page, sum up (with key financial numbers) the contents of your marketing plan. Use bullet points, short sentences and bold type for major points, and stay focused on the big issues. What does someone have to know about your plan to have any sense of it?

This summary gives plan readers a concise description of what your company plans to do in the coming year. It also forces you to boil your thoughts down to their rich and flavorful essence, which is always a good thing.

How To Write (Yes, Write) Your Marketing Plan

Here's a sample marketing plan summary:

The year 2000 marketing plan for Sumners and Associates has four main elements:

1. We review our existing competitive marketing situation. Overall, prospects look good for our company. Boulder is growing at a steady 4.2 percent rate, with new businesses starting at roughly 750 a year. No competitive bookkeeping and accounting firm has made significant marketing efforts, although Acme Bookkeeping did run a series of advertisements in the business section of the *Boulder Bugle*. Our gross sales were $145,000. We'll have to upgrade our software sometime this year, and this will cost us about $20,000, with associated hardware costs. Our supplier will let us spread these costs over three years.

How To

If you have a lot of marketing activities going on, you might benefit from using project management software, a sophisticated tool for keeping track of scores of events, people and budgets over time. There are a handful of programs available for both the PC and Macintosh platforms. Some are relatively simple; others very complex. But this type of software is only necessary for planning junkies . . . or for those with a sizable effort to run. For those people, it's indispensable.

2. We plan on marketing ourselves aggressively in the coming year. In addition to speaking and training engagements, we will prepare a series of three half-page ads to run on a six-time schedule in late summer and early fall in the *Boulder Business Bulletin*. We will also produce our first company brochure, which we will use as a handout at the training venues. Costs for production of the ads and the brochure and for placement of the ads will be $8,500.

3. We foresee the following results for the coming year:

    Gross Sales $154,000

    Net Profit $12,400

4. In the long term, we will explore the possibilities of opening a second office in the city. Over the next two to four years, we anticipate maintaining our historical growth of 5 percent to 7 percent per year. Toward the end of that period, we will hire at least one other employee and consider expanding our leased space.

Dream the dream. Your marketing plan should include a "blue sky" section in which you put your feet back and look to where you think you'll be in a couple of years. Especially in small businesses, it's a waste of time to formulate marketing thoughts that go out more than two or three years. But dreams are important—and they can be fun, too.

Your plan must address two different time frames: the short-term (one to 12 months) and the long-term (more than 12 months). Most of your document should focus on the coming year, which is the most important for the majority of small and medium-size businesses. Marketing typically demands the performance of a number of short-term actions planned in unison, which together bring about change. Once you've outlined the major year-end goals, the analysis will largely focus on the mechanics of media, mailing and promotion. But you shouldn't stop your serious thinking at year-end. Stretch beyond your business's immediate needs and envision the next two or three years. What are you ultimately reaching for?

Write this down, briefly and in general terms. Questions you might answer could include: How many employees do you envision adding over the next few years? Will your need for office space stay the same? Will there be major equipment purchases? Will you be able to hire a manager? Do there exist specific training courses or certifications you'd like to put your staff through? Will your profit margin stay constant, or do you think you'll be able to better it? Will you become active in local, regional or national trade groups? How will market demographics affect your business in the coming years? Keep track of how your larger vision changes over time as well.

Chapter 5

The Basics
Of Selling

OK, so you love your product. You've been around this market for a while, and—quite honestly—you've never seen a product so useful, so inexpensive, so long-lived and so visually attractive. Unfortunately, you're suffering from a condition that affects many businesspeople. Its principal symptom is a blinding lack of objectivity. If left untreated, it can result in the disappearance of entire businesses . . . company, staff and product, which fade till they become mere ghosts in the annals of business history.

Your customers remain proudly self-centered. They don't appreciate the glories of your product's reputation, the immense practicality of its design or the cleverness of its name. No, they're focused on their personal need. Maybe it's a car that's leaking oil. Or a child's sweater that needs mending. Or a bookkeeping system gone haywire. Or an old coffee pot that's died and gone to Colombia. What do they want? A solution to their problem, not a product. They want to be able to drive without dripping oil; they want something to keep their child warm; and they want an accurate financial report and a cup of java. You've got to present your product as the satisfaction to the need. As the scratch to their itch. That, they can buy.

Features Vs. Benefits: The Key To Marketing

In the Marketing Hall of Big Ideas, the distinction between product features and benefits sits on a raised marble pedestal in the center room under a ring of spotlights. This distinction separates marketers and everyone else in the business world just as sharply as the Berlin Wall divided Berlin into East and West. Many entrepreneurs talk about their product in terms of its features: its capacity, color, strength, durability and other technical capabilities. Marketers (that's you, now that you're this far into this book) are different. They speak of the product, often as dramatically as possible, in terms of how it will benefit the customer. They describe the need the product will immediately fulfill, offering a vision of the wonderfully satisfied customer living his or her suddenly carefree life. Marketers make a living by wish fulfillment (or sometimes, so I've heard, by just the appearance of wish fulfillment).

Some companies think "benefit talk" is beneath them: "That's for retail types," they say. High-tech businesses, generally selling to technically sophisticated customers, sometimes feel a full-voiced recitation of cutting-edge product features is enough to make the sale. Not so. Every per-

Jargon Alert

English is a resilient tongue. But sometimes marketers get caught up in their own enthusiasm and create twisted verbiage that they think makes their product or company more memorable. But most often, customers buy *despite*, not *because of*, the brutalized language. Service businesses normally don't have to worry about technical jargon, but they do need to avoid using tortured language to describe simple things. Ultimately, it only makes the sales process more difficult.

son responds most immediately to what he or she understands most easily—in this case, what the benefits of the features are. If you spell out the benefits to technical people, they don't have to calculate them themselves. Why make them work? You don't have to talk in baby talk. But be as obvious as you can. State your key competitive advantages as clearly as possible.

Some service businesses are also reluctant to think in terms of benefits—to their eventual calamity. Manufacturers at least have the physical product to talk about. Service providers don't, and they sometimes feel a deep-seated discomfort with the airy nature of what they offer. They often create esoteric jargon to glorify their "product" and make it appear more mysterious and complicated than it is. There's nothing wrong with this, except that when the jargon becomes *too* murky, it obscures the genuine value. As long as the jargon is benefit-oriented, no one suffers.

Benefits are the satisfaction of a need or desire. Let's take the example of a coffeemaker and study the difference between features and benefits:

Feature	Benefit
10-cup or 42-ounce capacity	Make a full pot and have fresh coffee for hours
Special filter switch allows pot to be removed while filling	Grab a quick cup during brewing without spilling a drop
Digital timer is programmable on a 24-hour basis	Wake up to freshly brewed coffee
High-impact polypropylene	If it breaks in three years, we'll replace it free
Uses paper filter #4: truncated cone 4.5 inches	Standard filter available everywhere
High-grade filter eliminates solids to 8 microns	Clean, smooth, great-tasting coffee

What you're doing is translating from a very accurate product description to the words your customer wants to hear. You're quite literally translating from one language to another. A parched Parisian won't respond to "Want some water?" but you'll get his or her attention with "Voulez-vous de l'eau?" It's the same thing when you mar-

A Diamond In The Rough

Perhaps the ultimate example of how to turn unlikely features into benefits (and of how to kick-start a stagnant market) comes from the well-muscled folks at Arm & Hammer. Working families had less time to bake, so baking soda sales had been flat for 20 years. One of their ad agency's copywriters (who are paid to explore benefits) considered baking soda's curious and little-thought-of ability to absorb odors. Not particularly useful, it had been considered. That changed when this copywriter suggested promoting Arm & Hammer baking soda as a "refrigerator deodorant." You know the rest. At last survey, most U.S. refrigerators contain baking soda. Behold the dramatic impact of an unexplored benefit.

ket a product: Customers may see you talking, but they won't become interested in what you're saying until you speak their language.

Study your product or service with this in mind, and then train your entire organization to appreciate the sometimes subtle difference in perception. The hydraulics engineer will boast of how many gallons of water a western dam holds, but regional residents will focus only on self-serving goodies like cheaper water, more electricity, fewer floods and more opportunities to take the boat out for a spin. Whenever you list a product's benefits, you're answering the age-old question: "What's in it for me?"

Once you master this distinction, you're halfway to becoming a marketing guru.

Insight

Think back to the last time you wrote up a resume (or evaluated one). The good resumes stress benefits to the hiring firm. The candidates emphasize how hiring them will benefit the company. "This job may be nice for me, but think how great it will be for you if I'm hired!"

Compiling A Key Benefit Inventory

What are your products' key benefits? You must first develop an exhaustive list of every feature for each of your products. Grill your product people until you've got everything. Now sit down with your sales manager (of course, this might be just you and a legal pad) and translate, one by one, each feature into a very short benefit statement. Some may not translate. If one isn't "benefitable" after reasonable effort, just cross it off. But experience shows that 90 percent of product features can deliver benefits to some market.

Does each benefit apply equally to every market for a product? Lightweight all-weather jackets might pack an enormous appeal to a serious backpacker, but brilliant colors might clinch the sale

Insight

While this ranking of benefits may sound mechanical, it's extremely important. You can't expect your customers to puzzle out what your product will do for them. That's your job. As you research the benefits for each market, you're basically setting your sales strategy. So you should do it right and stick to it. If you have salespeople working for you, they should be presenting the same benefits you are.

One Is Not Like The Other

Product Feature

Market A Benefit

Market B Benefit

Market C Benefit

Market D Benefit

A given product feature may present different benefits to different markets. Kitty litter's absorbency gives the homeowner (market A) a fresh-smelling laundry room. Service stations (market B) use it to soak up spilled oil. Gardeners (market C) use it to make soil for potted plants drain more quickly.

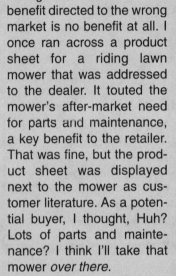

to suburban teens. Categorize the benefits by the markets they appeal to most powerfully. Then rank them by importance within each market.

Once you've solidified this listing for each product by market, you've created the most powerful tool your sales force can carry. In every customer contact, they should deliver the full key benefit message. This works for retail sales just as well as business-to-business. Each carefully crafted benefit will appeal to various clients unequally—that's life. Price may mean everything to one customer, while availability might be the deal breaker to another. You often can't know which issue might be driving a customer's decision. That's why it's critical to deliver the entire key benefit inventory at every sales opportunity—in sales presentations, in company literature, in displays. If you can't fit them all in (small ad, tight schedule or other reason), use the benefits by rank for the particular market you're addressing.

Key Appeal, Market By Market

Once you have your features translated into benefits, you've got to make sure that you know how important given benefits are to each type of customer. There are some things for which almost all of us are customers: restaurants, clothing, vehicles, watches and so on. Sometimes these items can be mass marketed: The manufacturer can apply the same appeal across a large number of people and be reasonably assured of the results. But more often, you're selling to several different people at once, and you must adjust your product's presentation to appeal to each of these differentiated markets.

Many times, entrepreneurs have trouble understanding that the exact same product has different appeals, depending on the type of customer you're selling to. Small advertising agencies and freelance writers often get instructions when creating a brochure to make it speak to two audiences, such as to both doctor and patient, when promoting a given medical device. Though both doctor and patient are looking for the same final result, their perspectives are unique. You must appeal to them differently, using different language.

Many middle-aged males suffer from what's called sleep apnea. It's a condition more prevalent among heavier men, and it basically prevents them from having a good night's sleep. They jerk themselves awake hundreds of times a night, arising exhausted in the morning. There's an operation to cure it, but it's expensive and intimidating to most patients.

But there's an alternative to surgery. A machine was invented that, under slight pressure, forces a steady stream of air down the individual's throat during the night. This keeps the man's air flow steady, and he gets a good night's sleep.

How would you market this machine? Well, if you're describing the benefits *to the patient*, you'll emphasize safety, ease of use, return of a good night's sleep, help with insurance paperwork, warranty and so on.

For the doctor (who'll write the prescription for the equipment), your emphasis will be different: The machine is so simple that the patient won't bother you with questions about its operation, it qualifies for insurance coverage, its efficacy is fully documented in research reports (so his or her professional liability is covered), it's adjustable to cover the vast range of patients, and so on. In fact, you will probably have to sell the doctor on the medical value of your equipment before he or she will even mention it to the patient (and give him your

How To

In tiered selling situations like the sleep apnea example— where you're selling to the physician and the patient— you must develop multiple sets of literature. To the patient, you will speak glowingly of the physician's skill and care . . . and of his or her sagacity in recommending this device. Your literature to the physician will speak of how well your equipment will take care of the patient and of how hassle-free it is for the physician to administer. A very different focus.

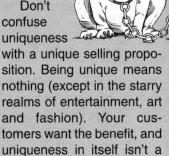

Danger Don't confuse uniqueness with a unique selling proposition. Being unique means nothing (except in the starry realms of entertainment, art and fashion). Your customers want the benefit, and uniqueness in itself isn't a benefit. What's in your product or service for the customer?

well-crafted piece of patient-directed literature).

What's Your USP?

When you market your product, you must not only appeal to the customer (and to each type of customer separately), but you must distinguish yourself from the competition. In fact, most products that compete directly against each other share many of the same benefits. No brand of ice cream tastes "unpleasant." No infrared spectrometer talks about its "inaccuracy." All the products in a given category are likely to make a large number of similar benefits claims. So why would a customer choose one over another? There can be many reasons, of course, especially convenience (it's right in front them). But often it's the USP, the unique selling proposition. It's the compelling benefit that shouts . . . no one else is like me!

What's unique about your product? What makes it stand out from the competition? What gives the customer a good and irresistible reason to select your product rather than those other fine products? If you're making ice cream, you can't base your whole appeal to the customer by simply saying "it tastes better"—unless you have some credible objective documentation that this is so. Perhaps you can claim that your ingredients are uniquely fresh, or that the ice cream is handmade in some particular way, which makes it taste "better" or at least different from other ice creams. Look at Ben & Jerry's: They don't just market their ice cream; they market the structure of the company itself and its commitment to making charitable donations. This helps give them a unique profile in a crowded market.

Many companies base their selling pitch on what's unique about them. For years, Ivory Soap based all its advertising on its claim of being $99^{44}/_{100}$ percent pure . . . so pure it floats! Domino's and its two-for-the-price-of-one pizzas. The unique Volkswagen look, which, thinking small again, has returned.

Once you've established your product's range of benefits and distinguished it from the competition, can you sum all this up in one phrase or brief sentence? Such as "When it absolutely, positively has to be there overnight," "Nothing runs like a Deere," "Better living through chemistry" or "Legendary engineering"?

If you can, then you are ready to take your case to the public. It's time to persuade them to buy.

Selling To The Public: The Four Pillars Of Marketing

An old marketing adage says that nothing happens until someone buys something—in short, sales drive every aspect of business. In every company, the salespeople are the front-line troops. In the rough-and-tumble of the marketplace, the slickest manufacturing processes, the shrewdest marketing, the brightest corporate reputations won't make the sale without the face-to-face (at least usually) meeting of seller and buyer.

This is personal selling, and it's the most important and direct aspect of the marketing process, but it is not the only way you appeal to the public and persuade them to buy. While marketing in the large sense involves every aspect of your company, the sales side of marketing is made up primarily of these four aspects:

- **Personal selling** is face-to-face salesmanship, when you have the prospect in front of you. It includes retail sales, much professional service selling and a healthy percentage of business-to-business sales.

- **Advertising** is paying for media space or time in which to sell your product at a distance.

- **Promotion** is a short-term activity, directed at either the distributor or the purchaser, to boost sales for a limited time through special pricing or other offers. Of course, you hope the short-term increase also leads to an incremental gain. It can include advertising and personal selling.

- **Public relations** is the unpaid (but, alas, not cost-free) marketing effort you undertake to expose your product to potential customers and other interested parties through the press, trade media and special media-related events.

Personal selling, advertising and most promotion efforts are direct activities: In a straightforward manner, you're saying "Buy me!" Public relations is the soft sell, in which you take a visible role in the community and increase the public's general awareness of you. The rest of this chapter and the next four will look at each of these aspects of marketing.

Business-To-Business: Giving An Effective Sales Presentation

Business-to-business sales usually involve giving a prearranged presentation, whether in person or on paper, of your product or service. This differs from retail sales to the general public, which is usually spontaneous and immediate. For more on retail sales and a discussion on sales staff, turn to Chapter 6.

In business-to-business environments, the selling and buying process is often not simple. Many times you'll never meet the person who will ultimately use your product, the person who'll authorize the purchase of your product, or the person who signs the check. If you're dealing directly with the buyer, consider yourself fortunate. You have to convince only one person of your product's suitability and of its superiority over competing products. If you've pulled together your product benefits properly, if you're talking to a buyer in a market that genuinely needs your product and if you've positioned yourself appropriately against the competition, you should be in good shape.

However, you may be presenting a proposal to a selection committee of a large corporation. Several of the people present may have competing agendas you don't know about, or you may discover after making your pitch that no one in the room has the authority to say yes. You may be speaking to a purchasing agent who makes the decision based on agreed-upon objection criteria. In that case, all you can do is prepare the best proposal you can, all the while focusing on making the description of your product and your company match as closely as possible the demands of the proposal request.

Despite these difficulties, the bottom line is the same: Personal sales makes commerce happen. And if you're the one making the sales pitch—or if you supervise those who do—fine-tuning your presentation techniques can pump up your bottom line. If you have a meeting with a company, you know that, at the very least, you're being taken seriously and that you have a reasonable chance of coming away with the order.

So what should you do? Here's a handful of tips from the experts.

Get Informed: Know The Buyer

Are you presenting to a company that can conceivably use or afford your product or service? Just as a real estate agent must qualify prospects, so salespeople must maximize their time by prequalifying potential clients and eliminating those who don't have the financial resources, who have proved themselves bad credit risks, who have a business that doesn't match up well with the strengths of your product and so on. Focus on prospective buyers whom you have a reasonable chance of winning . . . and who are worth winning.

Then, once you're at the stage where you're making an oral or written presentation, ask yourself whether the person you're presenting to has the ability to say yes. If the person doesn't, you may be better off trying to work around that person and presenting to someone who can give you the go-ahead. Once you've set up a serious meeting with customers who have purchasing authority, ask your contact who's going to be there and what their stake in the decision is. Get your hands on an organizational chart so you have a feel for the hierarchy. What are the people in the meeting likely to be most interested in? For instance, if the finance person is there, direct your comments on financial payback and return on investment to him or her.

We're talking business politics here, but that doesn't surprise you, does it? You've got to scope out the terrain of the sales battle before you can give it your best shot, and you'll have more success in the major meetings—with

Danger

If you sell to larger companies, you may be involved in "rogue meetings" or "commando purchasing operations" in which the corporate person looking to purchase products or services doesn't really have the authority to do so. He or she is looking to see what's out there, seeking a free lunch, trying to impress a superior, or just looking to wile away some hours. And if you're presenting to such a person, you're likely wasting your precious time.

Into The Great Unknown

An especially challenging kind of sale is the "concept sell," in which you have to sell not only your particular product but the entire concept behind it. In most sales, the concept of the product is self-evident. Bicycle manufacturers don't have to explain how a bicycle works or why you might like one. They only have to demonstrate why you would want their particular bicycle.

Imagine being the first person to introduce the Slinky to the market, the flavor straw or laser surgery for eye correction. You're faced with a large task. You have to educate your potential buyers on what your product is before they can decide whether to buy it.

Louis Rich Foods wanted to promote a line of turkey cold cuts—the product seemed like a natural. The American diet was moving away from beef and toward healthier sources of protein, and busy modern families were relying more and more on easy-to-prepare foods. But for most Americans, turkey was a once-a-year, butter-basted cannonball. Louis Rich had to spend millions of dollars convincing the consuming public that it was OK to eat turkey as a luncheon meat. After a concerted program of "educational advertising," consumer promotion, appearances on nutrition shows and articles in the trade press, they were able to make their case. Now turkey cold cuts own precious refrigerator case real estate in all supermarkets.

However, there are two major dangers inherent in the concept sell:

1. If no one has ever sold anything like your product before . . . er, maybe there's a good reason. This is not an appeal for an end to ingenuity and creativity. It's just a fact.

2. Once you spend the money and effort to create the market through buyer education, you've also laid the groundwork for your competition to come in and slurp up your carefully prepared customers.

significant dollars on the line—when you understand the situation you're confronting.

In addition to knowing whom you're presenting to, give some thought to *why* you're presenting. What is the company looking for?

What is the current situation that's driving their request for your presentation? Is there anyone else who works with you in your office who might have an insight into this company and why they're having you make a presentation? Are you presenting along with other potential suppliers, or is it you or nothing? Are there other noncompetitive suppliers who might give you some information on what's happening inside your target company? If you're able to ask clarifying questions before the actual presentation (this is common in governmental work), don't miss the opportunity to come up with some questions to ask . . . just to establish a working relationship.

If presenting is something you do several times a week, you may not need to do much research or rehearsing. Let's face it, after a few months of presentations, you'll have your pitch down pat, and you'll have a good feel for the terrain of most sales situations.

Rehearse Your Pitch

If presentations are not something you do regularly, then you need to rehearse what you're going to say and how you're going to say it. Work with someone in the office, a good friend or your spouse to smooth out the flow of information and make yourself as concise as possible.

Most of us have been in presentations when the presenter was out of touch with his or her audience, rambling on long after any audience interest had left the room in despair. Think in bullet points and headlines. You want the attendees to come out of your presentation with just a handful of clear benefit statements about your product. Don't drown your competitive advantages in a lot of chatter about your company, your history or your golf game.

If you use equipment to make your presentation (flip charts, computer printouts, PowerPoint on a laptop, interactive CD-ROM, interactive holograms, laser light shows), bulletproof your equipment and carry spares of essential parts like disks, bulbs and power cords. People tend to understand when you have a little technical trouble, but they do expect you to fix it. They're hiring you because of the resourcefulness of you and your products, right?

Get Some Sleep And Eat Your Wheaties

No matter how tireless your personality type, you've got to be your best when you're on stage. That means being well-rested, well-fed and relaxed. Get a good night's sleep beforehand, and eat breakfast. Get any materials prepared in advance, and proofread them carefully. Get near the presentation site early, relax with a cup of coffee or juice, and review your notes and your plan of action.

Once the meeting begins, you're expected to be the focus of attention. When people listen to a presentation, they're in a "receptive" mode—they expect to be informed and even entertained. You've got to deliver the goods with style and high spirits. You're the driver . . . make this vehicle go where you want it to. Don't come out of the meeting wondering if you were too low-key.

Sell The Benefits, Not The Features

We've been talking benefits for a while, and now's the time to put them to work. Key your entire presentation on the need your product satisfies, not on your superior technology, not on your well-trained staff, not on your wonderful reputation. What's in it for the people in the room? How will their company come out ahead if they choose to do business with you? What existing problem is this company wrestling with? This should lead your presentation. Your product is the answer.

Also, don't forget that the people you're presenting to also have a personal involvement in the sale. If they hire you or buy your product, will it be a feather in their cap? If they're at risk for choosing you over a better-known competitor, how can you reduce their exposure—extend a warranty, offer additional case histories, provide documentation to pass up the chain of command? Fine-tune your presentation to appeal to the individuals in the room as well as to the company they represent.

Insight

You'll score higher in a presentation the more you customize it. That can include personalized handouts or overhead screens. But go further. Build your presentation around the company you're speaking with. Make them forget you're pitching the skills of an outside company; speak to their concerns and interests, highlighting the ways in which their company will be enhanced by dealing with you. Think *them,* not *us.*

Invite A Dialogue

When you start your presentation, outline how you plan to organize the meeting—and make sure your audience understands that they have a role beyond merely listening. You expect them to ask any questions they have, raise any objections they feel, outline special applications they may have for your product, and explain how they'd like the product integrated into their operation. By inviting and encouraging their participation, you enlist their help in figuring out all the ways your product or service can benefit them.

Be Prepared For Any Objections

Sales objections give salespeople, especially new ones, the greatest difficulty. You're really rolling in your pitch. You think you're definitely receiving good vibes from the right side of the table. You're well ahead of schedule for your allotted presentation time. Then the mild-mannered fellow in the camel's-hair suit scrapes his chair, raises his hand and with fixed eye says: "I just don't see how this will work for us. The specs seem in the ballpark, but you're a new company, unproven, and this piece of equipment is too important to us. We've got to go with a proven provider, even if we give away a bit in capacity. It's just too risky."

The smoke from the explosion clears. Maybe some of the other people at the table climb on board and reveal similar feelings. Maybe you draw some sympathy. Maybe the meeting freezes, with no one set on how to proceed.

If you can't handle high-inside-fastball objections, you're never going to be successful selling. The sales experts counsel a calm approach:

1. **Hear the objection out.** Don't interrupt. Don't cut it short. Focus your attention on what's being said, taking some notes (without cutting eye contact for more than a brief period) so you capture all the details.

2. **Don't panic.** People who object are at least taking you seriously. When you get in a presentation where everyone smiles at everything you're saying, you're in trouble. When people object, they're looking for more information, or they want you to clarify their perception of your product or service. You should be prepared for every objection with a killer response.

3. **Find something in the objection to validate.** No matter whether it's well-founded or ridiculous, the objection must be taken seriously. You want to credit the questioner for mounting the objection. Acknowledge that you're a new and essentially unproven company, for example. In fact, you'd have the exact same objec-

tions if you were sitting where they are. If you need a few moments to gather your thoughts, respond to the objection with a clarifying question: "What kind of experience have you had with your existing equipment regarding downtime?" or "What's a doomsday scenario in your production? Let me see if I can address it." This technique will also help you zero in on the true nature of the objection.

4. **You've already developed a script with answers to every objection, right?** No? The section on page 94, "Overcoming Buying Objections," discusses how to do this in detail. Now's the time to pull that script up to the top of your mind and satisfy the objection raiser. Go through it calmly, getting your inquirer's assent at every step of the way. When you're done addressing the objection, make sure the individual feels comfortable with how you handled it.

Talk Money And Ask For The Business

You shouldn't end the meeting without addressing directly the issue of cost and terms. Some presenters hate to talk money, preferring to dance around the subject while focusing on the product and its benefits. I don't think that's effective. People want to know price, regardless of how little importance you try to attach to it. If your product is more expensive than the competition, make it a point to explain why, emphasizing the greater value the prospective customer will get from your product. If your product is less expensive than the competition, you should hammer away on that benefit, emphasizing how you're able to deliver top quality without charging a high price. Don't apologize for your price, either high or low.

Finally, you have to ask for the business. How does the sale happen? You can make the order form a part of your presentation kit and ask them to fill it out then and there. You can ask about which particular model they want to order. You can inquire as to which delivery time line they're working with. Make what's called the "presumptive close," by which you presume you've been successful and are simply making arrangements for delivery. This can push some buyers over the edge into making an immediate decision.

Fill Out A Call Report

All salespeople hate to fill out call reports. They often feel they're being checked up on, that no one back at the office has to know the details of how the meeting went. Even sole proprietors hate call reports, and they have no one to report to. There's just something so archival and so seemingly unproductive about them.

In fact, call reports are prime marketing ore for future efforts. Think for a moment of the value you can glean from 200 call reports of recent sales presentations:

- Which companies have been approached, when and by whom.
- What products they were exposed to.
- Who attended the sales meeting—and who is responsible for purchasing your product.
- Why they did or didn't decide on your company (assuming your salesperson followed up properly on a negative decision).

What can you do with this market intelligence?

- Study the successes to see what types of companies you're having better luck with. You can then intensify your efforts to make presentations to more of those companies.

Sales Call Report

Salesperson_____

Company visited_____

Date/Time_____

Clients in meeting (With titles)_____

_____

Reason for meeting_____

Topics discussed_____

Actions taken_____

Projects/Orders initiated_____

Action needed_____

Relevant earlier call reports_____

- Study the failures to see what you can do to make your product more appealing to those types of companies. With good, concrete follow-up, you can—over time—both enhance your product and alter your presentations for greater success.

- Use the unsuccessful presentations as a source for possible future sales activities. If you lost the ABC account pitch because your trucking firm didn't have enough experienced drivers, you can repitch the account when you get a little bigger.

- You know the people who hold key purchasing authority for your product. Keep them on a low-level direct-mail effort, to keep them informed of what's happening at your company.

All this is extremely valuable information. See page 93 for a sample call report form you can adapt to your company.

Overcoming Buying Objections

At the top of this chapter, you assembled a list detailing each of your product's benefits. That was the fun part. Now you have to look at the other side. What objections might you face in a sales call? Salespeople are like baseball players: Generally, their failures at the plate outnumber their successes. But like good hitters, salespeople raise their average by examining their failures and adjusting the next time they come to bat. Always ask yourself why a particular sale didn't happen. What kinds of remarks have you heard from prospective buyers that kept them from going with your product? These are the objections you weren't able to overcome in your sales effort.

You should be able to put together a list of the six to 10 most common objections that pop up during sales presentations. When you have that list, write down your best responses to each of those objections. Some responses may involve several different elements. Some objections may be hard to respond to in a positive way. You've just got to do your best in formulating your answers.

For instance, if the objection is that the speed of a piece of equipment is too slow, maybe you can focus attention on other strong points that more than make up for this: perhaps less downtime, lower error rate, greater ease of operation and therefore less training required, and so on. Until you come up with an adequate response, that objection will continue to kill sales.

Once you've developed your list of responses, you must be ready to use them on the spot. You can't call prospects back in four days to tell them, "You know, I was thinking about that bad reaction you had to the high failure rate of our pumps, and I think you're overemphasizing its importance." You have to have all that sales ammunition with you in the room when you're making the presentation.

Never forget that your job is not just selling the equipment or service. In the minds of the prospective buyers, you're the company, and they're judging the company by your performance. Respond smoothly to an objection, and they'll be impressed with your professionalism (and that of your company). But if you get flustered by an objection, or leave without giving an adequate response, you will create the opposite impression.

Objection Overruled	
If you hear . . .	**Then try . . .**
Your price is too high.	Re-emphasize the value of your product or service. If that doesn't work, then offer a slightly different (and less expensive) product or service. Or try discussing your available financing arrangements.
We're not ready to buy right now.	Ask what specifically is keeping them from making the purchase now. Address that objection.
Your product/service doesn't have a particular feature.	Ask why that particular feature is important.
	Suggest that the existence of another feature/benefit more than compensates for the missing feature.
We're not sure your product will work well with other products we have in place.	Find out what those other products are and get a testimonial on how well your product functions in that situation.

If you see the same couple of objections arising time and time again, make the smart move: Eliminate that objection before it arises. Build a preemptive strike against that objection right into the core of your presentation, so your prospects won't be distracted by the thought of an apparent weakness in your product or service. As you're able to refine your presentation based on experience, you'll be able to eliminate a good percentage of the common objections you run into. Only then will your sales effort really begin to take off.

Getting To The Dotted Line

Getting someone to say yes is not always easy. And, as anyone with any sales experience knows, everything can be cordial and positive during the presentation. But once it's time for a decision, once someone has to write a check, things can turn dark.

If you see some reluctance to say yes, get involved in helping them make the decision. An effective way to wrap the sale up—without appearing overly aggressive—is to recap why you're there, the need that the company recognizes, and how your product satisfies that need in all its aspects. If you've done your homework well and made a skilled and informative presentation, you should have left them right at the door of making the decision. Respectfully ask them what's keeping them from making the decision right now: Are there senior people who have to approve the decision? Do they have to evaluate a competitor who's yet to present? Is there something about your product/service that they're unsure of? By the process of elimination, you should be able to trim away the possible reasons for delay.

Of course, many business decisions based on a presentation take some time. More often than not, you simply can't force the decision while you're there. If you're told that's the case, learn when you can expect a decision. Then tell them that you're looking forward to the possibility of working for them, and immediately send them a recap of your presentation with some new material—whatever you can pull together to show that your desire to provide them service is still on your mind.

Some salespeople have had success unlocking a sale with the direct question: "Do you want to purchase this service?" Follow it with silence, and let the prospect take over the conversation.

If you sense a negative decision in the making, suggest that you'll send them a recap of the meeting with your final best offer in a day or two. This will buy you some time to come up with a "Plan B."

Finally, let's assume for a moment that you don't make the sale. Your immediate course of action should be to call your contact, acknowledge the inevitable, and then ask if he or she can help you understand why the contract went to another company. This provides you with a real learning opportunity, in many ways more valuable than (although not, unfortunately, as financially rewarding as) winning the sale. Make it clear you're not disputing the decision or trying gamely to alter it. Mention how you put some work into the presentation, and you'd appreciate the chance to use your loss to improve the way you make the next presentation. Was it price? Was it product issues? Was it a superior presentation by a competitor? Probe to get specifics, which you should write up in a call report for later analysis. If you learn why people don't buy, then take steps to remedy either your presentation or the product itself.

If you do get the contract, your job is just starting in two ways. First, you've got to make arrangements to have the product or service actually delivered. Second, you now have a relationship to tend, new people to learn about and perhaps a new application in which to test your product or service. Congratulations.

Chapter 6

Selling: Your Next Steps

In this chapter, we'll discuss various other aspects of the selling process. Since all of these areas don't apply equally to every business, here's an outline of what we'll cover:

- **The service sector:** How is marketing services different from marketing physical products?

- **Pricing:** This is an issue near and dear to every entrepreneur's heart, and one that stymies many new businesspeople.

- **Distribution:** What's the best way to move your product from your factory to your customer?

- **Your sales staff:** Every business needs someone who's selling your product or service, but which type of staff is best for you? What are general retail sales techniques?

- **Case histories and testimonials:** These may be the strongest weapons you have in clinching the sale.

Selling Services

You've doubtless noticed that I often mention "product or service" in the same breath. Every company offers at least one or the other; most companies offer both, whether they know it or not. If you're a manufacturer, retailer or dining operation, you're providing both a product (widgets, garments or tarragon chicken) and a service (quick delivery, large selection or a fine-dining experience).

The "work product" of some companies isn't as tangible or tasty as these. Accounting firms, law firms, architects, financial institutions, car rental companies, marketing consultants, chiropractors, psychologists, business brokers, real estate agents and many others in the business universe can't send you a box filled with a sample product.

As the century draws to a close, services move steadily to center stage. We are becoming a nation of services, with less and less manufacturing. Our manufacturing legacy in the heartland is now called the Rust Belt (although lately it's experiencing a resurgent glimmer with targeted marketing). Why the shift to services? Lots of reasons:

- More stringent environmental controls have made manufacturing (at least in the old way) more difficult. Companies are deciding: "The hell with this."

- More legal liability for manufacturers has increased the risk. (Want to buy a ladder-making company cheap? No? How about an asbestos manufacturer?)

- A strong economy means people can pay other people to do the things they don't

Insight

More than three-quarters of the American work force is engaged in providing services rather than making products. And the U.S. transition from manufacturing to service is steadily increasing. The old picture of the salesperson schlepping down the street with sample case in hand fades daily. Now it's a well-groomed professional, armed with a Pentium notebook and cell phone, selling services to help people do better whatever it is that they do.

want to do themselves. They hire fitness coaches, wedding planners, tax preparers, hair stylists, firewood deliverers and so on.

- Our entertainment and news media promote services constantly. We hear endless stories about massage therapy, dog psychologists, personal grocery shoppers, take-out gourmet foods and more.

- Low labor costs and relaxed environmental regulation overseas make manufacturing and assembly more affordable and less troublesome there.

- As more women have entered the work force, "family-related services" have stepped up to handle child care and other needs. Those families now have a second paycheck to compensate for their limited free time, and they spend it on lawn care, catering, travel and so on.

- New technologies have created totally new services, such as voice mail, computer dating, database researching, as well as an entire raft of online services.

When you have the money, and your free time is valuable to you, why not pay people to take care of time-consuming or tedious chores like tax preparation, housecleaning, investment guidance and so on? It makes sense.

The Difference Between Marketing Services And Products

Almost all service-oriented businesses share certain things in common that make them different from companies that mainly produce products, and these affect your marketing approach.

- **Services are typically tailored to the particular customer.** You can't mass-produce services as easily as you can physical products. An audit report for the Frogs "R" Us amphibian retailer can't be used for any other company. So the effort the service provider puts into developing the end product can't easily be used to spin off other similar products. This affects the marketing of the service.

- **Most services are personally linked.** Customers who buy services typically buy the skills, competence and attention of a particular person. If that person leaves one company and goes to another, his or her customers will often follow—because their loyalty is to the individual, not the company. This happens in brokerage houses, hair salons and upscale restaurants all the time. Service businesses are difficult to sell because they're typically owner-dependent, with little in the way of capital equipment (like manufacturers have).

- **Most services are also time-intensive.** In addition to expertise, what service providers mostly sell is time, and they typically bill using an hourly rate (as opposed to the per widget or per chicken-serving rate). You often make appointments to get your services rendered. For a service provider, time is literally money: If an hour passes unbilled, it's lost income, never to be recouped.

You can also look at services based on one of three qualities:

Professional Skills	Labor Skills	Equipment-Based
Financial	Household upkeep	Vending machines
Legal	Security	Taxis
Accounting	Janitorial	Airlines
Insurance	Beauty	Construction
Management	Lawn care	Auto repair
Medical		Flying lessons
Psychological		Dry-cleaning
Educational/ Professional		Printing
Marketing		Broadcast media
		Telecommunications

If your business is primarily a service provider, you have to approach marketing with some special sensitivities:

- **Service businesses depend on satisfied clients more than other businesses.** When you are marketing your services, you can't drop a product on your prospect's desk. It isn't easy to invite your prospect to compare your products with those of your competitor. So you have to market with a "satisfied client" list; they represent the best example of the quality of your service.

The catch here is that—for some businesses—companies don't want you publicizing their use of your services. If you provide counseling services to company X for help with its drug- and alcohol-dependent employees, the president of X might not want you trumpeting their employee problems across the market.

Solution: Develop client lists that don't mention the client. Describe your clients in ways that give the reader a "good enough" understanding of the types of companies you do business for. In your sales presentation, help prospects understand the need for privacy: Surely if they become your customer, they'd want the same discretion used in discussing your relationship with their company.

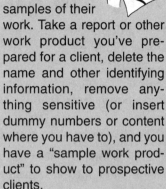

How To
Service businesses can still use samples of their work. Take a report or other work product you've prepared for a client, delete the name and other identifying information, remove anything sensitive (or insert dummy numbers or content where you have to), and you have a "sample work product" to show to prospective clients.

- **The sales process often takes longer, especially in business-to-business sales.**

Solution: Maintain a consistent sales effort, even when it's tempting to say you don't need it. If you lose a customer or two, you can't start from scratch to round up a few new clients. You should already have some prospects in the pipeline. This is another reason to keep up a year-round marketing program.

- **Services are more complex to price, to deliver and to evaluate than comparatively priced products.** Defining the quality of service delivery is very difficult. It boils down to whether the customer feels well-served.

Solution: When your business provides a service, you need to build a personal relationship. Your only job is to please your main contact. You'll need to conduct informal "How am I doing?" conversations on a regular basis.

- **Many professional services cover areas that are of extreme importance to the customer: legal, accounting, insurance, financial.** So customers tend to be very skeptical about changing their suppliers of these services, since they're intimate and revealing in a way most other services aren't. You need to make a very convincing case to get someone to switch from such a supplier.

Solution: When you market your service, stress the length of time of your relationships and highlight your sensitivity to the bonds of trust in your relationship with your customers. Offer prospects the chance to make a phone call to your current customers to allay their fears about changing suppliers.

Pricing: How Much Should You Charge?

Your product or service is worth exactly what someone will pay you for it. Finding out what that amount is has captivated generations of economists and millions of marketers. Customers want to pay as little as possible; businesses want to charge as much as possible. These are two sides in an eternal tug-of-war, which is as old as haggling merchants in a Middle Eastern bazaar and as modern as a long-distance provider weaving a web of words over different pricing programs.

Pricing is one of the most difficult tasks in any business. Many variables enter into any pricing decision. And the "manufacturer's suggested retail price" (has *anyone* ever paid this?) is only one of

Playing The Field

Stop into your local electronics store: In most product categories, there is an overwhelming range of offerings. When it comes to CD players, a single manufacturer may have a dozen different models on display, many of them only slight variations of the same machine. Why don't these companies reduce their product line and save on manufacturing costs?

Not so fast. One reason we see so many products with very subtle differences between them is that manufacturers want you and me to pick one that's a little more expensive than we might pick from a more limited selection. If we could choose from only two models, one at $89 and one at $135, many of us would choose the $89 model. But if we have five choices—$79, $89, $104, $135, and $189—the average price we are willing to pay will be considerably higher. The manufacturer wins, despite the increased engineering and manufacturing costs.

However, another reason for this plethora of merchandise is that manufacturers are also concerned with keeping up with each of their competitors' major products. Once a new product line is introduced, everyone rushes to get his or her own version on the shelves.

your decisions. You must consider quantity discounts, wholesale prices to retailers and trade discounts for distributors.

Here are three major points to keep in mind about pricing:

1. Your prices must fall between two poles:
   - A low price below which you cannot make money
   - A high price beyond which you cannot get customers

2. Customers also have a psychological comfort zone that falls between two poles:
   - A low price limit below which the product is perceived as "suspect" or "too cheap"
   - A high price limit beyond which the product is too expensive

3. Given the first two points, pricing (especially consumer pricing) is in large part psychological. Perceived value is what drives the exchange. If the customer thinks your product looks, feels or smells cheap, you won't be able to get a high price for it. If you're able to make the customer think your product is top-of-the-line, you can start counting the golden eggs. Pricing is not logical.

When you calculate prices, you must keep many different realities in mind:

- **Cost:** If you don't cover all your costs in making and delivering the product, you can't remain in business. So you must tabulate your *fixed costs* (overhead) and your *variable costs* (product- or service-related expenditures). Fixed costs stay relatively constant, no matter how high or low the production volume. They include management salaries; insurance; pensions; office, manufacturing or retail space; utilities; and interest expense. Variable costs are usually production related, but services also have a few variable expenses, primarily the time and costs associated with delivering the service to customers. Other product-related costs include raw materials, manufacturing equipment and production wages, packaging and distribution costs. You will, of course, need to raise your prices over time just as these costs grow to match inflation.

- **Competition:** Don't be too cost-focused in setting your prices. This is a natural tendency, since working with known internal and external costs can be comforting; these are items you can really nail down. They're a lot more reliable to deal with than the irrationality of the marketplace. Avoid this temptation.

Nothing For Something

I once took my desktop PC into a computer shop to have a larger hard drive installed. When I placed my order, I said that I wanted my existing internal hard drive left in place; I just wanted to add the new hard drive next to it. I had backed up all my files onto tape.

When I returned, my old hard drive was sitting on top of my CPU. Fighting hyperventilation, I asked what had happened. The technician explained that he thought it would run faster with just the new hard drive installed. I explained that I didn't want to have to restore all my files from the tape onto the new drive, updating Window registers and pointers and so on. I knew that would be nothing but trouble. He just bristled and said, "You know, our price for that hard drive is $20 cheaper than anyplace else in town!"

I smiled. There was just no sense in arguing with this guy. He didn't get it. The $20—at this point—meant absolutely nothing to me. The value was in getting what I wanted, not an extra sawbuck in my pocket. It took me two days to get my system up and running again. Sixteen hours earning $1.25 an hour.

You may have a hungry competitor eyeing *you* for lunch with an aggressive promotion designed to drain away your customers. You have to stay sensitive to the pulse of the marketplace. If a new competitor is coming into town, this is not a good time to raise prices. If, on the other hand, the other guy adds a new store and people start noticing that prices have gone up, drop your prices and buy baby a new pair of shoes.

- **Marketing mix:** Price is the easiest element of the marketing mix to change: You can do it almost instantly. But if your pricing strategy conflicts with your image in the marketplace, it can be counterproductive. Earlier, you decided how to define your company in the mind of the marketplace using the right mix of the Four P's—product, place, price and promotion. Keep this identity in mind as you set prices. If you want to be a low-volume, super-quality electronics operation, you can't rely on drastic price-cutting as a regular marketing strategy. You'll destroy your image. Conversely, if you've staked out the high-volume, low-price camp for your own, don't expect to have crowds at the doors when you raise prices and start acting upscale. Stay with your selected marketing mix.

If you want to make more money from your existing products, you have to raise the perceived value of your products: update their look, add new features, get quality endorsements, promote more heavily and so on.

- **Market environment:** The law of supply and demand governs us all. Are you selling in an up or a down economy (locally or nationally)? This impacts your pricing strategy. Are you selling lawnmowers during a severe drought? If your prices have been stable for some time, shake things up and move them around just to generate some market excitement.

- **Product life cycle:** For manufacturers, a new type of product—with high demand and no competitors—will allow premium pricing. An old warhorse—with established popularity, no start-up costs and no requirement for ongoing promotion—will allow moderate pricing to produce a steady profit stream (the much-admired "cash cow"). This principle also applies to service businesses: You must always be developing new services or novel wrinkles on established services to maintain interest and prices. No service can afford to do the same old things year after year, though sometimes this innovation amounts to just a change in terminology (especially true among management consultants).

- **Skim or penetrate:** These are two useful pricing approaches to keep in mind. Skim pricing means the commitment to maintain a high price and deal only with the top end of the market, which is least sensitive to price. You'll let your competition be the bottom feeders. Penetration pricing is a decision to lower your prices enough to make active inroads into a new market. You're willing to sacrifice your normal margin to "buy a market."

- **Higher prices not equal to higher profits:** Raising prices can sometimes cut your sales and leave you in worse shape than before. If your product or service is really needed by customers, and if there's no ready substitute, you may get away with it. But if the demand is elastic, your customers will decrease as your price creeps up. Don't be afraid to test higher prices for a time to judge the market reaction. If the demand stays strong, congratulations. If it doesn't, you can always return prices to their original level.

You can't, however, keep losing money for long, so you'll have to find other ways to increase profits.

Distributors: Friend Or Foe?

Happy are those manufacturers who sell their products directly to consumers. For them, the assembly line (through their retail outlets or direct-mail arm) empties right in the customer's hand, and the money paid goes right to the manufacturer.

For most manufacturers, however, life just isn't that simple. To illustrate the dilemma of distribution, let's put you into the tea business—as Tastee Tea. You purchase tea from all over the world. You make a number of delicious blends: some induce sleepiness, some a sense of well-being and some wide-eyed alertness. You mix those tea blends with a number of aromatic essences and flavors to produce,

The Circle Of Life

Every physical product has a life cycle—a movement from birth to death, as it were—that has four stages:

- **Introduction:** The product is new, so promotion and publicity are key. Often a money-losing stage.

- **Growth:** Sales volume increases, profits begin and competitors appear.

- **Maturity:** Sales grow and then level off. More competitors and more similar products. Price promotions often used to take customers from competitors.

- **Decline:** Market looking to new products and technology for need satisfaction.

Service providers don't face quite the same pressure for novelty as product manufacturers. But they have to stay on top of trends in their industry. Every service industry needs "juice"—the sense that "things are happening." For example, if you're an accountant, a financial planner, a fitness coach or a hair salon owner, you should see what others in your industry are doing to keep existing services fresh and then develop exciting and valuable products to build the future.

say, 12 different teas. When the tea is done, how do you physically get it to the customers?

If you sell your tea only to the local market, all you need to do is put a retail outlet on the front of your plant, plug in a cash register, run a few ads and there goes your tea, moving out the front door. But selling only to your local market severely limits the amount of tea you can sell. How far will people drive to get tea?

If you want to sell your tea in other parts of the country, how can you make that happen? You have several choices:

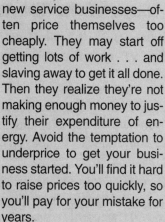

Danger
New businesses— especially new service businesses—often price themselves too cheaply. They may start off getting lots of work . . . and slaving away to get it all done. Then they realize they're not making enough money to justify their expenditure of energy. Avoid the temptation to underprice to get your business started. You'll find it hard to raise prices too quickly, so you'll pay for your mistake for years.

1. **Open Tastee Tea stores around the country.** Unless you've inherited jillions, you probably can't afford this. You also have to ask yourself two burning questions:

   - Will people come to a *tea* store? I don't know of any that just sell tea, do you? Even coffee shops are carrying more and more baked goods because coffee by itself doesn't draw enough traffic.

   - Is this really the most efficient way to sell your tea? Making tea doesn't give you expertise in running tea shops.

2. **Sell Tastee Tea through a mail order catalog.** This will prove very costly unless your teas are truly spectacular or you mail to the right list. Even in that case, you will need deep pockets.

3. **Visit coffee and tea stores around the country and persuade them to carry your Tastee Tea.** This is doable (and has been a successful paradigm for many products over the years), but it takes time and pulls you away from tea-making, which is what you're really good at and enjoy. While you're away making sales calls, who's keeping an eye on the Boysenberry Blend?

4. **Contact several key distributors and have them add Tastee Tea to their line.** If you can convince these distributors to carry Tastee

Tea, this is the easiest and most efficient way to get into the marketplace. If you select a distributor who carries products that complement yours (coffees, coffee and cappuccino makers, baked goods and so on), you can count on their help in lining up retailers.

Who Are These Distributors, And What Do They Do?

When you turn on your water tap, water happens. Wonderful, isn't it? You've got your hot; you've got your cold. It's clean, dependable and cheap. How does that water get to you? Chances are you haven't a clue—and you probably don't care. Depending on where you live, you have large-scale municipal water or a local or private well. It's the same with electricity and natural gas. These things make your life easier, but it doesn't make much difference how they get to you, just that they do.

Distributors in the American marketplace operate the same way. They're invisible to most consumers. Their names mean nothing to the people who enjoy the products they deliver. But they effectively (if not always efficiently) bridge the geographical gap between producer and retailer. Supermarkets and department stores couldn't exist without a complicated distribution system, capable of moving enormous amounts of product of every size and description.

Distributors add millions to the cost of the products we buy in the supermarket. But from the manufacturer's perspective, they deliver a lot, too.

- **They transport goods from large warehouses to the retail outlets.** The manufacturer can't afford to move these goods. The retailer can't afford to go pick them up. Enter the distributor, who serves as a superwarehouse, drawing goods from thousands of manufacturers, sorting them by retailer, and then dropping them off on the retailer's loading docks. Imagine the scenario if every

Jargon Alert

Distributors go by many names, depending on the part of the country and the market they serve. They may be called brokers, agents or jobbers, among others. Sometimes analysts make a distinction between distributors who actually own the product they deliver and those who merely distribute them without taking the title to them.

manufacturer had its own trucks delivering goods to every retailer in the country. The truck-building, highway and gasoline industries might encourage this type of system, but it would quickly create a disastrous and unproductive gridlock.

> **Insight**
>
> Some distributors offer terms of up to 90 days on paying their invoices. This is a friendly "float," which can prove very helpful to start-up businesses. Keep your payments to distributors on time, and you'll build a long and mutually beneficial relationship.

- **They warehouse materials in different parts of the country.** This storage role of distributors saves manufacturers millions in facility costs, since they don't have to build storage buildings to hold the goods that roll off the production line.

- **They handle the paperwork between the retail outlets and the manufacturers.** Retailers order their Twinkies from distributors, not from the manufacturer. This allows the manufacturer to focus on products, not on logistics, which is the strong point of distributors. Logistically, manufacturers can focus on a limited number of customers . . . the distributors.

- **They handle invoicing and collection.** This is an important service for manufacturers. It keeps them out of the collection business, especially for small accounts that the manufacturer wouldn't want to have to deal with.

- **They don't sell for you.** That's your job, through your advertising and promotion. Distributors put the product in the hands of the retailer. In many markets, you have to have distributors, but they don't relieve you of the primary sales responsibility.

From the retailer's perspective, distributors provide the following main benefits:

1. Access to a wide range of products from a single source. It wouldn't be practical for a retailer to order each of the products it carries from every single manufacturer.

2. Delivery. To the door, in the quantities and sizes needed, according to schedule.

3. Connections to the manufacturer's offerings of co-op advertising, promotional specials and special discounts.

Swimming With Sharks

You're a retail clothier. You've been carrying Trombone Boy jeans, slacks and shirts for five years. They make you some money, you have no problems, but you wish you could tweak your margin. However, the manufacturer's not giving an inch.

You're driving around one day and spot some new construction nearby. "What's going in there?" you ask the foreman. "New outlet clothing store," he replies. "Trombone Boy. Ever hear of 'em? Manufacturer-direct with great prices, they say."

Competitive pressures squeeze the distribution channel like never before, and new companies cast off the old rules. Supplier becomes competitor. Distributor becomes competitor.

Finding A Distributor For Your Product

The distribution channel you select for your product should be based on a careful analysis of the needs of your product in the marketplace.

How can you motivate distributors to carry your line? This can be difficult for companies and their products breaking into a market that's already flooded with other similar products. If you have an idea for a new plush toy, for example, you will have some tough sledding unless you can find something in your product that's genuinely unique and attractive to the consumer.

You can base your pitch to the distributor on a range of rationales:

1. You can offer relatively more money for the distributor than the competition. The percentage of sales distributors charge varies widely depending on the product and the market. There are no national norms—you might pay 5 percent; you might pay 20 percent. Talk to your local or regional trade association for guidance on distributor contracts.

2. You can offer more perks for the distributor than the competition. You can buy your way into the distribution chain with 20 extra cases of product for every 250 ordered by the distributor. You can fly the distributor out to your Hawaii sales conference to see what your company is about.

3. You can tie your product in with other products that you or other manufacturers create.

4. You can show the marketing campaign that supports your product.

5. You can demonstrate genuinely strong consumer appeal.

6. You already have a track record of introducing successful new products.

7. You've already secured other large retail contracts.

Remember, you're marketing to the distributor just as much as you're marketing to the general public. If you can't persuade significant distributors to handle your product, you'll have a very difficult time breaking into the marketplace in a big way.

You can probably find local distributors for your type of product in the Yellow Pages, but that's not the best place to look. When you need a new banker, lawyer or accountant, you usually look for word-of-mouth referrals, for the endorsement of someone you know and trust. It's the same with distributors.

Unleashing Your Sales Force

No matter what kind of business you run, someone had better be actively selling your product or service. As I've said above, there isn't a product or service, no matter how spectacular, that doesn't need to be marketed. For most products, that marketing activity must carry through to the immediacy of personal contact . . . selling. Retail stores obviously need an on-site staff to do this, but manufacturers can consider having their own staff or hiring outside reps. Service providers, since their businesses are typically built around individuals, generally handle sales themselves, without outside sales reps. Independent insurance agents would be an obvious exception to this principle.

Training Your Retail Sales Staff

If you're a retailer, the situation is simple, if very competitive. You need to convert a high percentage of the customers who walk in the door (or call on the phone) into purchasers. This book isn't the place to talk about how to set up a store physically to encourage your customers to buy. But you can train your sales staff in the fundamentals of face-to-face retail selling:

- Salespeople should be actively helpful and friendly, without seeming to exert sales pressure.

- They should listen to the customer, find out the reason he or she is buying your product and then try to help fill the need, not simply sell one particular item.

- Your staff should be well-trained in the psychology of dealing with customer—especially unhappy ones—as well as in the details of processing returns and in your basic sales philosophy.

- Salespeople should encourage cross-selling. If someone's buying a shirt, think tie. If a bouquet, think vase. If a particular CD, think other CDs by similar artists. It's a basic sales technique.

Selling in the business-to-business marketplace (or the professional marketplace) requires a more substantial effort. This is where business-to-business sales presentations come in (see Chapter 5). Typically, your customers are not walking in the door, the products are generally more complex, and they require a higher degree of customer education. However, more and more customers in the retail world are doing their homework, and they often come to you with a good background on the purchase they're about to make. If you run a shop, make sure your sales staff is at least as educated about your products as the typical customer off the street.

On-Staff Sales Force

There's truly no substitute for an on-staff sales force that's highly trained, well-motivated and experienced in the rigors of face-to-face sales. Any other form of sales effort is a poor second choice, although economics sometimes mandates the use of contract salespeople, especially for a manufacturing business. Service providers who use a contracted sales force must be firmly in charge of their activities: The boiler-room operations created by unscrupulous service providers (insurance, investment, home repair and so on) have given such sales efforts a black eye. If you're a small manufacturing company selling regionally or nationally, keeping a salaried sales staff on the road gets costly, but the advantages of using your own salespeople make a compelling case:

- **You make the hiring and firing decisions directly.** If you're displeased with a particular rep, changing him or her can get complicated.

- **You design and administer compensation.** This gives you great flexibility and the biggest of all sticks to ensure compliance with your policies.

- **You dictate accountability.** You can require and demand call reports, follow-up on trouble spots, greater use of cold calling and so on. With established manufacturer's reps, you may not have the leverage to dictate too many of the rules of engagement.
- **You handle the training, so your sales staff can be just as informed on your products as you want them to be.** With manufacturer's reps, you are one of many product lines.

There are disadvantages to an on-staff sales force as well:

- You hire them, you pay them. Salespeople are overhead, whether they're selling or not.
- To gain inroads into new markets, new salespeople are not an immediate icebreaker. They have no existing relationships, and they usually need at least a year to develop them.
- If you're working overseas, new salespeople fresh from the United States (no matter how energetic they may be) can be lost in the foreign market environment.

Contract Sales Force

Do you hire salespeople or do you have your products handled by manufacturer's representatives? Reps are typically self-employed inde-

Hired Guns Vs. Your Own Posse	
If your product is . . .	**Your sales/support should be . . .**
Company-based	Highly technical, requiring sophisticated service or application support
	A rare purchase, or one that's costly
	A critical product or service that's use is extremely important to the purchaser
Representative-based	Reps are easily trained on the product or service
	You sell to a broad geographic market and the price of your product or service is under $500

pendent contractors who specialize in a particular market and handle the products of several noncompeting (or *somewhat* noncompeting) manufacturers. They have an existing base of industrial or commercial customers whom they call on. They've often built up this list over years. Convince them to represent your line of products, and you have someone presenting your products who possesses an existing relationship of trust with your potential customers. This can be a good deal. Since reps work on commission, your costs will be minimal, other than expenses.

But in the same way manufacturers must persuade distributors to carry their line for eventual exposure to consumers, so manufacturers must also persuade reps to carry *their* line over someone else's. Reps can work with only so many lines, given that they have to develop a degree of product familiarity. And they don't want to appear to their clients as if they'll promote just any product that walks in the door.

Jargon Alert

In a case history, you tell a business story, demonstrating the problem faced by the customers and how your product solved the problem. They're often targeted at technical customers. You see them as stand-alone print pieces, as advertisements in the trade press or as recurrent themes in company brochures.

Good case histories are rich in detail, including explanatory charts and graphs. They use the real names of the players. And, of course, they end happily. A good target length for a case history is 250 words, or about one double-spaced typewritten page.

Testimonials And Case Histories

Not enough small companies take advantage of the powerful impact of detailed case histories or personalized testimonials. The impact of these documents on behalf of a small company is especially critical since smaller companies typically don't have the money that the big guys do to put behind marketing.

They say that word of mouth is the best advertising. It's true! And case histories and testimonials are the closest you'll get to having your customers calling their friends on your behalf. The reason companies often don't put them together is because they do take some trouble to assemble. However, your customers will generally be willing to talk about how pleased they are with your product or service. They'll often do so in writing. You just have to ask them and sometimes help them put the words together.

Make a point of doing both testimonials and case histories regularly.

For case histories, you'll need to alert all your salespeople (even if that's just you) to keep their eyes open for an interesting, amusing or revealing use of your product. Think about the benefit inventory you did for your product in the last chapter.

Jargon Alert

Testimonials are the words of the customer. They can range from brief kudos—"These guys saved my job"—to longer recountings of how the product or the company have performed impressively. Testimonials are often used in selling services. The more well-known the testimonial-giver, the more powerful its impact.

How To

Use case histories to close sales. Imagine you're in a sales situation where the prospect still isn't convinced you're the firm for the job. It's one thing to talk about all the work you've done in a particular field. But when you take out six or eight case histories—which detail the clients you've worked with, the projects you've tackled and the excellent outcomes—your prospect will be impressed. For those sales where you can't put an actual product on the table, case histories are invaluable.

How can you select case histories that reveal different aspects of your product? If the durability of your product is a strong selling point, get some case histories that illustrate it. Perhaps you remember John Cameron Swayze and the watch that just kept on ticking (Timex before they went digital)?

One accounting firm has a series of about a dozen case histories that detail the background of the client company, why they came to the accounting firm in the first place and how the firm was able to solve their particular problem. These case histories give the accounting firm the ability to highlight its expertise and build on its strengths.

A construction company that

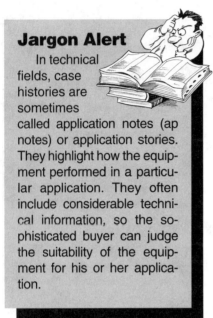

Jargon Alert

In technical fields, case histories are sometimes called application notes (ap notes) or application stories. They highlight how the equipment performed in a particular application. They often include considerable technical information, so the sophisticated buyer can judge the suitability of the equipment for his or her application.

specializes in assisted-living projects for seniors has created a two-sided sheet on a number of its projects, with color photos, details of the project planning and construction, and a very benefit-oriented summation of the construction company's role in bringing the project in on time and on budget.

Each case history should be brief and focused on just one or two benefits; don't make each one sound like all the others. Give them enough character and personality to make them readable, without sounding like a prepared advertisement.

Consider case histories an ongoing project. This is especially important for small companies since you can't invest the dollars in advertising and public relations that create a grand public image. You have to work with more modest tools, which in fact prove just as effective. Every three months, each salesperson in your company should submit a list of client projects that may make interesting case histories. There's nothing like 'em.

To begin a case history, gather the core facts, along with the best contact for a follow-up interview. Then assign it to someone on your staff with a knack for writing (or hire someone outside your company to write the case history). Use photography or charts where they'll help underscore the magnificent performance of your product. Include direct quotations from your client. And if you can attach some numbers to the performance of your product—boosts in production, more satisfied customers, increased retail traffic counts and so on—it will make your case history even more compelling.

Testimonials are typically shorter comments by a customer on your product or service. They don't dwell at length on a particular application, but they make general positive "sound bites," which lend themselves well to advertising or presentation in proposals. If you have a satisfied customer, ask him or her to say something nice about your company or your product in writing. If the customer's too busy, have someone on your staff interview the customer over the phone and draft the testimonial for the customer to approve and sign. This isn't dishonest, just a time-saving technique to move things along.

Any company worth its salt should have dozens of testimonials in its marketing files. They can prove effective in presentations to companies in the same field as the testimonial giver. People tend to rely on the implicit endorsement that's part of the testimonial's appeal. Develop them all the time, and use them whenever you get the chance. And avoid the temptation to complete a dozen and then feel you have enough. You never know when the next testimonial will clinch your next client.

Chapter 7

Targeting Your Advertising To Your Business

Now comes the fun part. After all the heavy lifting of strategizing and market analysis, of benefit generation and marketing plans, of market positioning and demographics, you're at the point where you're ready to make some ads.

But wait. Not all products lend themselves well to actual advertising. You don't see much advertising for funeral homes, for example, or for advertising agencies (hmm, that one's worth thinking about). Many business-to-business firms (like contractors and distributors) don't advertise, even in the trade press. If your product is a sophisticated high-end product with a very small audience, your actual advertising needs are minimal. That's a market better served by very targeted personal selling or informational direct-mail solicitation. You may use some ads to "soften up the market," but your sales will require more work than a few ads.

How To

Make an ad larger or run it more often? Every small-business person wants to get the most out of an ad budget. But this common question is tantalizingly difficult to answer. Experience says you should run no ad less than four times. It takes that many times for your audience to take notice of it. If you have a publication that's targeted very precisely at your market, then you should go for the larger ad running fewer times. If you're running in a more general market publication, where your customers make up only a small percentage of the readership, go with a smaller ad and run it more often.

The vast majority of businesses, of course, benefit by advertising, whether it's to the general public through the mass media (nationally or locally) or through very targeted publications (some with circulations in the four digits) that speak directly to the people who make the buying decision.

Advertiser trends come and go. For years, we saw no advertising by hospitals or doctors, by lawyers or accountants, by dentists or psychologists, by banks or credit unions. Those that tried it were sued or bad-mouthed by their peers. Many didn't think it was appropriate for their image: "People will think we're just a business soliciting customers."

That's all changed. The financial and medical communities now make up a large percentage of advertising at the local level. Loosening of regulatory pressures has accounted for some of this emergence of advertising, but so has competition. In major metropolitan areas, television spots for lawyers blanket the airwaves, promising quick and lucrative settlement of injury cases, offering help with establishing job-related injuries, and guaranteeing a painless entry into the world of contemporary personal bankruptcy.

Of all the different aspects of marketing we've looked at so far, creating and placing advertising costs by far the most money. Most of what you've done up to this point in your marketing has created only internal costs—salaries and overhead. Maybe you've gotten involved with a consultant or two on market or customer surveys, but your wallet hasn't yet been seriously damaged.

Once you get into real live advertising, you must take out the checkbook and start signing your name. In Chapter 5, we saw that some buyers get squeamish at the close of a sales presentation, when it's time to place an order and pony up some cash. You should feel the same way about advertising. Is your product or service one of those that actually benefits from advertising in the print or electronic media? Can you reach your best buying audience for a reasonable dollar through paid advertising? Can you objectively justify your advertising choices? Where does your competition advertise . . . and why?

The Basics Of A Good Ad . . . In Any Medium

OK. Let's say your market is very reachable by advertising. You've selected the media that speaks most directly to your prospective customers by asking them which media they're most likely to read, watch or listen to. You've also reviewed media kits and studied the demographics of each media's audience. You've found some venues that focus quite well on your target audience: They don't give you a lot of "waste"—audience members who wouldn't be interested in your product.

Speak To Me, Baby	
If you're selling . . .	**You should consider . . .**
Skateboards	Hippest radio station in town
Classical music CDs	Concert programs for classical performers
Financial services	Upscale city magazines, business pages of the local newspaper and radio or television financial programs
Business cleaning services	Local business magazine, business pages of newspaper
Family dining	High-listenership radio, newspapers, local shoppers, billboards, transit (buses)
Home health-care services	Newspaper, radio and TV shows with older audiences, shoppers, specialty elderly newspapers

Insight

You can't buy steak with a hamburger budget. But at least buy good-quality hamburger. You probably can't afford to run a full-page color ad. But the very small ads (page after page of them) in some publications don't have much of a chance to make an impact. Go with fewer publications and fewer insertions to pump up your ad size and get noticed.

But what should the ad say? If you say everything you think needs saying, you'll need four pages. With all the thinking you've done about your product and your customers and how they use your product, you're brimming with persuasive arguments on why certain people just gotta buy what you've got.

The first thing you have to contend with before you're ready to put together your ad is the public's resistance to advertising itself. Most Americans see hundreds of thousands of ads each year. We've all become immune to a lot of advertising as a self-protective adaptation. If we didn't, we'd go crazy. So we don't really hear the commercial message blasted in our ear when we're on hold on the telephone. We rarely notice the ads on the side of city buses, on bus benches, on shopping carts at the grocery store, or circling the stadium as the local university takes to the gridiron. When we read magazines or newspapers, we skim over the ads vying for our attention, noticing the pictures perhaps but not ingesting the message to buy. It's as if we are continually creating internal computer security measures while hackers, the ads themselves, keep trying to break in: the more innovations one side comes up with, the more quickly the other side develops a countermeasure. It's a constant tug-of-war.

You must become a hacker. Your ad must break through the advertising clutter and the self-protective apathy of your potential customers. An advertisement has a simple task, really. It's designed to get the reader, listener or viewer to do (typically, buy) something. It can compel this behavior by persuasive information or by emotional appeal.

How an ad does this is represented by the operatic acronym AIDA: attention, interest, desire and action. First you get your prospect's attention, then you build interest, this swells to desire, and it culminates in action.

- Hey, that's a neat picture of a tall, cold beer.
- Boy, a day like today's a great one for a beer.
- Say, it's 85 degrees out there, and I'd really like to have one myself right now.
- Honey, I'm driving down to Steve's for a six-pack. Be right back.

In this case, quenching your thirst is the benefit that's being sold. But not every ad relies on selling benefits. A lot of consumer advertising sells an appealing "lifestyle," and it establishes a link between the desirable lifestyle and your product. The consumer is attracted to the lifestyle and becomes drawn to your product. This "transference" forms the basis of celebrity endorsements. C'mon—how much does Michael Jordan know about batteries? Or Jim Palmer about mortgage financing?

Despite this, most advertising relies on carefully crafted benefits, set like diamonds in an entertaining and informational format.

What makes a good ad?

Many long books have been written on just this topic, and some good rules of thumb have emerged from all this head-scratching. But remember, there are always notable exceptions to each of these "rules." Recall that marketing is part science and part art, and ads may be the most mercurial ingredient of all.

1. **An ad must be clear.** Many creative types in the advertising profession don't always buy this, but if your reader doesn't under-

Head Case

Here are some sample headlines. You want short heads (usually no more than 10 words) that will typically work with a visual. They should have a benefit in them. And they should be customer-focused. (For advice on writing body copy, see the "Creating Good Ad Copy" section on page 128.)

- Quick And Painless Preparation Of Your Taxes. Guaranteed!
- Enjoy A Beautiful Lawn For Pennies A Day. No Sweat.
- The Flavorful Bounty Of Italy . . . Come!
- Mexico: More Affordable Than Ever Before.

stand your cleverness—or has to work to figure out what you're trying to do—you've created a poor ad. Don't make the target audience work. Amusement and entertainment are fine, but not at the cost of clarity. Make your message unambiguous. Think of the old restaurant signs: They didn't say "Cosimo's Trattoria" or "Pierre's Bistro." They just said "Eat." Hungry?

2. **An ad must be simple.** This flows from rule number one. Don't fall into the trap of trying to put eight different benefits in an ad. If you get your reader or listener to remember one thing from an ad, you've done a fine job and you should take the rest of the week off. If the person remembers two things, you should enter the Advertising Hall of Fame.

Hone your appeal down to its simplest form. Go for unity of impression.

For instance, in a print ad, make your headline short and powerful, promising an important benefit. Then have the body copy pay off the headline, explaining how possessing your product will deliver the benefit to the user. Of course, you want to make the advertisement interesting and engaging, but informative and compelling are critical. Get their attention, get their interest, kindle their desire and move them to action. Then you get their money. It's a good thing.

Taking Action

You get action by increasing urgency. Stress the short-term nature of the opportunity. Underscore how simple it is to get the benefit of the product . . . with just a phone call. Offer additional information for a phone call or returned coupon. Connect a benefit directly with the action line.

- Our smart copiers will change the way your business handles paper. Call now for more free information.

- A full-body massage won't just make your day . . . it will make your week! Set up an appointment today.

- Make a decision now to change the financial path of the rest of your life. Give me a call today.

- These special-value prices will last for only three more weeks. Don't miss out.

3. **An ad must impel to action.** You want your customers to do something after reading or hearing your ad. Maybe you want them to go to your restaurant for dinner next Saturday. Maybe you want them to call your 800-number to order multiple truckloads of foam floor padding. Maybe you want them to cut out the coupon and redeem it for a discount on a basket of variegated geraniums. Maybe you want the home handyman to look for Tightman pliers the next time he's in the hardware store. We'll talk about "institutional advertising" a little later, in which the "call to action" is less strident. But in most cases, you want action. That's what you're spending your money for. Especially for a small business, you can't be running advertisements that aren't single-mindedly focused on generating a response. When the reader/listener/viewer has finished your ad, what does he or she feel compelled to do? Make sure you're not simply providing information.

4. **An ad must be intrusive.** You don't penetrate advertising clutter by looking like everyone else. You have to stand out in some way: with an attention-getting headline, with an intriguing visual, with an eye-catching graphic, with attractive design or with the striking use of color.

Never run an advertisement in any medium without studying the ads already running there. Such a survey will tell you several things:

- Who thinks it's a good place to advertise

- Who doesn't

- The level of "ad design": Is it *Pipefitter's Monthly* or *Architectural Digest?* Run a cheap-looking ad in an expensive publication and you'll get little response. You won't look trustworthy.

How To

If you can afford only a small ad, make the most of it:

- Don't fill it up with teeny copy.

- Add even a small visual for impact.

- Use color if you can afford it.

- Use a heavier border or a bolder typeface for your headline.

- Make it a different shape.

- Use more than one small ad on the same page.

- Use artwork that makes your ad look like someone's circled or highlighted it with a marker.

The size of typical ads: For many publications (trade, business and consumer), a partial page ad (called a fractional) puts you in the back of the book. Buying a small ad can prove to be a false economy.

You measure intrusiveness, then, by the ad environment in which you'll be appearing. Producing spots for local television can cost less than a thousand dollars in a smaller market. But placing a cheap spot (which will still be plenty expensive) on a major TV network will make you intrusive in the worst sense of the word. You'll be the trailer park on Rodeo Drive, the Hawaiian shirt on the Champs Elysée.

While the "Ad Strategy Work Sheet" (on page 129) isn't the best way to teach creativity, especially in creating print and broadcast advertising, it helps you think clearly about what you want. We've all seen wonderfully inventive ads at the low-budget, small-market level, as well as remarkably inane ones at the high-budget, full-network level. Creating advertising isn't easy, especially when you're pressured to be innovative.

Creating Good Ad Copy

Simply put, an ad should be interesting to read. This is, obviously, easier said than done, but keep the four basic elements of an ad in mind (clarity, simplicity, impulse to action and intrusiveness), and follow these basic guidelines from advertising copywriters:

Ad Strategy Work Sheet

This work sheet will help you solidify your thinking about your ad, whether it's for print or broadcast. It will keep you from simply throwing something together to meet a deadline. Ad ad gives you the opportunity to make a brief presentation to your prospects. Don't you want to think a bit about what you'll say?

1. What's the target audience of this ad?

2. Why are you running this ad?

3. Which media will run this ad?

4. Which products are you featuring in this ad?

5. What benefits do you want to communicate to the target audience?

Continued

Ad Strategy Work Sheet, cont'd.

6. How do you support those benefits? How do you convince the reader the benefit is true?

7. What do you want this target audience to do?

8. Other important information (size, colors, length, other campaign elements and so on):

1. Use an active voice, not a passive voice.
   - "This vacuum sucks up dirt." **Not** "Dirt is removed by this vacuum."
   - "Everyone will love this dish." **Not** "This meal will be enjoyed by everyone."
   - "These roses will beautify your home." **Not** "Your home will be beautified by these roses."
   - "We'll return your car good as new." **Not** "Your car will be returned in excellent condition."

2. Use energetic verbs and phrases, not dull or tepid ones.
   - "These training techniques will transform your business." **Not** "These training techniques will effect a change in your business."
   - "Pack a lunch and come for the day." **Not** "Bring something to eat; the seminar will last past lunch."
   - "Make the cash register ring." **Not** "Increase gross revenues."

3. Be specific, not general or abstract.

   - "Saves you $75 to $100 every time you use it." **Not** "Saves you money."

   - "Lasts for 20 years on a typical home." **Not** "Long-lasting."

   - "You can use it every-where." **Not** "This principle is adaptable to a range of situations."

4. Use "you"—speak to the customer. You're explaining a desirable benefit to another human being.

   - "Your family will see the difference." **Not** "Most families are able to notice a difference."

   - "Boost your profits in the next quarter." **Not** "Typical users realize an increase in profit."

   - "We'll bring you information you can use." **Not** "Information will be provided to all subscribers."

5. Make your ad no longer than it has to be. And how long is that? As long as it takes to communicate your key benefit to your customer. Technical products typically need longer copy than consumer products. But post-Seinfeldian companies like Lands' End and J. Peterman have made millions by extolling the arcane in lively and lovely writing.

   You can probably write both a successful long ad and a successful short ad for your product. If you think that's true, opt for the short ad—at least initially. It will be cheaper (because it takes up less space) and less likely to zip by your customer unnoticed.

6. Keep headlines short. Don't dilute the impact of the headline's larger type by diffusing it across too many words. A headline should be no more than 10 words. If it's longer than that, it's not a headline, just an overambitious lead paragraph.

   Let's take the headlines from the sidebar on page 125 and look

---

Jargon Alert

"Copy" is the word advertising agencies and media use in talking about the words in an advertisement or press release. The people who write copy professionally are called copywriters. Don't confuse this with copyright, the legal right of ownership to an artistic or intellectual product.

at some body copy for them. Remember that the body copy has to pay off the promise offered in the headline.

- Quick And Painless Preparation Of Your Taxes. Guaranteed!

  Supporting copy: Tax season is here, and you're probably feeling the heat. New rules from Washington. The April 15 pressure cooker. Financial penalties for mistakes. Hours locked up with piles of receipts and endless government forms. There's a better way.

  Johnson Tax Service takes the pressure off your shoulders. We've been making taxpayers smile for 11 years, with quick, patient and economical tax form preparation and filing.

- Enjoy A Beautiful Lawn For Pennies A Day. No Sweat

  Supporting copy: You can have a luscious, weed-free, family-pleasing lawn with just a single phone call. Our climate isn't easy for grass. Growing a rich, beautiful lawn takes special knowledge and lots of hard work. If you just want to enjoy your lawn, call Berger Lawn Services for a free estimate on a season of lawn pleasure—without a drop of sweat. Call before March 10 and get free reseeding of trouble spots!

- The Flavorful Bounty Of Italy . . . Come!

  Supporting copy: Take the family on a little trip . . . and taste Italy's rich flavors in delicious pasta dishes, specialty pizzas, hearty homemade soups, chicken parmesan and a wide range of healthy salads. And don't forget our Italian desserts! Cappadona's specializes in families, so you can feed your entire crew for a modest price. And everyone loves our Italian specialties, from the grandkids to the grandfolks.

- Mexico: More Affordable Than Ever Before.

  Supporting copy: Air fares to Mexico have dropped dramatically in the last six months. So you can take in the sites, sounds and tastes of the exciting Mexican culture at bargain prices. The flight that

How To

Use advertising's "magic words" to ensure your ad's impact

We all react positively to the tried-and-true nuggets of persuasion: "free," "new," "now," "improved," "easy," "extra," "special," "proven," "value," "sale," and "limited time."

Tricks Of The Trade

One trick designers use to organize an ad visually is to use what's called the "grid system." Imagine placing a tic-tac-toe grid over your ad so that two vertical lines run from top to bottom and two horizontal lines run left to right, dividing your ad into nine sections. Where these lines sit is not important; they can slide one way or the other.

What is critical is that they provide a *visual organizing principle*, like the street grid in a city. Align all the elements of the ad (visual, headline, body copy, logo, address) so they are balanced in the grid. This keeps the elements from looking randomly placed.

costs $249 in August costs just $155 if you book your flight by the end of April and fly within 90 days. And we at M. Breen Travel will throw in our "Enjoying Mexico" booklet at no extra charge. Take that vacation you deserve and spend your money *there*, rather than *getting there*.

Creating Clean Ad Design

The elements of effective advertising design parallel those of strong ad copy.

1. **Your design should be clean and uncluttered.** Let the design lead the eye of the reader through the ad without distracting the reader from the flow of the visual and the copy.

2. **Make the visuals large enough.** If you're going to use an illustration or photo (which is usually a good decision), make sure you make it large enough to make an impact. Small photos don't create much of an impression. The eye reacts more strongly to bold pictures.

3. **Steal ad designs that appeal to you.** Yes, you're authorized to steal—not the ads themselves but design styles. Most of the large ads in trade publications are put together by professional designers. Imitation is the sincerest form of flattery, so flatter them royally and use variations on their designs to make your ad look good. If you're working with a designer or ad agency, don't be afraid to show your team ads that you like.

4. **White space is not wasted space.** Avoid the temptation to pack every centimeter of your ad with copy and visuals. Readers won't know what to focus on, and it can be too busy. Leaving some "white space" around the important parts of your ad will highlight them, and it gives the reader's eye a chance to rest.

5. **Be conservative with type.** The enormous assortment of neat typefaces can be intoxicating to businesspeople new to creating their own ads. The best ads don't use more than one or two typefaces, often just one for the headline and another for the body copy.

Do You Need An Ad Agency?

Advertising agencies contain specialists in marketing, advertising creation and media analysis and placement. Large companies, with budgets in the millions, almost always use advertising agencies, often more than one. In popular culture, ad people are often stereotyped as hucksters, but sober marketing types at the nation's most conservative companies choose advertising agencies with straight faces. What do they see in ad agencies? They see smart professionals who, at their best, know how to connect to an audience and persuade them to buy.

Here are the main benefits of using ad agencies:

Jargon Alert
Commercial artists usually start designing an ad by doing "thumbnails"—tiny rough versions of the ad, perhaps the size of a playing card (perhaps artists' physical thumbnails used to be bigger). Should the visual go here . . . or here? It's a cheap and easy way to experiment with the basic structure of the ad.

1. **You get professionals.** Your product benefits from the skills of people who market and advertise for a living. When you market and create advertising for yourself, it's a part-time job. Your main job is running your company, manufacturing stainless-steel sinks or retailing jelly beans. You don't have the background you'll typically find at an ad agency.

2. **You get experience.** Agency professionals have marketed and advertised for hundreds of clients in all sorts of markets. Just as you've become

Talking About Your Business (Stage 3)

Here's another chance to take a quiz on your business and its marketing.

1. How many different advertisements have you prepared for your company?

2. For each ad, list the publication in which it will appear and why.

3. For broadcast media, why have you chosen a particular station on which to advertise?

4. Which customer segments have you not yet produced an ad for? Why?

5. Which products or services have you not yet produced an ad for? Why?

an expert in your business by working with all sorts of product challenges, so the ad pros have learned a few tricks along the way that they can turn to your advantage. If you're lucky and you choose wisely, you can get an agency with strong experience in the very market you're selling to. This can be an absolutely tremendous advantage.

3. **You get connections.** Most advertising agencies have deep connections with the media, certainly on the local level. They know

Does The Shoe Fit?

Advertising agencies come in all shapes and sizes. Most have fewer than 10 people; some have thousands. Your tiny local ad shop may be quite excellent, while a large high-profile agency may be lackluster. A number of small agencies are "boutiques," which rely to some degree on freelancers (often moonlighting from larger agencies) to do the creative work. And design studios will often portray themselves as "full service" agencies. Don't get more agency than you need. If you have "bicycle needs," don't hire a "Mercedes."

All advertising agencies offer creative services, account management and media buying. Most offer some public relations and market research. Shop around when you are looking for an ad agency, ask questions to find out the nature of the company you'll be dealing with, and make sure that the services they offer match your needs. Do you see some local advertising you like? Call the advertiser who created the ads. Many communities have a local advertising federation that can also give you a list of agencies to consider, although they don't typically give referrals.

how to buy broadcast media effectively and efficiently. They know the media representatives from the stations. They know the printers who create your brochures. They know the publishers who put out the newspaper and city/regional magazines. They know marketing research firms that can bring you insights into your target audience. If you're traveling in a strange land, it's very helpful to have a knowledgeable local to make the arrangements for you.

4. **You get a team.** The ad agency has people to make a campaign or project run smoothly: writers, designers, marketers, traffic people, media specialists and support staff. They know how to work together, and they know how to schedule.

Of course, ad agencies get a bad rap. They are known as smiling generalists with no discernible skills—just a bunch of order takers and commission grabbers who don't know the meaning of hard work. But they are no different from any profession: largely trustworthy and competent but not without flaws. The advertising profession suffers from some marketing problems of its own in terms of public perception.

Targeting Your Advertising To Your Business

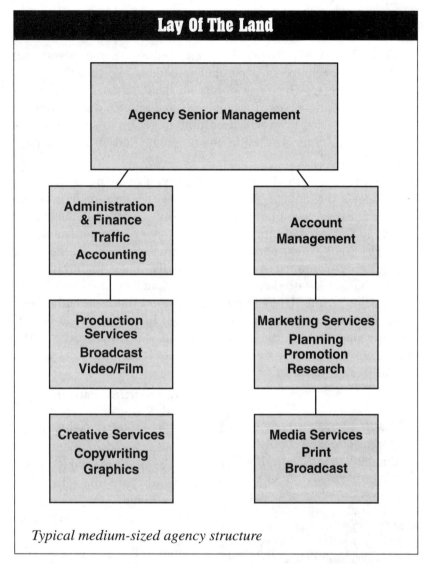

Lay Of The Land

Agency Senior Management

Administration & Finance
Traffic
Accounting

Account Management

Production Services
Broadcast
Video/Film

Marketing Services
Planning
Promotion
Research

Creative Services
Copywriting
Graphics

Media Services
Print
Broadcast

Typical medium-sized agency structure

Ad agencies can raise your blood pressure with some common downsides:

1. **They're expensive.** Sticker shock doesn't just come from automobiles and houses. Creating a brochure can run thousands and thousands of dollars before it even reaches the printer's door. Developing a marketing plan will also involve hundreds of hours at hourly rates ranging from $75 to $200, depending on the market. Small businesses especially are often thunderstruck at how inflated agency bills can become . . . and how quickly. Here is one

criticism that is largely true: Ad agencies don't do a good job of preparing their clients for costs or of justifying them after the fact.

2. **Their broad experience is often shallow.** Some advertising agencies specialize in a particular market, like technology, finance or retail. But most don't. So their expertise, like South Dakota's Platte River, is a mile wide and an inch deep. Even the smartest agency team will need time to get up to speed on your product and your marketing environment. And guess who pays for that time?

3. **You may get the B team.** Unless you're a big advertising spender, you may be delegated down the line to the newest, most inexperienced people at the agency. Agency management may have these people work on small, marginally profitable accounts (like yours, perhaps) before trusting them on the more profitable accounts. Ad firms typically make their pitch for your business with their most seasoned, most capable, most impressive people. If you sign on the dotted line, suddenly those people don't show up at the meetings. Instead, you get bright, shiny people long on enthusiasm and short on street smarts. You've taken on a training assignment for the agency. And you're paying for it.

How To

Want to get your readers to notice your ad? Use the testimonial of a current customer speaking of the virtues of your product or service. It works with celebrities, and it works with people on the street. People are leery of advertising, but they believe what someone tells them, which is the essence of a testimonial. Put together a testimonial by a typical product user and watch the results.

4. **Ad agencies can be "yes men."** Because advertising agencies are typically much smaller than their clients, they can exhibit a natural tendency toward paranoia. To keep their clients, they may tend to go along with whatever the client wants to do—too timid to disagree or argue the opposing point of view. If your agency can't lead, they shouldn't be your agency. You shouldn't pay expert's prices for less-than-expert advice.

5. **The language barrier.** Not only are discussions about marketing communications particularly prone to mis-

understanding, but in working with an agency, you will also typically be communicating through several layers of people. Your main contact is usually an account representative; you normally won't talk directly to the staff writing or designing your materials. Then you're telling an ad person what you think of your market and how you think the ads have to work. Will the agency person come back to you with ads you think are marvelous? Or, as often happens, especially in new relationships, will the painful climb up the learning curve commence?

> **Insight**
> The larger your print ad, the more likely it will be noticed. But you'll pay more for a larger ad. In general, go for the largest ad you can afford. It will increase the impact of your ad and lead to a greater response. It also gives you more room for information on your product or service—along with that eye-catching visual.

Freelancers Vs. Agencies

If you spend less than $25,000 a year on advertising, you're probably not a good candidate for an advertising agency. You'll either be too small for them—in terms of how much gross profit they can make from your business—or you'll be too unimportant to them after they do take you on as a client.

At this spending level, you should use freelance talent to produce your materials and campaigns. It's not hard to find competent freelancers who'll work with you on an hourly basis; expect to pay $40 to $90 an hour for experienced people. It's like building a house. If you hire a general contractor, you've got to pay him or her money to keep everything running smoothly. If *you* hire the individual contractors (plumbers, carpenters, electricians and so on) and act as the coordinating general contractor yourself, you'll save a lot of money . . . but you'll work for that money you save.

If you want to handle things yourself, get your thinking done first (market focus, customer selection, benefit inventory and so on). Then talk to your friends and colleagues in business for referrals to freelancers. Use the Yellow Pages as a last resort. Once you have some candidates, interview them to see how they fit with your needs. You're looking for people who know what they're doing, so find out who they've worked for (and call these references), review work samples, ask them how they price and look at some projects that are representative of their pricing (ask specifically how much they charged to write or design each brochure or sales letter). Make sure your writer and your designer can work together (or you'll regret it). Introduce them to each other (although they'll likely already know each other) and have a three-way discussion of the project and possible approaches. You'll be able to tell the chemistry pretty quickly.

Another low-cost alternative—which entails a little extra risk—is to contact a local technical college or art school and have some students work on your materials as a project or as a way to gain experience. You can also contact small newspapers in your area and ask if any staff members do advertising copy or design on the side. If you go this route, provide lots of focused input and be prepared to be patient. But you'll save a fortune.

If you spend more than $100,000 a year, you ought to have an advertising agency, for marketing consulting and creative work, if nothing else. With that amount of money going out the door in marketing, you need high-level thinking behind your efforts. And unless you're a very large company, you can't justify the salaries of marketing and advertising specialists on board. Even the giants with large and professional marketing departments use layers of ad agencies to refine their internal thinking, bring them new ideas and execute their plans.

If your marketing spending is in the middle ($25,000 to $100,000 annually), you fall in the gray area. If you want to save the 20 percent of your budget you'll probably spend on an agency and do the strategic thinking and creation of materials yourself, give it a try. If you'd rather rely on experts to do the job for you—with all the risks that involves—then try an agency relationship for a year and see how you feel about it. Some people wash their own cars; others take them to the carwash. What kind of person are you? Either way you decide about an agency, you bear the risk.

If you decide on a detailed relationship with an advertising agency, they will probably want to be appointed as the "agency of record," a term much valued by ad people. It means that they're your official agency, and that you won't give significant projects to other agencies. In your favor, it also indicates a level of commitment on your part that will (or should) stimulate the agency to invest some time (unbilled) to building up their expertise on your market and your product line. It also gives them a warm, fuzzy feeling that makes them more comfortable in contracting for advertising space and printing costs on your behalf. Nearly every ad agency has been stung by non-paying clients and forced to pay media bills out of their own pockets. The "agency of record" relationship has something for both sides.

Danger

I've worked in ad agencies and as a freelancer for 20 years, and I know from experience what happens when clients aren't able to guide agencies or freelancers in doing their work. When ad agencies don't understand the chain of approvals for creative materials, and they're locked out of the company budgeting process, bad things happen: spoiled relationships, wasted money and poor marketing.

But don't let the "agency of record" moniker be used against you. Some agencies come to believe that they have a monopoly on your advertising and marketing budget. You don't want that. For most small companies, a one-year contract is plenty. It gives the agency some security, while the client company can move to another agency within a year if it's not satisfied.

Here are some tips on working efficiently with advertising agencies or with experienced freelancers:

1. **Insist on detailed written communications.** This includes meeting reports, in which the agency recaps the results of meetings between your company and its representatives. You review the report to make sure what's there is complete and accurate. Document your phone conversations. Use e-mail or faxes when appropriate to document decisions and agreements.

   I'm not implying you should mistrust the agency. But marketing is a complicated and expensive business, and the relationship between client and agency must stand up to the stress of the marketplace. Documenting paperwork keeps both sides confident in the integrity of the other. Agencies or freelancers don't want clients claiming they never gave the go-ahead for television production; clients don't want the agencies placing media buys without their approval.

2. **Decide on frankness up-front.** Like all business relationships (including the one between you and your customers), this connection depends on the idea of a fair exchange. Both of you have to get something out of the relationship. You have to be willing to communicate the good and the bad to your account executive. Yes, you like this brochure design; no, you don't like this ad. And then give reasons.

3. **Be willing to pay for good work.** In a good agency relationship, you're getting talented, experienced people devoting their time to thinking of ways to help your business grow. It's the same with seasoned freelancers. You've got to pay them for that time. While you should scrutinize all bills closely, don't nickel-and-dime your agency unless you've seen indications that there's trouble brewing. If you're satisfied with the product, don't balk at paying a fair price.

4. **Be clear about your needs, and be open to feedback.** You have to manage your freelancers or your advertising agency. You need to guide them—communicating with them clearly, making decisions and giving them reasons for your decisions. An ad agency can't do its job properly if it isn't sure what you want, doesn't know whose opinion to follow and doesn't know why things get changed or canceled.

   Conversely, if you insist that your agency always agree with you, you don't need professionals—you need servants. You have to be prepared to be told things you don't want to hear. You must listen to presentations objectively, with your clearest thinking. You are, of course, the one who signs the checks, but if an ad agency has earned your respect enough for you to hire them, then you should listen to the professional advice and experience they have to offer.

5. **If you don't understand your market, chances are your agency won't understand it either.** Especially in the initial stages, an agency or freelancers are going to depend on you for some start-up guidance. Don't even think about bringing some creative people in if you don't know what your market is. If you're at a loss to identify it, you need a market research firm or some professional trade seminars, not an agency.

The Wonderful World Of Media

Most small businesses tend to restrict their actual advertising to the print or broadcast media. Indeed, these are the best and most flexible media in which to send your message, and this section discusses them in detail. However, there are other less-common options you might consider for special situations, such as billboards, transit advertising (bus benches), and site advertising (bowling alleys and ball parks). If any of these secondary venues strike you as right for your market, call the local billboard or bus company or site manager. They'll be more than happy to share their advertising possibilities.

Insight

Paradoxically, this rise in specialized print media takes place at the same time that we all can't help but notice that "people don't read anymore." Audiobooks, *People* magazine, stagnant book sales, Gen X/MTV—people may still be curling up, but it's not with printed matter as much as in the past. So the golden age of print specialization is taking place in a stressful time for the overall print medium.

Print Advertising

Print advertising, depending on your product and market, gives you a wide range of options, including newspapers, shopping circulars and a wide variety of magazines. All these avenues, however, are facing pressures (good and bad) due to changes in technology and the explosion of advanced database marketing capabilities. This is not a good time to be a general publication: They're the ones facing tough times.

Publishers can now make money with smaller press runs than they could in the past, and advanced databases give them the ability to target very particular slices of the market. In the past, a general sports magazine might be designed to appeal to all men ages 25 to 45, and that was it. Now there are scores of magazines targeting different portions of that same demographic and subtargeted by sport.

So let's say you're a jogger who's also interested in rock climbing and world soccer. You can subscribe to several publications in each of those interest areas. Soon you're getting five magazines that speak directly to your interests. Where does that leave the general sports magazine, which unavoidably includes a share of articles that don't appeal to you? Nowhere—certainly not in your house. Magazine evolution mirrors animal evolution, with more and more specialization as time passes.

So the large-circulation magazines are under pressure from more specialized media. This is good for small business. Smaller circulation magazines are cheaper to advertise in, and more magazines speaking to more precise targets is a very good thing for businesses like yours.

For print advertising, you have five broad choices:

- Newspapers
- Shoppers
- Consumer magazines
- Business magazines
- Trade magazines

Newspapers

Newspapers are a good medium for local retail advertising because of their "hometown" focus, and most food coupons are carried by newspapers (Tuesday is traditionally coupon day). Below are the basic pluses and minuses of newspapers as a medium:

Newspapers are generally eager—perhaps too eager—to work with new retail accounts, giving them a bewildering range of advertising space contracts from which to choose. You buy space by the column inch: one column by 1 inch is 1 column inch. A 10-column-inch ad can be two columns by 5 inches or four columns by 2½ inches. Some newspapers have gone to a "modular format," which restricts the size and shape of the ads they'll carry. Get a rate card from the newspapers you're interested in. The newspaper masthead

Newspapers	
Plus	**Minus**
Low-cost (compared with other options)	Lots of waste circulation (unless you're retail)
Large circulation (big percent of some demographics)	Poor production quality (color still risky)
Targetable by section (business, sports, local and so on	Little long-term effect (an ad hits the birdcage on day two)
Quick impact (within a week)	Easy for your ad to get lost (much clutter)

will give you the number to call. The rate card will give you demographic information on readership, as well as a complete picture of their advertising rates. The rate card will show you which sizes and shapes you can use. Color has become much easier for newspapers; even the establishment *The New York Times* now proudly bears a color photo on the front page of each edition. The quality of color printing in smaller papers has been improving.

The more space you contract for, the lower your rate. The big local advertisers—food stores, car dealerships, electronics retailers—enjoy sweetheart deals because of their big spending.

If your target is the general consumer, newspapers should be in your media plan. They reach a lot of people, most of whom are looking for things to purchase (cars, vacations, a restaurant experience, groceries, camera equipment and on and on). The newspaper advertising department can provide you with more information than you can read on the buying habits of their readership.

If your target is businesses, the business section of the local paper provides a reasonably good vehicle for your advertising if used in conjunction with other approaches. Local businesspeople typically have no place else to go, since broadcast media is notoriously weak in business at the local level. But remember, your ad dollar is buying the entire circulation. If your product appeals to many area businesses, it's a good deal. If your product is specialized with a tightly focused appeal, you should probably look elsewhere.

As the print media specialize, we're beginning to see some specialized newspapers, especially in larger towns and cities. Entertainment publications have grown enormously in popularity, as have periodic newspapers speaking solely to the elderly market. If you're

How To

The Yellow Pages isn't a consumer magazine, but it's a print advertising medium you should seriously consider. It can be expensive, but for many businesses, it means a steady stream of new customers. If you run a restaurant, home-repair business, medical service, heating and cooling repair shop, body shop, car dealership or other business that deals with Joe and Jane Consumer, you should be there. Go with the prime Yellow Pages for your area. Avoid all the me-too lookalike books.

Shoppers	
Plus	**Minus**
Very low cost	Very low readership
Complete household circulation	Poor production quality
Fosters hometown connection	Little long-term effect (an ad hits the bottom of the birdcage on day two)
	Easy for your ad to get lost (much clutter)
	Image buster unless handled carefully

looking for a younger, more active demographic, the entertainment newspapers are excellent, and they have a loyal readership. If your product appeals to the elderly, you can't beat the modest advertising rates of their specialty papers. Larger metropolitan areas or business regions sometimes feature business newspapers; don't miss them in reviewing the media available to you.

Shoppers

I don't know anyone who reads shopping circulars, but they've been around for years and appear like clockwork in my mailbox. There are thousands of them nationally, generally advertising low-end items or basic services to the consumer marketplace, in addition to the extensive—and sometime anthropologically interesting—classifieds. They can also serve as a venue for some shotgun public relations activities at the local level. As an advertising vehicle, they're an inexpensive way to reach your entire geographic area, but actual readership may be low. If you're a local business advertising your restaurant, car repair, home improvement or repair service, real estate agency or financial service, they're worth a try.

Consumer Magazines

Publishing technology has led to an explosion in the number of magazines targeted to the American consumer. At the current rate, we should each have a personal magazine by the year 2007. From the "shelter" publications like *House & Garden* through the galaxy of hunting and fishing journals, and zooming past the distaff cosmos of *Mademoiselle* and *Ms.*, publishers have microtargeted us like never before.

Consumer magazine circulations are audited by the ABC (Audit Bureau of Circulations). Publications usually carry their ABC-audited circulation in their media kits. If you're dealing with a non-ABC-audited publication, you have to take their word for it. And you should be skeptical.

Standard Rate and Data Service (SRDS) has a full list of all 2,700 U.S. consumer publications—at the national, regional and local levels—in 75 different subject categories (see the "Appendix" for contact information). At the national level, these are expensive publications because of their lush print formats and their large and desirable circulation. Locally (in city and state magazines), they provide a nice alternative or supplement to newspapers and broadcast. About a hundred urban centers have a city publication worth investigating. If your market is the upscale general public (the core demographic of these publications), this is a good option to investigate.

Consumer Magazines

Plus	Minus
Reasonable cost locally and regionally	Expensive nationally, and more expensive despite slowing growth
Range of precise targets	Not always easy to match to your target audience
Possibilities for PR connection	Competing with many moneyed advertisers with contracts
Excellent production quality; they look marvelous	Ads separated from editorial material
Some pass-along/waiting room readership	Very long lead time
National magazines allow some regional customization	Need several different magazines to really cover a large market

You'll buy by the page or spread (two facing pages), with half-page, quarter-page and eighth-page (and other more exotic) options. For most, full color is an option if you've got the budget.

For all of these publications, request a rate card from the publisher, which—in addition to costs—will tell you deadlines, special issues, ad material requirements and lots of good information on who reads the magazine. Magazine rates used to be non-negotiable. That's no longer true, especially if you have some ad budget firepower. If can't get a lower rate, push for better position: the closer to the front of the magazine the better, and even better—next to an article on your industry. You can also push for appearance in special issues, like the annual overview or directory issue. Remember, to the magazine, you're the customer. And the customer is always right.

If you're convinced you need to run an ad in a particular publication but haven't had the time to create one, almost all business publications can help you create a plain vanilla advertisement. Just make it good plain vanilla.

Business And Trade Magazines

For business magazines, you have national, regional and local options, with a total of more than 7,500 publications. The last decade

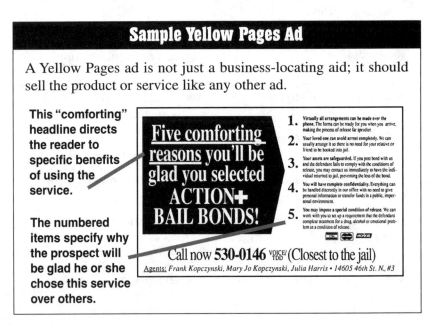

Sample Yellow Pages Ad

A Yellow Pages ad is not just a business-locating aid; it should sell the product or service like any other ad.

This "comforting" headline directs the reader to specific benefits of using the service.

The numbered items specify why the prospect will be glad he or she chose this service over others.

Five comforting reasons you'll be glad you selected ACTION+ BAIL BONDS!

1. Virtually all arrangements can be made over the phone. The forms can be ready for you when you arrive, making the process of release far speedier.
2. Your loved one can avoid arrest completely. We can usually arrange it so there is no need for your relative or friend to be booked into jail.
3. Your assets are safeguarded. If you post bond with us and the defendant fails to comply with the conditions of release, you may contact us immediately to have the individual returned to jail, preventing the loss of the bond.
4. You will have complete confidentiality. Everything can be handled discreetly in our office with no need to give personal information or transfer funds in a public, impersonal environment.
5. You may impose a special condition of release. We can work with you to set up a requirement that the defendant complete treatment for a drug, alcohol or emotional problem as a condition of release.

Call now 530-0146 VOICE/TDD (Closest to the jail)

Agents: *Frank Kopczynski, Mary Jo Kopczynski, Julia Harris • 14605 46th St. N., #3*

Rate Roundup

Most print rate cards are similar. You get discounts for the size of your ad and for the frequency with which you run it. The rate is per black-and-white ad. These figures are for a well-produced Midwestern city magazine with a circulation of just under 20,000.

	one time	four times	six times	12 times
full page	$2,235	$2,125	$1,970	$1,790
half page	$1,720	$1,380	$1,280	$1,165
sixth page	$560	$530	$495	$450

If you run four sixth-page ads in a year, you'll pay $530 each, or $2,120. If you commit to a longer contract, you'll get a correspondingly lower rate. If you don't run all the ads you're supposed to, you'll get "short-rated": Your ads will be recalculated at the appropriate rate. If, for example, you committed to a 12-time half-page rate in a year and then ran your ad just four times, you'll pay the short-rate difference—you've "shorted" the publication on insertions. Instead of four ads at $1,165, you'll pay for four ads at $1,380: a difference of $860.

has brought a boom in business publications at the city and regional level, paralleling the explosion of subnational consumer magazines. For major business-to-business approaches, these provide a prestigious, though expensive, venue.

The major national "executive" publications (*Business Week*, *U.S. News & World Report*, *Fortune* and *Forbes*) have very large circulations and are read avidly by business decision makers around the country. This business magazine category also includes smaller-circulation publications like *CEO* that speak directly to senior management, regardless of industry. Smaller, and in some ways more powerful, publications like *Chemical Engineering* and *Aviation Week* are major forces in their well-defined marketplaces. Circulation in the top thousand business publications is audited by the BPA (Business Publications Audit of Circulation). As with the

Business And Trade Magazines	
Plus	**Minus**
Most of the same pluses as the consumer publications, plus:	Most of the same minuses as the consumer publications, plus:
Very finely targeted; some reach virtually your entire target market	If you're a small, first-time advertiser it's easy to be over looked by the publication and the readership.
Many linked opportunities such as trade shows, promo-motional publications and sophisticated inquiry tracking	You're probably running advertisements among competitors with deep pockets . . . and really, really big ads.

ABC, publications typically carry their BPA-audited circulation in their media kit.

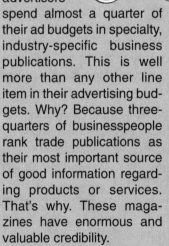

Insight

Business-to-business advertisers spend almost a quarter of their ad budgets in specialty, industry-specific business publications. This is well more than any other line item in their advertising bud-gets. Why? Because three-quarters of businesspeople rank trade publications as their most important source of good information regard-ing products or services. That's why. These maga-zines have enormous and valuable credibility.

You should know that much of the trade circulation for busi-ness magazines is unpaid— they're complimentary. These publications make their money through advertisers, not through subscribers.

The business press represents a very important avenue through which to reach companies that may buy your product. Business-people read, use and keep their publications more than con-sumers do theirs. Harry the iron foundry manager may not store his *Horse World*, but you can be sure he has a tall and well-thumbed stack of *Iron Age*. This means you can reach the exact people who make the buying de-cisions on your product, and you

Reservation For One, Please

Booking an ad is a two-part process:
1. First you sign a "space contract," which commits you to the number of annual appearances and the appropriate rate. It formalizes the agreement between you and the publication. Dates are typically left fluid for later periods in the contract.

2. When it's time for the ad to appear (months before issue date), you place an "insertion order," which commits you to a particular issue and size/color ad. Usually you'll send this in with the materials the publication will use to reproduce your ad (floppy disk or print films). Make sure you get the technical details right on the format the publication needs for your materials. This can be very confusing for the uninitiated.

can trust that they'll actually see your ad if you choose your venue wisely. This kind of certainty is worth good money to advertisers. And publishers know it.

Rate cards for business publications are similar to those for consumer publications, although the business pubs offer many more "fringes" with their advertising contracts: prime spots at their trade shows, increased acceptance of press releases and listings in various directories. They may also list you on their "bingo card"—the tear-off card that lists all the advertisers and assigns each a number. Readers return the card to the magazine with numbers checked for the companies on which they'd like to receive information. The magazine processes the leads and passes them along to you.

Broadcast Advertising: Radio And Television

Broadcast advertising used to be too expensive for small businesses. But media pressures are working in your favor. There are a rising number of radio stations for you to choose from. And cable (and the Fox, UPN and WB networks) are putting the heat on the traditional three TV networks.

Radio

For the retailer, radio is a wonderful medium. It offers the lowest "cost per thousand" (CPM) of any media, and it's done so for over 10 years. This low-cost reputation has also led radio to be underre-

Radio	
Plus	**Minus**
Mobile and everywhere	Scattered market, too many stations
Very low cost, both in air time and production	Background noise; not really heard
Timely, can be on the air in hours	Need many repetitions to make an impact
Listeners are loyal to their favorite station	Skimpy research on audiences/ listenership
Allows considerable creative flexibility	No visuals and no holdover; once heard it's gone it's gone
An excellent support media	

spected as a positive marketing force. It's generally run along with television and print, rarely by itself.

Radio sales reps sell advertising spots in dayparts:

Morning drivetime:	6 a.m. to 10 a.m.
Daytime:	10 a.m. to 3 p.m.
Afternoon drive, prime:	3 p.m. to 7 p.m.
Night:	7 p.m. to midnight
Late night:	Midnight to 6 a.m.

Stations sell listeners to their advertisers. While TV advertisers often choose specific shows for their particular demographics, you choose a radio station for its overall listener demographic— country western, middle-of-the-road, jazz, talk, classical, blues, progressive rock, you name it. All U.S. stations subscribe to the Arbitron rating service, and you can see how the various stations stack up in drawing various age groups

Jargon Alert
CUME (or cumulative rating) counts the number of listeners who are tuned in for part of any quarter hour.

and genders. You can find older copies in your local library; more recent listings will be provided by any of the stations. If you have a product or service you know has a strong appeal to people who also like religious music—or easy listening, or top 40—then radio should be in your marketing mix.

When you're looking into buying radio, talk to some businesspeople you respect who already do some radio advertising. Get the name of a trustworthy media rep from a friend in the business com-

> **Jargon Alert**
>
> AQH is average quarter-hour share. This is a radio station's listenership as a percentage of the total audience in a given area. Take a mental snapshot of who's listening at any one time during a quarter hour and that's the AQH.

munity or a colleague from a local service organization. Or just call one of your favorite radio stations to get the process started. A rep usually handles just one station, or sometimes an AM and FM pair of co-owned stations. Although the media rep profession has its share of scoundrels and ne'er-do-wells, there are some fine professionals out there who recognize the benefit of helping a new customer come to grips with a confusing business. A good rep will help you understand the language of radio, with its CUMEs and AQHs. In exchange, look to see if you can work the rep's station into your schedule . . . or tell him or her right away that it can't happen.

> **Jargon Alert**
>
> CPM is the standard measurement to compare one advertising option against another. It's always used in broadcast media, sometimes in print as well. It stands for cost per thousand. That is, how much does it cost you to reach a thousand people one time?

Most radio advertisers buy what is called a rotator or a TAP program (pronounced "tap"; stands for total audience participation). You contract for a given number of spots in a week, which the station will distribute over an agreed-upon number of dayparts at an agreed-upon percentage.

For example, you might buy 30 spots in a week, to be distributed among morning drive (45 percent), daytime (20 percent) and afternoon drive (35 percent).

You can also move one step up in targeting (and budget) by sponsoring a particular program that might appeal to your potential customers. This is common on talk- and feature-heavy AM stations.

Finally, if you're thinking beyond the local market, investigate radio networks, which are staging a comeback these days. You can choose from around 40 networks, which might offer you the selection of stations, markets and programs that will bring you mouth-to-ear with your customers.

Radio, perhaps more than any other media, is the land of deals. You can trade some of your product or service to a station for extra ad appearances. You can have one of the popular DJs do a "live read" of your advertising copy to give your product a personal push. You can make your product or service the prize for a station giveaway. An experienced radio rep has more angles than a hall of mirrors. See what kind of special deals (and prices) you can negotiate.

Television

Television has become the ultimate advertising medium. It glitters. It teems with celebrities hawking wonderful items. It's born anew each season with exciting new shows and stars. It's come to mean America in a large part of the world.

As an advertising medium for the small business, television provides great value at the local level. By local, I mean affiliates of the big three networks (ABC, CBS, NBC) and Fox, UPN and the WB. You can produce a modest spot (using the station's in-house producers) for under a thousand dollars. And you can get on the air with a reasonable schedule without venturing into five-figure territory. This may not be something you'll do each week, but—at certain times of the year—it may give you a traffic boost like no other medium.

Television	
Plus	**Minus**
The visuals, the visuals, the visuals	Television is very expensive to produce
As many different audiences as there are shows	Flashy visuals can impede sponsor name retention
Good viewer information	Networks losing ground; mass market disintegrating into cable and satellite chaos of hundreds of choices
Total flexibility in creative concept	Zappers make commercials disappear
Perhaps the best way to reach a mass audience	Floods of ads as networks and affiliates sell maybe too much ad airtime
"As seen on TV"—a distinctive place to advertise	
Local stations are very competitive, and you may be able to take advantage in negotiating rates.	

You buy television like radio, but differently. You can insist on airing during (or adjacent to) certain shows, or you can let the station make the selection with specified dayparts.

Television has different dayparts than radio does:

Morning:	6 a.m. to 9 a.m.
Midday:	9 a.m. to 4 p.m.
Fringe:	4 p.m. to 7 p.m.
Prime time:	7 p.m. to 11 p.m.
Late fringe:	11 p.m. to 1 p.m.
Late night:	1 a.m. to 6 a.m.

Prime time rates are highest, generally followed by morning and fringe. This depends to some degree on the part of the country and the season.

More than radio, television is also seasonally dependent. The fourth quarter (October to December) is busiest because of Christmas advertising. The second quarter (April to June) is next busiest, with the coming of spring and warm weather. Then the third quarter (July to September) chases people outside and demand drops. The first quarter (January to March)—the dead of winter after the flurry of holiday advertising—is the deadest (and cheapest) time in TV advertising. In election years, national or local, all media reps just *love* politicians, a major source of advertising dollars. By the way, shrewd media tradition dictates that politicians always pay their media bills upfront.

Here are some reasons why you might want to use local television:

- To draw ongoing retail traffic, especially if your product is visual (gift shop, restaurant, tourist attraction, home furnishings)

- To create a special promotion for an event, sale, grand opening or personal appearance

- To be proactive in combating new competition, which may soon be advertising itself

- To build a local brand name through a long-term, consistent advertising message

As with buying radio, I recommend you work with a responsible

Through The Wire

Cable television is a medium in its infancy, and it offers great opportunities to small businesses like yours. Cable is hungry for advertisers *and* for content. So if your business is one that can put together an occasional segment to educate the public (home decorating, landscaping, investing, real estate, physical therapy, computers for normal people and so on), you can get airtime *and* a bargain on advertising rates. Do not miss talking to your local cable stations. They represent a land of hidden opportunity. Look in your local newspaper television listing (or the Yellow Pages) for a listing of what's available. And check out the stations yourself to see which station matches up best with your potential customers.

station rep about whom you've heard good things. Buying TV time is complicated, and mistakes can be very costly.

Measuring The Effectiveness Of Your Advertising

There's no topic of more interest to advertisers of all sizes than the measurable impact of advertising on sales. Advertising is expensive, and small companies want to know they're not wasting their money.

There are a number of ways to measure how well your advertising is working for you. None of these methods is foolproof. And none of them will work for all types of businesses. But try a few of these on your advertising efforts, and you'll get a sense of how well they're doing and whether the expenditure is giving you a satisfactory return on investment.

1. **Mechanical measurements:** When you have your customers bring in a coupon or a copy of an ad to qualify for a special discount, you have absolutely clear evidence of how well your ad has drawn. You can even code your coupons to the precise appearance (publication and date). This will also work with phone calls, when you code your ad with a particular "operator number" or have callers ask for "Mr. Henderson."

2. **Before and after survey:** Sometimes your advertising isn't selling some specific item; it's designed to increase traffic generally or increase market awareness of your company and its products. You can conduct a market survey testing for the level of awareness of your company and products as compared with the competition and its products. After your awareness campaign has run, you would then retest for awareness of your company and its products. Barring outside influences, you can attribute the difference in awareness to your advertising.

3. **Customer query:** Instruct your staff to simply ask customers why they're there and how they heard about you. Tally the answers, and you'll see the effect of your advertising.

4. **Revenue measurement:** Lots of factors can impact your gross revenues, no matter what kind of business you run. But counting the till every day before, during and after an advertising campaign can tell you in absolute terms if you're doing something right.

When you make your judgments on this, allow for mitigating factors (look at the last few years, for example, to see if there's normally a seasonality to your business).

5. **Split runs:** Run two different versions of an ad—with different prices, different products and different time applicability—and measure the difference in responses. This will also allow you to learn which appeals work best with your target audience.

Chapter 8

Sales Promotions: The Turbocharger

As your marketing efforts move your company forward, you'll have times when you want to produce a heightened customer response. You might want to simply increase sales temporarily, move some inventory that's backing up, finish up with an old product before getting in a new one, try a little harder on a particular submarket—there can be lots of reasons.

Advertising is one way to do this, but a surer way is sales promotion.

The Tools Of Sales Promotion

Sales promotion works for cereal manufacturers and car makers, for magazine publishers and cigarette packagers, for lawn mower companies and brewers. All these industries and many others use the immediate impact of sales promotion to transform potential customers into actual ones, or to turn low users into moderate users. How do they do it? They bribe the customer. It's perfectly legal bribery, of course. The customers beam as they pocket some extra dollars. And the company grins about the increased volume, the new products introduced and the new market exposure to the product line.

Students of advertising define and analyze sales promotion in a number of different ways. Here we'll look at several fairly clear categories:

1. Coupons
2. Special pricing
3. Point-of-purchase promotion
4. Contests
5. Trade incentives
6. Cooperative advertising

Later in the chapter, you'll meet trade shows and specialty items (giveaways), two other types of promotion sometimes put in with sales promotion.

Jargon Alert

Although the word "promotions" is used loosely to mean almost all arenas of marketing, most professionals apply it to short-term, direct and quantifiable sales-inducing activities, often including a discount or special value offer. Examples include coupons, contests, premiums, rebates, free samples, point-of-purchase displays and incentives to the distribution channel.

Coupons

Retailers use coupons to spur sales of specific items, at specific times, among specific audiences. Coupons have become an enormous business in America, but like the airlines' frequent flier miles, they are also something of a "Frankenstein's monster"—a creation that their creator wishes had never happened. To put it another way, retailers have climbed on the back of this tiger and ridden it enjoyably for a long time. Now they're unable to dismount.

Coupons have been around for over a century, and advertisers this year will distribute more than a quarter of a trillion individual coupons. Most are distributed as inserts in the Sunday paper, but redeemers find their mailboxes flooded with special coupon packs as well. The grocery stores themselves produce a wide range of coupons, both through the newspaper and in special in-store publications.

Coupons are a proven, effective technique for making product introductions, for persuading buyers to switch from one brand to another, and for getting consumers to test products they haven't tried before or to make larger-sized purchases. It's a money thing: Use the coupon to save 35 cents when you purchase

Jargon Alert

An FSI (free-standing insert) is the glossy, full-color sheet or group of sheets that fall on your lap when you open up the Sunday newspaper. They're typically provided to the newspapers by large FSI production companies for insertion by the local newspapers. Most of the coupons are placed by large national advertisers. Ninety percent of all coupons appear through FSIs.

four rolls of product X. The expiration date on the coupon allows the manufacturer to put an end-date on the price promotion.

Grocery stores have a love/hate relationship with coupons. They like the extra sales they generate, but they hate the logistical hassle of dealing with them. Wrong coupons cause bad feelings, lines are slowed, checkers get confused and so on, though scanners now read the bar code printed on the coupons and speed the process along. Stores receive compensation for redeeming the coupon, both for its face value and a handling fee.

As with all promotions, the product must succeed or fail on its own merits. A manufacturer can get a consumer to try a product by offering cents off. But if it doesn't taste good, a few cents off won't bring the customer back.

One reason coupons continue is because it's easy to judge their success. Within weeks of a coupon's appearance, a manufacturer can tell you how many have been redeemed across the country. And they can calculate the incremental increase in sales over time through the periodic use of such coupons.

If your business lends itself to coupons—grocery store items, health and beauty products, restaurants, retail music, florists and entertainment venues like theaters, bowling alleys and roller rinks—they're worth a try if you're able to clearly delineate your goal. Make them the exception rather than the rule. Track their impact on your bottom line carefully. You can track coupons by coding them with their source. For coupons that will appear in the Sunday newspaper on August 15, for example, put a little 8/15 down in the corner. You'll be able to track exactly how many coupons were redeemed from that particular promotion. Coding coupons over time will tell you which publications, and which issues of those publications, work the best for you.

To cover your cost, tie the coupon purchase in with another purchase: "Two dollars off on a coffee mug when you purchase a pound of beans." What you make on that other purchase will help defray your promotional expenses. In many retail trades, this is called a "loss leader."

Special Pricing

This category of sales promotion covers a range of terms and applications: rebates, mail-in coupons, buy three and get four, and general sale pricing. The retailer wants to convince the buyer to act *now* by offering a special monetary concession with an immediate purchase. This avoids the paperwork morass of coupons, and it's generally linked to higher-price goods.

We've all seen stores that seem to make a living by offering things at sale prices. Most Americans have become very callous about the reality of "sale prices," especially when we're told that the sale "must end absolutely on Monday evening . . . so you've got to make you're mind up right now."

While an occasional discount period seems to do no permanent damage to price integrity, overuse of sales leads the consumer to avoid purchases until a sale arrives. Obviously, this defeats the purpose of the sale from the offerer's point of view. When buyers *expect* sales, they soon *demand* sales. And then your carefully crafted market pricing careens out of control.

When to use special pricing:

1. To counter special competitive situations—the opening of a new store—or to take advantage of a competitor's high prices

2. To move merchandise you've purchased on special pricing arrangement with the manufacturer

3. To establish a loss leader, when your offer mandates that consumers purchase other products at the same time

4. To increase volume: Offer a 10 percent discount on all purchases over $150

Point-Of-Purchase Promotion

You use point-of-purchase or point-of-sale (POS) promotions at the actual place where people do their buying. The thinking here is simple. Take an impulse-type item, one that doesn't require research or comparative shopping. Place an exciting, high-energy display near the items on the aisle or at the checkout to get customer attention. Appeal to the basic instincts—hunger, thirst, sex, humor, greed, whatever. Boom, you've hooked them.

Insight

Constant couponing and product sales can hurt you. Some large retailers are shifting to an "everyday low pricing" strategy to avoid the endless treadmill of price-cutting and sales. While cutting prices does bring in the customers, it also costs you money, both in the discounted price itself and in the costly mechanics of "handling" a store sale: informing cashiers, coupon appearances, changing signage and so on.

Research shows this "crude" advertising is very effective. People buy many more items in stores than they plan to buy. A lot of color and design research has gone into assembling POS displays. Supermarkets look like Christmas year-round with their colorful displays of all sizes. They now have little flashing machines on many shelves with blinking lights. They hand you a coupon. Pull it out and another appears. Eerie. Personally, I much prefer the nice ladies handing out cracker and port wine cheese samples.

By itself, point-of-purchase advertising works. When it appears along with similarly themed advertising, the combination is dynamite. Run a radio spot telling listeners to take a pizza picnic. They buy the pizza at special midday prices and you throw in the soft drinks. Place a newspaper ad with a picnic graphic and the same theme line. At your pizzeria, have a poster facing the front door to remind them of the promotion. And have each of your employees wear a "Had a pizza picnic lately?" button.

Contests

Contests (a competition that requires some skill) and sweepstakes (which are chance-based) can work for small businesses, but you have to watch the way you run them. Government regulators at the state and municipal level monitor contests and sweepstakes avidly since they are based on a blatant appeal to the latent greed in all of us.

At the national level, advertisers undertake such "events" because of the attention they draw, both from consumers and the media. Make the prize big, glamorous or intriguing enough, and you draw attention.

The McDonald's chain has mastered the art of running sweepstakes based on ingenious tie-ins with popular culture. Its youthful market joins in enthusiastically, the resultant publicity garners major press coverage, and a few more french fries meet their inglorious and McDividend-enhancing end.

Any such activity you undertake should focus on drawing your customers' direct attention to your site, and on getting press coverage to magnify its impact. Have a drawing to give away a trip. Offer all purchasers in a given time period a chance at a drawing for a new camera. Put the good ol' jar of jelly beans in the window and request guesses

When Push Comes To Pull

"Push-pull" is a term describing two complementary ways that a manufacturer creates a promotional demand for a product. In a "pull" promotion, you, as the manufacturer, create demand at the consumer level and have them "pull" your product through the marketing chain. If you run coupon ads or a flight of TV advertising to generate response, you're engaged in "pull" advertising. If you're hitting the end-user with a heavy message frequency, you're counting on the public to go to the outlet and "pull" the product through the retailer.

"Push" promotions take place between manufacturer and distributor. You provide incentives to the middlepeople in the distribution chain—giving them heavy discounts, cooperative advertising money, deals on related products, all-expense-paid trips to the Cayman Islands and so on. They "push" the product through to the end-user with in-store advertising, favorable positioning and other help.

for a prize. If your prize is a gift certificate, you're guaranteed to get the winner into your operation at least one more time.

Trade Incentives

In the same way that manufacturers give price breaks and coupon discounts to consumers, so they take care to treat their own distribution channel right by offering rewards for help in moving their products.

Manufacturers recognize that distributors and retailers control the far end of the hose. They are the point of interaction with the consumer. If the distributors and retailers aren't on a particular manufacturer's side, then they're in someone else's pocket. Since distributors and retailers buy in much greater volume than does the individual consumer, so the rewards to the distribution channel are accordingly much larger.

Danger
Before you get far in your plans for a contest or sweepstakes, check with local authorities to get up to speed on the local rules governing them in your home market. Typically, your secretary of state or the State Department of Commerce can help you (names vary by states). If you think you've got an idea that will really attract some attention, give your attorney a call. A little time and money spent upfront can save you an enormous amount of expense and embarrassment if things go wrong.

Getting on the shelves is a life-and-death struggle for all manufacturers of retail products. If they can't get *on* the retail shelf, they can't be bought *off* the retail shelf. In some sense, the manufacturers are held hostage by the far end of the chain. This is especially true for new manufacturers who are trying to break into a distribution network, which is always interlaced with complex and mutually supportive incentive arrangements.

Distributors may get a paid trip to an exotic vacation locale for boosting product volume over a specified period of time. A retailer may benefit from price breaks above a certain sales volume, a discount that can amount to sizable dollars on strong sales. Finding out what's the standard for your industry involves some sleuthing. It's a murky area, and every industry is different. Contact the trade association that deals with your industry, and talk with someone there about industry practice in compensation and discounts. Speak to noncompetitive people in your business about how they handle distributors or retailers. Ask payment questions directly.

Working with the distribution chain is a throwback to earlier times, and you have to do some investigation to find out how things are handled in your industry. The guiding principle, of course, is that you've got to be competitive: Distributors and/or retailers must have a reason to carry your product. You're renting shelf space and you're paying the rent to the retailer, and you pay the distributor to "move you in" to your rented space.

Cooperative Advertising

This form of promotion indirectly rewards the lower end of the distribution chain for promoting a manufacturer's product. "Put my name and logo in your ad in at least 12-point type," says the manufacturer, "and I'll pay 50 percent of the ad's cost when I receive a copy of the invoice."

The concept of cooperative advertising offers major advantages to both manufacturer and retailer. The retailer gets money, of course, as well as the connection with a prestigious brand name. The retailer's media friends love cooperative advertising, since it expands the budget they'd normally get from the retailer. For the manufacturers, they get local exposure and local appreciation from the retailer. And the market's customers see ads in their local newspaper carrying the manufacturer's national brand logo.

Cooperative advertising goes mostly into newspapers, although many manufacturers encourage their retailers to use broadcast and direct mail as well. The accounting behind cooperative advertising can get complicated, but if you have a manufacturer offering you money to run ads, take it and run. If you're a manufacturer and want retailers to give your products greater visibility, offer to pay for 50 percent of the advertising in which your company name and logo appear. This will get them thinking about you! Spell out very clearly what type of appearance in the ad will earn the cooperative dollars, lest a misunderstanding leave hard feelings.

Trade Shows And Exhibitions

When entrepreneurs start up a business, their knowledge of the industry varies widely. Some have worked for firms for years and know the market and the competition very thoroughly. Others have wandered into their particular field from afar, and they spend their first few years trying to grow a business and build their expertise at the same time. It's a tall order.

For both these business owners, trade shows and exhibitions provide a tremendously valuable opportunity to learn and to sell. Getting hands-on competitive intelligence is never easy, but it's as easy as pie at a trade show. A little creative self-identification can get you a complete review of the competition's product line. You can then ask what they think of your products (of course, they can't know who you really are). It's . . . er . . . enlightening to hear how your competition speaks of you to prospects. This is competitive research at its grittiest.

A walk around the exhibit hall will earn you a sackful of literature on suppliers, distributors, the trade press, new market concepts—a 2-pound synopsis of the market that you can review at your leisure when you get back home. You can also have yourself put on mailing lists, participate in market surveys and earn complimentary subscriptions to a handful of journals. Not to mention more coffee cups, laminated business cards and free golf balls than you'll ever need.

If you're selling business-to-business, exhibiting and walking around at a major trade show lets you accomplish several important tasks at once:

1. Show off your product to people who are hyper-qualified as buyers (they've gone to the trouble of showing up).

2. Meet your current customers, and get a feel for how your product's really performing.

3. Spy on your competition, and either gloat over your superiority or gnash your teeth at their achievements. Some people say that looking at the competition is what such shows are really all about.

4. Connect with distributors, wholesalers, brokers and others in your product distribution channel.

Jargon Alert

When attending trade shows, many businesses host a "hospitality suite," a group of rooms at a nearby hotel to which they can go with prospects, respected suppliers or just friends in the industry. It's a place away from the hubbub of the exhibition hall, where parties can talk business and generally get acquainted. It's commonly supplied with food, drink and sales tools.

5. Build a mailing list for follow-up contact. This is why you're there.

6. Schmooze with major prospects at your company's booth or hotel hospitality suite.

7. Make small or major presentations to attendees under the auspices of the show's organizers. This boosts your credibility and enhances the seriousness of your product.

8. Meet the movers and shakers in your industry's trade press. You'll never have a better opportunity to chat with the top editorial staff.

9. Sell some product!

Here is a list of tips for making the most of trade shows:

- **Pick the right show.** Especially for small companies, the trade-show circuit can be a budget-buster. It's expensive to fly staff and materials all over the country, especially when the return may be marginal. Before you start reserving booths, look at the trade show scene in your industry strategically. List the major shows, their location and venue, logistical considerations, anticipated attendance, costs, competition typically in attendance and distribution channel involvement. Most respectable show organizers have detailed information on past attendees and exhibitors. Talk to some of your noncompetitive peers in the business and get their take.

Once you've laid this all out in front of you, let your overall budget make your decision. Experience suggests it's better to have a strong presence at one important and expensive show than a mediocre impact at several smaller, inexpensive shows.

> **How To**
>
> You'll find major trade shows listed in the publication *Tradeshow Week*, as well as in the major publication in your industry. Attend the biggest trade show you can to stay in touch with the best thinking in the industry. Exhibit at the best trade show you can afford.

- **Get an attractive, portable, versatile booth.** The display industry has a range of good-looking booth arrangements that are sturdy enough to travel well without showing their miles. You'll want a setup that gives you the room to display literature, show visuals of your product and its manufacture, take names and addresses, and put on a modest show of bustle and enthusiasm.

Don't go the bargain-basement route in show booths: If you're trying to convince important prospects you offer a quality product, you don't want the letters peeling off your signs and your tables looking like pioneer-day school desks. Do not, repeat, *do not* use plywood: It shows every impact it will unavoidably absorb. And then it falls apart. It also makes you look like a hand-to-mouth organization, which is never a good thing (with all due respect to the much-admired American plywood industry).

How To

It's not hard to get on mailing lists without giving away who you're working for. Crafty businesspeople have some business cards printed up with their home addresses and a foggy title like "market consultant" or "distribution analyst." They may use their son's or daughter's first name. You get competitive literature sent to your home without your opponent identifying you and purging you from the list. Oh yeah, and make sure to drop the card unnoticed on your target's table so you don't get spotted and identified at your own booth later in the show.

- **Decide what you want to accomplish and stay focused.** Do you want to sell product? Some shows make that an emphasis, but most don't. Shows are contact points, like the trappers' rendezvous: Everyone in the area comes together to see what the other folks have been up to—and incidentally to trade some furs. Trade shows provide a good venue for many tasks:

  1. Introduce new or enhanced products to the market
  2. Distribute surveys to develop better market understanding
  3. Make strategic or key personnel announcements
  4. Bring together key players on the sales staff for networking, training and morale boost
  5. Build your contact list

- **Have your literature ready.** If you have a gap in your printed materials, plug it before show time. For large shows, companies often prepare special brochures or flyers speaking directly to attendees, perhaps offering special terms or discounts. If you know you're attending a particular show, mention that fact (and give your booth number) in advertising leading up to the event.

- **Give your display energy.** A card table with technical product sheets will not have people backed up in the aisles. What can you do to generate excitement?

    1. **Show your product working.** Many computer-based products are live-linked at shows, so prospects can see the systems actually working on *their* problems.

    2. **Bring visuals to make your booth eye-appealing.** Use charts and graphs on the curtains, use larger-than-life scale models to show technical details. Have a continuous-loop video of your operations running throughout the conference. Use logos of large companies you've served. Show antique versions of the equipment you're introducing. Your prospects are human beings with an interest in your market—what will get a rise out of them and make them elbow their way to the front of the crowd? In the trade show, *you are the ad,* and you must break through the clutter of all the other "ads" to hook the interest of your customer.

    3. **Don't be afraid to get silly.** Attend a few shows and you will see: People dress up in strange costumes and clown makeup, feed mice to cobras, recite product benefits at a machine-gun pace, print prospects' names on old-time newspapers with heroic headlines, and anything else to create interest. However, unless you're in a remarkably retro market, avoid the classic bimbo in a bikini. It will hurt you.

    4. **Food and drink never fail.** The more unusual the better. Rattlesnake hors d'oeuvres? Camel jerky? But avoid messy items.

- **Allow the opportunity for serious business.** Most people who come to your booth will be tire-kickers. They'll grab a handful of pistachios, cherry pick your printed materials and move on to the next booth. But every once in a while, you'll bag a live one. Know how and where you will talk to this person at length. Will it be a spot in the rear of the booth, a nearby conference room, a table in the concession area, a later meeting at your company suite?

- **Select the right cast.** Get the right people at the show. Introverted types don't always do well in the hustle and bustle of in-your-face show-booth selling. Enlist your most experienced salespeople.

Throw in key marketing staff so they can refine their understanding of the market and help you sell better. Give yourself enough crew to get the job done. Prospects won't wait around for someone to break free from a conversation.

- **Capture business cards.** You want to leave with as many leads as possible, so bait your hook with a tasty morsel. Set up a drawing with a prize. Tell people you've got earthshaking material stalled at the printer that will be available next week. Offer them a market report that is too bulky for you to take to shows. Set up a follow-up contact by your applications specialist, who will have special knowledge of the prospect's market challenge. Give out newsletter subscriptions. Offer imprinted premiums that will be shipped to the prospect's office in three weeks.

- **Follow up.** Before you go to the show, you should have decided what to do with the leads you generate. Most companies divide them into categories: hot prospect, recontact in 60 days, put on mailing list, send specific materials and so on. You've got to move promptly and efficiently on this, while the prospect's memory of you is fresh. Many firms fax or e-mail leads and literature requests from the show to their home office, the support staff handles fulfillment, and the literature is sitting on the prospect's desk when he or she returns to work. It makes a good impression.

Speciality Items

Specialty advertising has been reborn of late. For years, it was the land of trinkets and kitsch: marginally usable imprinted calendars, blotters, miniature flashlights, piggy banks, baseball caps, refrigerator magnets and imprinted pens and pencils. Times have changed.

The $5 billion specialty item business has upgraded its toys. To attract new business, companies now offer to throw in expensive tool kits, clothing (almost a quarter of current sales), premium food items and attractive art objects for home or office. Thousands of advertising specialty businesses have grown up to supply the demand. They draw on hundreds of manufacturers who in many cases have established separate divisions to handle the corporate specialty business.

The market is growing for good reasons. Here are four of them:

1. **People like getting stuff for free.** And they feel obliged to you for giving it to them. That sense of obligation may lead them to consider you for a bidding opportunity in return. For ongoing customers, it makes them feel you genuinely appreciate their business.

2. **Specialty items have a long shelf life.** Your gifts (often with your logo) will be worn, used, looked at or ridden for an extended time.

3. **You can be creative with your gift.** One company gives each of its major clients a striking art vase produced and signed by a local (but nationally recognized) pottery artisan. Fruitcakes may not have many fans, but specialty smoked salmon or gourmet cheeses are very popular, especially around the holidays.

4. **You don't have to engage in shameless self-promotion.** Some firms give gifts (especially sportswear) imprinted with the name of the *recipient's* company. Talk about appreciation.

In a business-to-business market, you can use advertising specialties to thank customers for their business (and to remember you the next time they need a product or service like yours). When you're targeting your specialties toward a business, you can spend a little more—since your clients' list is smaller than the phone book. When your product is a service, delivering a specialty product with your name on it gives your customers something to look at. You can employ advertising specialties as a promotional strategy to reach the general public (radio stations do this all the time).

When you're considering purchasing some specialty items, ask yourself the following questions:

- How do these specialty items fit into my marketing plan and budget? It has to make economic sense. Not all your customers need to get something.

- Whom do I want to give these items to and why? Limit your list, so you can spend more on the customers that are important to you.

- Do I lose anything by *not* giving them? What is your competition doing?

- What reaction to my company will these products trigger? If someone is an important customer, you don't want to give away a cheap-looking trinket that will do more harm than good. The greater the sale per customer in your business, the more impressive the advertising specialty should be.

Sales Promotions: The Turbocharger

- What items have a natural connection (however indirect) with my company's business? Here's your chance to be clever, but don't get carried away and give your client something he or she doesn't know what to do with. You want the customer to be thankful and come away with a heightened impression of you and your business.

Chapter 9

Public Relations:
The Softest Sell

Public relations represents a greatly underused opportunity in marketing your firm. Most small companies don't do any public relations, even though it's among the simplest of market-enhancing activities you can undertake. Even "amateurs" can have a powerful local impact. In fact, local media sometimes prefer working directly with the "newsmakers."

Public relations is the fourth horseman of marketing. We've already covered the first three—personal selling, advertising and promotion. But public relations moves by a different tactic. It's the king of indirection. The "Buy me" message is whispered very softly in the ear of the prospect, while the more visible part of the communication proceeds through the reportorial objectivity of the news media.

In fact, the various marketing techniques reinforce and complement each other. News has credibility, but with PR you can't dictate its appearance or message. Advertising puts you in control· of appearance and message, but the public views it as less credible. Promotion further entices people (who've come to know of you through PR and advertising), and personal selling finalizes the exchange.

The Importance Of Public Relations

What is the task of public relations? Quite simply, to trade on the inherent credibility of the nonpurchasable news media to enhance the visibility and desirability of your product.

Public relations isn't aimed solely at potential purchasers. This seems counterintuitive at first, but think about it: You want everyone to have a favorable attitude about your product and company, right? In fact, as we've seen, marketing includes everything that impacts the exchange between you and your customer. All exchanges occur in an environment alive with other players who can impact the exchange—either working to make your sales effort easier or dooming it to failure. Public relations provides you the opportunity to influence these "environmental factors" in your favor.

Some of the marginal players you may want to influence include:

- Legislators (who have the power to make laws affecting your business)
- Local government leaders (who can affect zoning and many other areas)
- Community leaders (who impact the social environment in which you work)
- Potential suppliers (who can decide whether to work with you)
- The general public (you never know when individual members may drift into your marketing target audience)

Public Relations: The Softest Sell

- Shareholders (if you're a publicly held company)
- The financial community (especially if you're not publicly held)
- Regulatory agencies (who can inspect or audit you until you're sore)

Public relations includes a range of activities, from press relations to lobbying federal lawmakers. It also encompasses corporate communications (stockholders, SEC relations and so on), visitor relations (if you're enough of an institution to merit visitors), and even non-sales-oriented Web sites.

Companies aren't the only entities that engage in public relations. It's used very effectively by tourist groups (which have a special, almost symbiotic relationship with the travel press) and municipalities (for tourism, funding and overall spin control). Trade and professional associations (the National Association of Manufacturers, the Advertising Council, the American Plastics Council) conduct highly structured public relations at the national level. They are the 500-pound gorillas of PRdom.

For your company, public relations provides some unique wrinkles in the marketing mix:

- **Credibility:** You speak to your markets or your public in a forum that's explicitly more believable. Readers or viewers trust the media (consumer or business) more fully because of its implied endorsement of what it says about your company. In fact, most people don't understand the role that companies play behind the scenes in creating news about their products. This is now a well-established system, and the news media are neither innocent victims of shrewd PR opinion molders nor fully complicit co-conspirators in the manipulation of the American public. They're somewhere in between, balancing their own integrity against their own needs and their ties to corporate America.

  Any shrewd observer of the network evening news or—even more blatantly—the morning news programs can see the telltale fingerprints of corporate public relations specialists at work in many of the light news segments. And let's not even talk about the use of the media by politicians . . .

- **Affordability:** Public relations generally costs far less than advertising. Of course, if you have people who do nothing but public relations, you have salaries and expenses to cover. But out-of-pocket costs are very modest, especially compared with the whopping print space or airtime costs of the *paid* media, particularly if your target audience is local or regional. PR impact typically far outweighs its expense.

- **Precision:** You can select specific media. Just as with paid advertising, you can direct your PR efforts to particular media. Television, for example, reaches the greatest proportion of the general public and obviously lends itself well to visuals. If your product appeals to a broad market and makes for an interesting visual demonstration, television can be a prime media for your public relations. If your spokesperson is attractive, comfortable and credible on camera, put him or her in front of the cameras at every opportunity. You pick the media that highlights your product most convincingly. You may not be successful at getting exposure where you want, but you're free to take your story where you want to.

- **Lasting impact:** It leads to a long-term relationship. As you establish contact with the local business press, keep the big picture in mind. You know what you want from them; they know what you want from them. It should be a relationship based on mutual needs. You need exposure; the media needs news. It's important to the media to look in touch with the business community.

Local media is often criticized for being business-illiterate and unfriendly. Let's face it—the press (once you get away from the major markets) tends to rely on relatively inexperienced and low-paid young people for most of its work. TV stations and newspapers have some senior people, but the younger generation handles the front-line reporting. This is good for you.

Young reporters—especially business reporters—can always use a hand understanding the details of the marketplace. Provide reporters with a source

How To

Integrate your PR and ad schedules. No company has enough money (OK, maybe Microsoft does) to do all the advertising it wants. To put your name out there more often—without breaking the bank—schedule your PR efforts to maintain media visibility in your market when your ads aren't running.

for insightful, candid and not blatantly self-serving information, and you have a contact for years.

Be honest in your efforts. Give your media contacts good, solid press releases and credible news conference announcements. Don't pester them with non-news issues and blatant product puffery. If you establish yourself as someone who knows and plays by the unwritten rules of press/PR relations, you'll gain the respect of the media folks. You'll ultimately benefit from this respect. (See the "How A Newsperson Thinks" section on page 180 for more on this.)

- **Marketing linkage:** Public relations can further your marketing goals. Make your public relations effort an integral part of your marketing plan. If your marketing goal, for example, is to introduce a new lightweight but damage-resistant attaché case, you select your markets, pick your media and prepare your advertising materials, just as we've outlined in the preceding chapters. But you include public relations (the news/entertainment media) as another outlet for your message. You send a free attaché case to well-known business travelers and ask for their reviews. You have the case "reviewed" by editors of local business publications, including the business editor of the largest newspapers. You create an "event," whereby the attaché rides the local airport luggage carousel for 24 hours straight to demonstrate its sturdiness. All this is built into your marketing plan. You combine the news dimension with the paid advertising portion of your overall marketing effort. Public relations enhances advertising—together they make marketing successful.

Insight

Be sensitive to the time constraints affecting the media. Broadcasters and newspapers reporters work on very tight schedules. Contact them two or three weeks before the event you want publicized to allow time for a second contact before the event itself. With the trade press, you need to think months ahead. Get a copy of their editorial calendar, which is normally prepared at least a year in advance, before contacting them. Try to tie your release or article in with the issue that relates best to your subject.

How A Newsperson Thinks

You won't get anywhere with the business press or consumer media if you don't "market" to them. If there's one thing you've learned so far, it's that you have to get inside the head of the customer. Public relations provides another group of noggins to penetrate—media news directors.

If you're running advertising, all you have to do is hand your media rep the check and you're on. Not so with public relations. You don't choose where to appear. The media decide whether to allow you to appear. So you have to understand what they like and don't like to run in their pages or on their airwaves.

Consider the newsperson's job. He or she has pages of newsprint or precious air time to fill. If it's a busy news day, there's no problem finding stories of interest. Sometimes a single enormous story—Kennedy's assassination, the World Trade Center bombing, the Olympics—will dominate the news completely. But for every day like that, many others dawn with few good stories to report. Newspapers can't put out a six-page newspaper since readers would revolt and advertisers would sue. TV news programs can't simply run public service announcements or station promos—their audiences would defect, and they'd never make payroll.

Every reporter is part marketer. He or she writes or shoots stories with the audience in mind, adding style or looking for content that is appealing and/or interesting. After all, news is a product, no matter how much of a veneer of "importance" the media may put on it. The media hold a public trust to be informative and objective, but they are also a business. If a newspaper doesn't give readers what they want, the paper won't sell, and eventually it will fold—as so many afternoon papers have done with the emergence of the two-earner family as the norm. The network news operations battle fiercely for audience share and the resultant advertising dollars. And the local news directors are driven by forces just as demanding.

This is not to criticize the Fourth Estate. The dedication and integrity of many members of the press do indeed help keep democracy breathing. But they exist in a capitalist environment that requires bottom-line success.

The day-to-day reality looks something like this: The editor, whether in print or broadcast, pushes his or her reporters to come up with something every day. If the editor's smart, he or she has a number of stories on the back burner that are not so time-sensitive and that can fill in the inevitable blank spots. If you can provide the media with a story they perceive as news to their audience, and you can offer it to them in a form that's easy to work with, yours may become that slow-day story—and you will be way ahead of the game in gaining public relations exposure for your company.

Your PR goal is to think of stories that will make the media outlet look good to its audience. Follow the same feature-benefit equation you used to figure out how to sell your product to your customers. What benefit does your news release or feature story offer to the media? If it doesn't offer them anything, then why should they run it?

How To

When you talk to the media about your story, highlight the benefit the media itself will gain from the appearance of your story. Will it help the media outlet:

- bolster its local business credibility?
- scoop the competition?
- provide a strong visual for television?
- tie to a holiday or local special event?
- build on existing local interest?

Newspeople look at their subject matter as either hard or soft. Hard news is timely, detailed and likely to be of immediate interest to a sizable portion of their audience. They feel they *have* to run it.

Soft news is less time-sensitive. It is often turned into feature-oriented human-interest stories: the pregnant cat that crawled into the basement window to have her kittens. The insurance agency with a handful of crazy explanations of car accidents. The civil engineer with a story of the toughest highway in the state.

The media doesn't *have* to run these stories. But if they're appealing enough—if they're cute, clever, intriguing or unusual—they'll run them to entertain. In fact, before the days of computerized typesetting, newspapers had books of little squibs—interesting facts in varying lengths (now called factoids) they could use to fill out a column.

Chances are your business doesn't generate many hard news stories. Some examples of such hard news stories:

- New product

- New plant or office
- Hiring/promotion
- Major contract/government project
- Stock offering
- Ownership change
- Business alliance

Each time you're lucky enough to score a success in one of these areas (keep the failures to yourself, of course), you write a press release and forward it to your local business press contacts. If the story is of greater interest than normal—a very large contract, hiring a local celebrity, a major new product—you might get both business news and regular news coverage, which is a coup that quickens the pulse of every PR person.

While your hard news stories may be rare, your company offers a never-ending supply of soft news stories. One of the most powerful tools you have with soft news is the well-developed anecdote. Find an interesting and/or amusing and/or heartwarming use of your product, and then weave a short feature story from it. Most companies never exploit this part of their business . . . the human part. But it can pay nice dividends because everyone—the general public, your current customers, your prospective customers, the media itself—is a sucker for a good story.

The hardest issue here is finding these anecdotes. Your sales staff doesn't think "anecdote"; they think sales. Your engineers don't think "anecdote"; they think application. You've got to get them both to slow down for a second, tip their chairs back, and talk to you about some of their stories. I've never met a business that didn't have some good ones. Play on your people and your product in an unusual situation or "with a twist":

- Medical equipment that saves a life
- A computer tape drive that maintained data in the midst of a flood
- An insurance agent dealing with a tornado
- A restaurant's freezer failure
- The double life—home health-care provider and model-train builder, financial planner and orchid expert, software developer and cross-country bicyclist, cleaning service owner and jazz musician, receptionist and repertory actor

Public Relations: The Softest Sell

Sample Pitch Letter

March 15, 2000

Leonard Thompson, Feature Editor
Blankville Gazette
1234 Main Street
Blankville, AA 33333

Dear Mr. Thompson:

I run a car detailing business in Blankville, with three shops in town and two others in southern Ohio. My company has detailed more than 550 cars in the last three years. Business is booming, as more and more people are getting into taking extra care of their vehicles. We know the secrets of supercleaning them so they look like new.

I'm proposing to write a series of two 800-word articles on how car owners can maintain the value of their cars by using some simple cleaning tricks. I know you have a car section coming out in about four months, and that might be a good place to put the first article (or both of them). If you need more, I can write more.

I'll explain some of the techniques car detailers use to restore cars to their showroom luster:

- The best polish to use . . . do the quick polishes work?
- How to get your chrome to shine and stay shining
- The right products for getting your upholstery clean . . . and then sealing it against dirt
- Some simple ideas for keeping the driver's seat area clean and uncluttered
- How to evaluate windshield treatment to repel water

I've enclosed several copies of my company newsletter, as well as an article I wrote for the national *Detailers* magazine. I can also provide relevant photos to support the articles.

I look forward to your response. Please give me a call to discuss any aspect of this proposed series. I think your readers will enjoy them.

Sincerely,

Jack Ferreri

- Reactions to related national events
- Interesting overseas sales

Within your company, set up an informal procedure for gathering anecdotes. Assign a marketing-savvy staffer to poll each employee with customer contact every 60 days. Look for case histories and testimonials (see Chapter 6 for more on these) and search through PR raw materials—job site photos, meeting reports, job status reports, information on trips abroad and so on—anything that you might grow into a news story.

When you have your story idea, formalize it in a pitch letter and send it off (see page 183 for a sample pitch letter).

Your Company As A News Resource

There's a second type of soft news you can use to highlight your professional expertise to your target market. Whatever your business is, you know more about it than any news reporter. How can you leverage your expertise into press exposure?

- **Write a periodic column.** CPAs do it leading into tax season. Investment professionals do it all the time, providing potential investors with helpful advice on how best to invest their funds.

Insight

You can also become a radio star. Many smaller community radio stations and public radio stations have regular guests on a very wide range of topics, from dealing with sick animals to car repairs, from getting crab grass out of your lawn to finishing your basement. What regular features (weekly or biweekly) does your local radio market offer? Offer yourself as an expert guest.

Massage therapists do it in early summertime as people start to ruin themselves with exercise. Nursery owners write columns of regular gardening advice. What can *you* write a monthly column about?

- **Establish yourself as an interview resource.** With a media kit and personal background information, demonstrate your knowledge to the local media. When a story dealing with your expertise emerges (either locally or nationally), write your press contacts offering your insights from a local perspective. You can offer your experience across all media, print and broadcast.

1. After a large fire, talk about what's involved in cleaning up. This works for specialized damage restoration services, regular house cleaners, painters, remodelers and paperers.

2. Before the Tour de France bicycle event, explain the basics of buying and maintaining a bicycle (works for bicycle shops and sporting goods retailers).

- **Teach courses/workshops/ seminars at local colleges, extension campuses, tech colleges or for evening classes.** No doubt you could probably teach "Starting Your Own Business," "Writing a Business Plan," and "Hiring the Best People," in addition to

Talk The Talk

You'll do a better job of promoting your company if you become comfortable talking to the media. It can be intimidating, since we've all seen news clips of ambush interviews set up to make businesspeople look bad. But media people are regular folks just making a living. Help them do their jobs and you'll do fine. Here are a few tips:

- **Be prepared to respond quickly.** If you're called for an interview, they won't want to talk to you next month. More likely tomorrow morning. Be flexible with your timing. It will probably be a phone interview, since timelines are so tight.

- **Talk with simple phrases and short sentences.** Also, keep examples clear and straightforward; don't use abbreviations or trade jargon.

- **Be as colorful as you can.** Remember, the media wants everything compressed into bite-sized nuggets and sound bites.

- **Give some thought before your meeting of how to make your business entertaining and illuminating to the general public.** What interests people about your business?

- **Speak forthrightly.** Answer questions directly, without a lot of qualifying phrases. If you don't know the answer to a question, tell the reporter you'll find out and get back to him or her. Then do it.

Insight

When you send in a release and encourage the editor to call for more information, be prepared for the call. What additional information do you have to give out? If you're shrewd, you'll put only the basics in the initial release, but make it enough of a tease to encourage the editor's call. Have background information already prepared. Putting things in a Q&A (question and answer) format is easy, and it simplifies the job for the editor or reporter.

courses in your particular field. Ours is a country filled with self-improvers. My mailbox is filled with educational offerings from all over the country. These sessions serve a double function:

1. You get the chance to impress potential customers with your knowledge.

2. You get up close and personal with present and future customers. It's instant market research that will serve to keep you in close touch with your market.

- **Give speeches at the local level to service and luncheon clubs.** Look under associations or fraternal organizations in your Yellow Pages (think Rotary, Lions, Kiwanis, Optimists and local civic organizations). If you're a people person, this can be great fun. If you're not, think of it as "mass prospecting." Many community groups look for speakers to give them 35 minutes to 50 minutes of information on almost every imaginable topic.

The Press Release

The press release is the basic currency of public relations—it's the one-dollar bill. Almost everything that happens in public relations starts with a press release. A press release announces news. People who receive press releases expect them in a certain format. While creativity is normally a great ingredient in marketing, your press release should follow press release standards. It still gives considerable range to your cleverness.

The Five W's

Your press release must be concise and complete, and it must answer journalism's five W's: who, what, when, where and why. If you don't cover the fundamental information, save your stamp and just throw the release in the recycle bin.

News editors are busy people. They want the key information in a press release revealed in the headline and the first two or three sentences. People who write releases tend to offer more information than the editor can use . . . or wants. So be sure *your* release gets to the point immediately.

Don't use negatives. Do use active verbs and concrete language. Pepper your release with relevant facts and figures that support its newsworthiness, but don't overdo it. More is not better. In press re-

Sample Press Release

January 9, 1999

FOR IMMEDIATE RELEASE

NEWS

For additional information, contact:
Jody Milstead
(999) 999-9999
Fax: (999) 999-9998
Jody@PR.com

HULMSLET OPENS DEKALB CONSULTING OFFICE

Hulmslet Consulting Group will open a two-person office in the Water Street Complex in DeKalb in late December. The DeKalb office will focus on Hulmslet's experience in consulting with nonprofit organizations on gaining funding from state, federal and local governmental and private entities.

"We're happy to be in DeKalb," said Hulmslet Director of Operations John Meyers. "It's a community with a healthy arts and community organization network that matches up well with our strengths. We hope to add to our new office in the next 18 months."

Hulmslet Consulting Group is a 12-person consulting firm based in Decorah, Iowa. Hulmslet works with arts groups, social welfare groups, political organizations and lobbying groups in the areas of proposals, fundraising, organizational structure and administration.

Full press kit available upon request.

See Hulmslet Web page at www.hulmslet.com.

How To

Sending out a press release is never enough. Follow up with a phone call to the editors, and ask if they've received it and whether any decision has been made on when it will appear. You don't want to be a pest, but you don't want to be ignored either. Be persistent. After you send out enough releases and make enough follow-up phone calls, they'll know who you are. Make your follow-up phone call within 10 days of sending out your letter. That gives them time to receive it but not to forget it.

leases, more is worse. If an editor's really hooked by your release, you'll get a call for additional information.

A press release should never exceed two pages, and the one-page release seems to be the standard. Tighten your writing until you pack the information onto a single page if at all possible.

Your most important information—the five W's—goes up front. Then provide minimal background, perspective and more general narrative. The editor will use it (or more likely rewrite it) as he or she feels is appropriate.

To humanize your news, put in a brief quotation from a big player. Make the quote lively and dynamic—avoid business jargon if you want the quotation included. Make sure you fully identify the speaker.

The final paragraph of your release should be a succinct, one-paragraph summary of what your company does for a living. This will remind the editor of who you are. It may appear in the final news story but not likely.

Some other press release elements:

- **Date:** Always date your press release. Most releases also carry the header line "For Immediate Release." Use it if it's relevant.

- **Contact:** At the top of the release (which is always issued on your letterhead), put the name of the person at your company you want the press to contact, along with the appropriate phone number, fax number and e-mail address. If you have a Web page, list it.

- **Photo:** If your story benefits from a photo, include one in black and white. Put the caption at the end of the release and tape a copy of the caption onto the back of the photo.

How To Hook The Media On Your Story

Business news editors receive scores of releases each day. Many are from ad agencies and public relations firms trying to do the same thing for their clients that you're trying to do for yourself. To be noticed above the fray, sometimes it helps to be resourceful. Here are some ideas:

- **Talk to your friends who run businesses and ask if any of them have a contact at the media outlet in which you're interested.** Ask them to share the name or put in a good word for you.

- **In addition to sending the release to the business editor, also mail a copy to a business staff member.** You can often find the names listed on the newspaper's masthead.

- **Follow your mailing of the press release or feature-story pitch with a personal phone call.** Explain that you're checking to see if the editor got your piece, if there were any questions and so on. You'll probably get the bum's rush when you call, but you won't hurt your cause.

- **Review the last few months of the business pages (or broadcast venue) and see which companies appear to have more-than-average luck in getting coverage.** Give the company a call and ask to talk to the individual in charge of public relations. Explain that you've noticed their PR success, and you'd like a few tips on how you can emulate it. Don't call a competitor, of course. People like to be recognized for their success; you'll likely learn a trick or two.

Publicizing Special Events

As you build your relationship with the media, you'll be able to use it more and more to promote the news potential of your business. When your business makes bona fide news—has a grand opening, conducts a special community event, passes a milestone anniversary, makes an important new hire, moves to larger offices or gains an important new contract—you need to let the media know. If you've really got some news, you're what the media exists for.

When you're planning an event, talk to the media early—with a preliminary press release and a phone call. You want coverage of your event. You'd like a reporter to show up with a photographer to take some photos, interview some attendees and write a glowing

Insight

For local television, consider a video news release (VNR) for news with a visual component. Provide the station a printed release supplemented by video footage on cassette, which they can run as background to the news reader vocal. Show your machine kerchunking, the marathon runners sweating, the international visitors smiling. Even if the video quality doesn't meet station standards, they can at least *see* what you've got. They'll re-shoot if they're interested.

story for the Sunday paper. After the event, if you don't get on-the-spot coverage, send the editor some photographs and a press release on the event. Something is better than nothing.

One of the surest ways to receive coverage is to team up with high-visibility organizations in your community. Children's groups, community organizations, religious groups, tourism centers, arts groups: All these have a built-in interest the media like to tie in with. Think of visuals when you're staging your involvement; television lives for pictures. Make your event both newsworthy and community-enriching:

- Sponsor a quarter-mile run for kids.
- Coordinate a fund-raiser for seniors.
- Take some underprivileged young people to the local zoo.
- Take part in a career clinic for high schoolers.
- Have your business play a role in county fairs or other community activities.

Pick The Right Media Outlets

Bacon's Publicity Checker is the PR industry bible. It lists all the PR outlets in the country, including newspapers, electronic media and trade press. You get double-checked names and addresses, as well as information on whether the source accepts photos and other details. A one-year subscription is several hundred dollars, but it includes a year's worth of updates. Check your local library to see if they've got a copy. Call the local newspaper and ask if you can use their copy.

If you've hired a new receptionist, don't send a release to *Business Week*. You have to be realistic in your public relations expectations, especially when you're just getting started. Look at your marketing plan and your target markets—who should receive messages about your company's activities? Some likely targets:

- **Local media:** This helps reinforce your strength in your local market. It also aids in recruiting employees from the local labor pool and from your competitors. And each positive story you can place serves as a partial reserve of goodwill in the event that you earn some bad publicity. Targets would typically include the local newspaper, city magazines, local business publications, television and cable stations with news or business interest, and your local chamber of commerce.

- **State/regional media:** This depends on your target markets. Most regions have a number of business publications in which you'd probably like to make an appearance now and again. Get inside the head of this editor—Why should your story run in a statewide or regional publication? What's the benefit to the media outlet?

- **National media:** Unless you've really got something remarkable happening—a celebrity connection, verifiable contact with a remote alien civilization, recent Elvis testimonial—stay local and regional. The national audience is the playground of the big dogs.

- **Trade press:** Most companies would benefit from a relationship with their trade press and the resulting connection with colleagues across the nation and the world. Even if your market is small-time local, there's no downside to getting known at the other end of the country. You never know what can happen.

Tell The Whole Story: The Press Kit

If you're just getting into organizing PR activities for your business, you probably need a press kit. The press kit expands on the company information included in the final paragraph of your press releases. It usually consists of a folder with one or two pockets, designed to hold a changeable array of company information:

- Company history, with trade association memberships
- Overview of products and product lines
- "Capabilities brochure"—your single most comprehensive piece of company literature that describes your firm's overall capabilities
- A guide to the marketplace for your product

- Biographies of principals (with CEO photo)
- Samples of advertisements and background news features
- Most recent product press releases
- Organizational chart

The press kit should accompany your first press release to a new media outlet, but don't send it each time a release goes out, as that gets too expensive. Although you might mention in your release that "a full and updated press kit is available for your review."

A press kit should be on hand anytime you stage a press conference or meet with the business press.

Chapter 10

Be A Good
Corporate Citizen

You're positively beaming with marketing vision by this point. You've got your market targeted. You've thought through your marketing plan in detail, and you've cleverly segmented your markets into logical categories. Your marketing plan sits proudly in a three-ring binder behind your desk. Time to check off the "Marketing" box on your to-do list, right?

But there's more. If you're in business for yourself, you know—of course—that there's always more. Entrepreneurs can fall into the trap of self-absorption very easily. We devote almost all our energies to our business, and then we keep the little remaining time we have left to ourselves and our families. Our work demands are tremendous, causing us to guard our off-the-job time (you've heard of that, haven't you?) zealously.

"If I handle the marketing well, won't business take care of itself?" you may think.

No business is an island. You run your shop surrounded by thousands of other organizations, businesses and individuals no matter where you live and work. They're all conducting *their* businesses, living *their* lives, trying to build *their* community. Leaving aside your marketing connections, what relationship does your business have with the community at large—beyond the business arena? Can you succeed in the long run keeping yourself aloof from the society in which you hope to flourish? Not likely.

By their very nature, small businesses depend more on their local communities than do large corporations. You don't succeed in a community without getting involved. It's good for business, it's good for the community, and, ultimately, it's good for you. To enhance your job satisfaction and enjoyment of your local community, you and your company should become good corporate citizens.

Becoming a good corporate citizen may be an obligation, but it doesn't need to be a burden. It really isn't one. It's personally very enjoyable, and it can help your company assume a respected role in your local and larger community. This is a good thing. Being a good corporate citizen means putting good word of mouth to work for you.

Making your company a good corporate citizen gives you a range of rewards:

1. It brings personal satisfaction, since you can really choose the public service arenas in which you and your company will become active.

2. You'll meet other business leaders and get to know them face to face, often outside their normal "business personalities." This "beyond the suit" interaction can be personally rewarding—and it expands your network of business contacts. The commercial marketplace is a community, and we all tend to do business with the people we know. It's natural; it's human.

3. You'll enhance your understanding of your community. My Rotary Club meets once a week. I've been a member for 12 years. In that time, I've heard perhaps 500 presentations about all sorts of things, from social welfare issues to politics, from new technologies on the local scene to living in Croatia, from a major referendum on a convention center to mass transit issues. I'm richer for all this insight.

4. You'll keep from becoming too one-dimensional through your work. If you don't *have time* for community involvement, you *need* community involvement.

5. If you're running your own business, you've likely been luckier than most on the way up. Making your company a good corporate citizen is a way to "give something back," to repay society for the benefits you've enjoyed . . . no matter how hard you've had to work to earn them. The French have an expression for it: *noblesse oblige.* Nobility has its obligations.

6. When businesspeople go out of their way to make an impact on the community, that's news. You may garner positive press coverage for your efforts. But there's no guarantee.

How To
Make your company into a company of tomorrow. These times are spawning a new kind of company—firms that try to respect their employees more than companies of the past, to treat them better, to share a brighter vision with them. You see these companies in the news, with their innovative on-site daycare centers, their profit-sharing plans and their commitment to openness. These companies play an active role in their communities, both with their employees and beyond.

7. You can increase the quality of the people you draw to your company. Your high-minded community commitment will attract other hard-working, like-spirited people to your company. And don't underestimate the impact of vigorous corporate citizenry on your current workers. Your company's visibility and good name will make them proud to work there and eager to refer their friends to you as potential employees.

Don't misunderstand: This isn't the same thing as doing a good deed and sending out a press release. If you approach it that way, you'll likely do more harm than good. It's akin to "enlightened self-interest." Approach the task with a spirit of helpfulness, with a genuine resolve to benefit other members of the community.

Of course, you'd like to get some business benefit from your commitment of time and resources, but you shouldn't be directly self-serving. Let the publicity come to you rather than set your PR machine in motion. You'll benefit in the long run.

Make The Business Connection Clear

Your goal with this "white hat" activity is to benefit the community while keeping yourself in the peripheral vision of the public eye. You want your name, the name of your top people, your company's name and the names of your product to be part of the public's consciousness. Companies like RJ Reynolds and Texaco spend millions sponsoring art and opera because they feel it's the right thing to do— and it earns them some recognition and kudos from influential people.

Decide early on whether your community involvement will spring from your time or your checkbook. The size of some companies, or the intensity of the workload, makes it difficult to get active community involvement from staff members. In that case, checkbook involvement is better than none.

If you have some business seasoning under your belt, consider involvement as a board member:

- **Community boards:** school boards, arts organizations, social welfare organizations

- **Professional boards:** Your line of work has a professional organization at the local, regional and national level. Get involved in building the strength of your trade. Offer to serve locally and eventually at higher levels. You'll make valuable contacts, you'll expand your understanding of the nuances of your business, and you'll have a hand in mapping the future of your industry.

- **Affinity boards:** No matter what your interest (model railroads, fly fishing, corvettes, Thai cooking, orchid growing), play a role in meeting local and national people.

How To

Join a service club. You'll meet local businesspeople, help your community and have fun. Don't fall for the ancient stereotypes of cigar smoke and dirty movies. Today's service clubs are filled with vibrant, people-oriented individuals of all ages and genders. Some options: Eagles, Elks, Jaycees, Kiwanis, Lions, Masons, Optimists, Rotary and Sertoma. Look in the Yellow Pages under "Organizations," "Associations" or "Clubs."

Be A Good Corporate Citizen

You can also use board connections in reverse. Create an advisory board for your business, with key suppliers and clients. You can use this board (perhaps with biannual telephone meetings) to advise your business on strategies, industry trends and so on. Of course, you'll choose members of this advisory board who can benefit your business with more than advice. You hope you're building a bond between your company and the companies of the board members.

Insight
City hall and county government can impact the way you do business and certainly affect the way you're perceived on your home turf. It's good to have them on your side.

Be forewarned: Don't be transparent in your creation of an advisory board. If you're just doing this to curry favor with influential people, you're going to get turned down (these people aren't stupid, after all), and you'll damage your relationship. Choose your advisory board members wisely . . . and use the board intelligently and respectfully.

Social clubs are another opportunity. Most communities have social organizations to which you apply for membership. Large cities have layers of them. To promote the growth of your business in the long term, make an effort to get involved in these circles. For some people, this social networking provides great joy and satisfaction. For others, it's torture. You know which kind of person you are.

Networking is especially important for service businesses because of the personal source of the business. You're not selling a product, just your own time and expertise. The better known you are in your community, the more recognized your product.

If there's a statewide association for your trade or profession, at the very least you should be a member. You're almost always more successful as a member than as an outsider. For many businesses, it also makes good sense to join the local convention and visitors' bureau. The more convincing an impression you give of being a "team player," the more likely you'll benefit from commercial alliances and "inside handoffs." If you're a manufacturer, join the local or state manufacturers' association.

Depending on the size of your company, consider creating a speaker's bureau—a contact person within your company who will coordinate requests for presentations by you (or another senior person) about your company or industry. The contact person can prepare a slide show to go along with the presentation, and he or she will coordinate all other details: which group you'll be speaking to, length of program, venue, requirements for visuals, types of interest and so on.

Consider joining organizations as a supplier (or associate) member. Printing press manufacturers and ink suppliers, for example, frequently join printers groups. Again, you're spreading your name around, going to a few meetings, meeting individuals who might turn out to be customers sometime in the future. Such affiliated organizations can also give you insights into the business market you're trying to serve.

Involve Your Company
And Its Customers

How can you get your company involved? There are no end of good causes that can use a helping hand. Every community—no matter how small—offers scores of avenues for an organization to get involved. Here are just a few ideas that might work for your company:

- Join an adopt-a-highway program.

- School intern program: Offer high school or local college students the opportunity for some real-world experience.

- Food for the elderly or homeless: Help financially or by serving meals.

- Audio books for the blind: Audiotape producers are always looking for readers and funding.

- Sponsorship of broadcast public service announcements: Pick a cause you believe in—ideally one that has something to do with your line of work. You sponsor the socially beneficial message.

- American Red Cross blood drive at your place of business.

- Help with fund-raising for any number of good social causes.

- Get involved with the high-profile telethon for local public television.

- Invite service clubs and youth groups to visit your offices or plant. Show them your product and how you make it, giving some idea of your impact on the local economy. For youth groups, prepare a token visit remembrance.

Be A Good Corporate Citizen

- Every major disease has a walk, run or bike these days. Get your family, your employees and your clients involved.

- Let a spokesperson for Big Brothers or Big Sisters speak at your workplace.

- Encourage on-site breast cancer screening.

- If you're in the food business, donate excess food to homeless shelters.

- If you're in the music business, arrange for small free concerts at homes for the elderly.

- If you're a financial person, offer to give some counseling at a neighborhood center on budgeting or debt management.

- If your business provides an infrastructure-related skill—plumbing, electrical, construction and so on—you have ample opportunities to satisfy your community improvement urges.

- Promote adopt-a-pet programs from your local Humane Society.

- Have employees contribute old clothing to give to the needy.

- Work with a local environmental group to clean up a neglected nearby natural area.

- Work with a local neighborhood center and take some needy kids to a ballgame.

- Print up some T-shirts and do some construction work for Habitat for Humanity.

- Get involved with causes that are favorites of local print, TV and radio outlets. This will assure you the cause is legitimate, and you have a better chance of coverage. The causes might differ by station or publication, but they will most likely be related to kids, schools or the environment. It doesn't take

Insight

A group of businesses and service organizations run a Paint-a-Thon program in Dane County, Wisconsin, in which each year some 20 to 30 homes of elderly or disabled citizens are painted—all on one Saturday. The paint is donated, while the groups and businesses pick up some incidental costs (like lunch, brushes, ladder rental and so on) as well as supply all labor. Each group works on its own house, so a great group spirit develops. Press coverage is considerable. And everyone has a great time.

much research to find out what causes your local media is involved with—all you have to do is read, watch and listen.

- Approach a service group in your community and ask them to develop a project for your umbrella sponsorship.

- Consider sports sponsorships, especially for teams from disadvantaged neighborhoods.

- Promote literacy programs in connection with schools or community organizations.

- Young people these days need mentors, an adult who can teach them about life. Look into existing mentoring programs.

- Talk to your local social service people. They can steer you to hundreds of additional worthwhile opportunities.

Limit your involvement to a few ventures. It's far better to work with two or three causes where you can make a difference than to spread yourself so thin that your money or your effort have little impact.

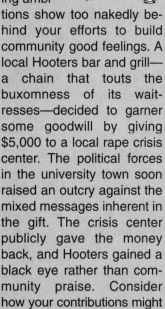

Danger

Don't let your marketing ambitions show too nakedly behind your efforts to build community good feelings. A local Hooters bar and grill—a chain that touts the buxomness of its waitresses—decided to garner some goodwill by giving $5,000 to a local rape crisis center. The political forces in the university town soon raised an outcry against the mixed messages inherent in the gift. The crisis center publicly gave the money back, and Hooters gained a black eye rather than community praise. Consider how your contributions might be viewed by people who may disagree with your business.

Chapter 11

The Internet: Marketing At The

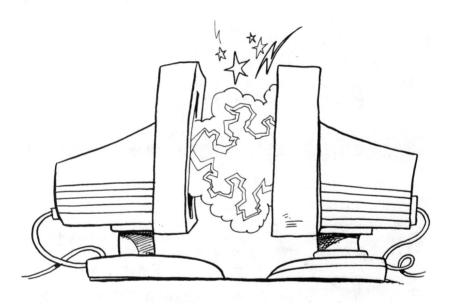

The Internet is expanding and gaining capabilities so quickly that by the time this guide is published, much in this chapter will probably be out of date. But even if many of the details contained herein quickly gather cobwebs, you'll learn enough to get started on your own exploration of a truly interesting and unique place to do business—one with marketing possibilities galore!

According to a recent study, Web commerce hit $10 billion in on-line transactions in 1996, and it should grow to nearly $30 billion in 1999. For this reason, and the ability to contact customers and co-workers around the world, the Internet is just too tantalizing a prospect to ignore for many small businesses. If you make use of only a tenth of its capabilities, you gotta be there.

Compared with other marketing avenues, the Internet offers some outstanding advantages:

- You can establish a basic presence without a large investment.
- You can talk to the online world across borders and around the clock.
- You can establish yourself as an informational resource in the prospect's mind.
- You can speak directly to interested prospects. Depending on your markets, it may be a popular avenue for sales.
- You can look bigger and more professional than you are (always a big plus for the small business, right?).

Most owners and managers of small entrepreneurial businesses usually don't need to be sold on the bright promise of the Internet. Many have worked with computers for years and aren't afraid of using their technology skills to explore some new terrain. If you are leery of venturing out onto the Internet, relax. It's a different marketing terrain, to be sure. But your basic marketing skills will support you surprisingly well.

Jargon Alert

Whichever ISP (Internet service provider) you choose, make sure to check out its reputation. You will be vitally dependent on this supplier; it will be your computer phone company. Ask the company for a list of current business subscribers and call them to ask about their experiences. How often does the system crash? How about busy signals and access delays? Can you get service support when you need it? Will the ISP grow as you grow, in size and technology?

The Internet And The World Wide Web

As you may know, what's come to be called the Internet started as the Arpanet back in the '60s. Originally designed as an Armageddon-proof communications network for the military-industrial-academic complex, it soon outgrew its original purpose. While a few savvy vendors, such as CompuServe, began offering e-mail to the masses even before the advent of the desktop computer, the Internet blossomed dramatically in the early '90s with the implementation of the World Wide Web.

The Web made the Internet much easier to navigate for "civilians" and others not accustomed to the sacred hieroglyphics of mainframe communications. It was more visual since the internal computer operations and communications could be accessed through a graphical user interface (what techies call a GUI), not unlike the Macintosh or Windows operating systems. Most of the recent surge in activity on the Internet occurs through the Web. The wealth of information available on the Web is how most people access and use the Internet.

To establish a link to the Internet, most small businesses have two options:

Jargon Alert

A Web browser is an application program (like a word processor or spreadsheet) that enables you to work on the Web—to navigate, view graphics, visit newsgroups and adjust general settings for how it works. In some cases, you may even be able to use it to send and receive e-mail. The two most popular ones—now engaged in a very public struggle to the death—are Netscape Navigator (the former leader) and Microsoft Explorer (the onrushing behemoth).

1. **Hook up with an Internet service provider, or ISP:** You dial one of the ISP's local phone numbers with your modem, using your computer's communications software. The ISP's server computer answers your call, recognizes you and then connects you to the Internet. Many ISPs provide e-mail as part of their package, along with access to newsgroups (more about that later). ISPs typically charge a flat monthly rate ($15 to $30) for unlimited Internet access.

   Some large and sophisticated ISPs offer a broad range of support services, including Web hosting services, through which you can establish your own company Web site. CompuServe, The Microsoft Network (MSN) and America Online (AOL) are three examples of ISPs that cater to a nationwide market. They may be more expensive than the bare-bones ISP provider (which basically just charges an entrance fee to the Internet), but you'll have more support for putting the Web to work for your business.

2. **The second and more expensive option is to become your own ISP by purchasing a server computer for your company.** Since the Internet is really just a whole bunch of these servers (called hosts) connected together over the phone lines, larger companies often cut out the middleperson (the ISP) and buy their own hosts to handle their Web access and e-mail.

To access the World Wide Web, you must have a Web browser. Generally, ISPs provide you with this (which normally includes e-mail), but the larger commercial ISPs—such as AOL, MSN, the Baby Bells and other major companies—also offer a wide range of other services and goodies. Several, such as MSN and AOL, are their own online "communities," providing members with customized search services, news and information services, online technology and software support, and any number of special-interest forums, chat rooms, and newsgroups for business, finance, sports, arts and entertainment, games, and anything else people want to talk to each other about. These are normally designed to be more user- and family-friendly than the benign chaos of other areas of the Internet, which can be more difficult to navigate.

These larger services have grown dramatically over the past 10 years. Like many other ISPs, these services also give you the capability to put together your own Web site. Another added benefit of these large ISPs is that many have local numbers you can call to access their service nationwide and even worldwide. Once again, be sure to do some research. Bigger isn't always necessarily better, and sometimes the smaller services will be slightly cheaper or offer other perks to get your business.

E-Mail And The Communications Revolution

E-mail is worth the cost of admission to the Internet. It has become a business necessity, and every day you spend without e-mail is a day you're sacrificing communications efficiency. I can't say it any more boldly than that. E-mail will revolutionize the way you communicate within and outside your company. If you are not a believer already, let me list some of the advantages it has over traditional communications:

1. The technology has proved itself stable, easy-to-learn and user-friendly—once you get used to it.

2. Messages are automatically time-stamped and saved, so you have a "paper trail" of communications on a project. It allows you to organize your messages (outgoing and incoming) by topic: You can open folders in which to store messages related to colleagues, clients, projects, suppliers, general topics and so on.

3. You can forward to one person e-mail you receive from another. This is a tremendous time saver and can speed up project and committee work.

4. You get all messages in electronic format, so you can edit an e-mail you receive before forwarding. Get an e-mail message, make substantive or formatting changes, and send it on. Again, great for team projects.

5. You can send and receive lengthy written documents via e-mail as attachments. You can edit what you receive with any word processor.

6. You can sort or search for e-mails by date, time or subject. This can help you pull together a range of information quickly on a given topic or reconstruct a chronology.

7. E-mail is essentially free. It's part of your ISP charge, and you pay no extra charges per message.

8. You can maintain an e-mail address book of all the people you need to stay in contact with. As addresses change, you simply update your book. A mouse click prepares you to send an e-mail to a person in your address book.

9. You can send the same e-mail to one or to thousands of people with just a few mouse clicks.

10. You can send and receive e-mail when you're on the road. Accessing the Internet

Insight

Can you really make money on the Internet? Yes, if you do it right. Amazon.com is the "virtual bookstore" that—right now, at least—dominates book buying on the Internet. Its sophisticated Web site includes the latest technology—and very good prices. Amazon.com gets 4 million visits a day. While such a system is complicated and expensive to set up, with it you can easily sell goods and services over the Internet to users around the world. Think of the potential of 4 million visitors a day!

with a laptop from motel rooms has grown commonplace in working America.

11. It's very efficient. Many professionals spend a lot of time at their computers, and they find e-mail the preferred form of communication; it avoids the annoyance of call-backs, voice mail and phone machines. Once you send the message, it's sent—and you *know* it's been sent.

E-Mail Communication Tips

Sending e-mail seems very similar to dashing off a quick note at the computer and zipping it off magically without printing it out. But it's not. Here are some insights into some unique aspects of e-mail you should be sensitive to:

1. **Written communication is forever.** No matter how well you know the person on the other end of the computer exchange, be prudent. Don't say things you can't afford to have get around. This is especially true if you're communicating with a company whose procedures for screening e-mail you're unfamiliar with. You don't want the Secret Service, local SWAT team members or paramedics with big hypodermics and a straitjacket lined up outside your office. You also don't want to explain messages containing bad taste or bad judgment to your colleagues . . . or to an opposing attorney under aggressive cross-examination.

    As some government officials have found to their regret, deleting e-mail from a computer system won't necessarily make it disappear. Technical wizards can resurrect it from the network's server, the main computer that runs the system.

2. **Make your messages short.** People are busy, but the ease of e-mail sometimes seduces us into long-winded rants about irrelevant topics. Save that for elsewhere. Short messages get read, and they'll earn you a reputation for concise communication and clear thinking. Don't write long sentences or paragraphs; break them up for faster reading. By the way: Don't use all caps. IT'S CONSIDERED BOISTEROUS OR ARGUMENTATIVE SHOUTING.

3. **Keep your writing informal, but not sloppy.** Don't get hung up over perfect grammar and flawless sentence construction. But don't let the ease of e-mail degrade the quality of your communication. Unless your message is very short, read it through again before you send it and make clarifying edits.

4. **Are you sure you want to send that e-mail?** If you're upset or angry about something, it's a little too easy to create and send a blistering e-mail. If, half an hour later, you cool off, there's no "unsend" button to bail you out. Consider the impact of your message and the *way* you say things. Remember, e-mails can be forwarded. If you're mad, it's prudent to wait before you send that e-mail and then reread it when you've calmed down.

5. **Don't become an e-mail junkie.** E-mail is not a substitute for face-to-face or telephone communication. Don't hide behind the monitor. And please don't become one of those people who finds something funny, cute or grossly obscene on the Internet and insists on sending it to everyone with whom they've ever swapped an e-mail.

6. **Look before you click.** We habitual computer users have grown accustomed to moving quickly on the keyboard and clicking the mouse. When we see a dialog box, we don't always read it—we just click or hit Enter. With e-mail, this can get you into trouble. A high-profile legal case was thrown into turmoil when someone on the defense staff sent an incriminating statement to the prosecutor instead of to a hired investigator: All it involved was a simple mouse click on the wrong recipient. You can easily send the wrong file to the right person as well. 'Tis better to have looked and clicked than never to have looked at all.

How To Set Up A Local Network

This isn't the place for a technical treatise on computer telecommunications, but we can cover some basics. To have a network up and running in your office, everyone you want on the

Danger

I've seen offices where the computers weren't networked and where the "e-mail" computer stood on its own in the corner of a large room. The staff were supposed to check it now and again for individual e-mails, but I've never seen this setup come close to working. One solution in smaller companies is to give every computer Internet access. Rather than being connected to a local network host, each person can send e-mail through the ISP (a local phone call) and check for messages a few times a day.

Caution: Dangerous Surfing Ahead

It's a brave new world, and the advent of e-mail and the Internet have brought with them whole new sets of problems. Or, perhaps, they're only new arenas for age-old workplace issues.

You need to set up guidelines about privacy, standards of decency and the levels of acceptable usage for e-mail and the Internet. Ideally, you shouldn't have to worry about these things, but experience suggests they can become a problem unless you lay down clear guidelines upfront.

The most common issue is employees surfing the World Wide Web for personal chuckles on your time. You can establish any kind of guidelines you want, as long as they're consistent for all employees. Your network consultant can give you some tips on software that will let you track employee access usage. Expect your staff to do a little wandering, especially after the network is first installed, but that should taper off quickly. If it doesn't, act soon to make sure recreational surfing doesn't become a habit.

Expand any company handbook you have to include standards of decency and the Internet. Spell out that Internet work on office computers does not include sexually oriented sites. If you're worried about problems, a few commercial software vendors offer programs that can be installed on your server that allow you to limit access to certain kinds of Web sites.

Do you as an employer have the right to read an employee's e-mail? The law is still evolving on this, but the current state of the law says you do. In your new-employee briefing, you should make it clear that office computers are company property and, such as, files and messages on them belong to the company. You might say explicitly that you have no objection to a modest amount of personal e-mail messaging at work, but the law doesn't view these messages as the employee's private property. Ask for their cooperation in minimizing personal computer time and in keeping privacy issues from becoming troublesome.

network must have his or her own computer. Your installer will run cabling connecting each computer with the server, a dedicated computer whose job is to run the network. You install networking software (which includes messaging—e-mail—capability) on the server and each individual computer. Users sign on to the system with a password, which enables them to get their e-mail and send e-mail to others on the system. As mentioned earlier, the server itself must be connected to the outside world to allow the network users to send e-mail outside the company or to browse the Web, and your phone system will also have to be set up to handle this.

Don't trust yourself to set up a computer network. This is not what you're good at, and there's no reason you should spend your time and energy getting good at it. Look in your local Yellow Pages, and you'll probably find a busload of suppliers eager to help you out. Check out their references before you use them, give them plenty of time to understand what you need, and get a detailed estimate. Because of the technology involved, you're vulnerable. So proceed cautiously.

Jargon Alert

A newsgroup is a discussion group on the Internet. You'll find newsgroups devoted to many, many different subjects. Newsgroup postings don't show up in your e-mail box; you go to the newsgroup portion of your browser to review messages.

Some of the companies that sell network server computers (IBM, for example) will also sell you a support subscription along with the computer. When the computer arrives, a support person comes along and takes care of installing the network, and he or she will also be available to fix any problems you have once it's all hooked up.

Networking software is complicated. Give yourself and your network supplier a month to get the bugs out of the system. And appoint one person in your office as the network administrator or guru. This individual will handle problems your staff discovers and then work with your network supplier in getting them solved.

Having all your computers networked allows your staff to communicate instantly with one another via e-mail and to store files on the remote server so they can be accessed by everyone. The network will also allow you to back up all company files from the server onto a backup system.

Once you get onto the Internet, the borders of your e-mail disappear. Now you can exchange e-mail with anyone on the planet who's connected. You can do it anytime, and you can send messages carrying attachments with text or picture files.

Listservs And Newsgroups

You have two other Internet avenues that offer you the opportunity to listen to and, to some degree, talk with your market: listservs (sometimes called mailing lists) and newsgroups. Each of these Internet features gives you the opportunity to observe the rough-and-tumble nature of the electronic marketplace.

Most software companies have newsgroups—some official, some not. If you're interested in what people think of a given piece of software, the company newsgroup will let you sample that reaction in no uncertain terms. And you get to witness company support staff trying to please their sometimes irate (and sometime just marginally sane) customers.

All newsgroup messages are linked by topic; they're "threaded." This allows you to read a lengthy sequence of messages (called postings) on a given theme. Your browser's newsreader software lets you visit, read and post messages in any newsgroup that appeals to you. It will let you view a listing of thousands of newsgroups, many of which introduce you to different communities and even galaxies. Newsgroups frequently host discussions that become, shall we say . . . spirited.

A newsgroup is more freewheeling than a listserv since they're often unmoderated: Anyone can say anything about anything. If you manufacture cooking utensils, for example, you can sit in on discussions by avid cooks on the advantages or disadvantages of existing products. You yourself can get involved and invite people to contact you directly through e-mail so that

Jargon Alert

A listserv is an electronic mailing list devoted to a particular topic; you subscribe to it via an e-mail message and then receive messages via your regular e-mail. Thousands of listservs cover topics of all sorts, from the practical to the inane. You receive all mail that members of the group send to each other. Some listservs deliver just one or two messages a week; others deliver hundreds of messages each day. Many listservs are moderated—someone "monitors" (some say "censors") communications to reduce off-topic postings and general rowdiness. Visit www.onelist.com for a listing of listservs.

you can have them try out a new product, fill out a customer survey, give you reactions to competitive products, or comment on different pricing strategies.

Unless your product or service primarily targets people who are also avid Internet users, newsgroups and listservs are better at providing you with market information than with actual sales. With newsgroups and listservs, you know at least one strong interest of the people who post messages. But how can you make use of these groups?

Danger

In the rec.travel.europe newsgroup, members frequently ask specific questions about logistical details in European cities. One travel agency answers such questions thoughtfully and then steers readers to the company's Web site for additional information. Aim for helpfulness, not self-promotion. Regular users of this group can smell an overaggressive self-marketer a mile away and will tend to ignore you. Make your appearance noteworthy for genuine, detailed knowledge, not for horn-blowing.

1. **Read the FAQ (the list of "frequently asked questions").** Most people in the newsgroup or listserv will have read these. If you don't, you're likely to post a message that makes you look either stupid or insensitive to the group dynamics. Most FAQs are only a few pages

Who's Surfing?

Some key facts about Web users from the Georgia Institute of Technology's ongoing online user survey:

- Of the 31 million current users, two-thirds are male.
- Two-thirds of all users are between 25 and 50 years old, and one-fifth are between 19 and 25.
- The mean household income of users is $58,000.
- Of all users, 30 percent are in computer-related work, 14 percent are students and 10 percent are in education.
- Sixty percent of users access the Web from home.

Jargon Alert

Because of the fluid nature of the Internet audience, most newsgroups and listservs have FAQs—frequently asked questions. Some are simple; others are quite elaborate and structured. Find out where the FAQ document is kept, download it (or read it online) and learn the answers to basic newsgroup or listserv topics. To avoid looking ignorant, always read the FAQ before contributing.

long—they'll give common abbreviations, background info on the group, identify some legendary posters and generally orient you to what the group's about.

2. **Lurk for a month or two.** Lurkers are people who read without posting. Get to know the terrain. Again, you want to use this forum with the utmost of courtesy.

3. **Wait for a question or comment to which you can truly add some good comments.** Write a concise posting and mention your Web site or e-mail for more information.

4. **Be especially helpful to the opinion leaders of the group.** Their impressions of your knowledge and capabilities will influence all other readers.

5. **Since you can respond to newsgroup messages by either a newsgroup posting or by private e-mail (and to a listserv posting by group mail or private e-mail), consider posting a survey via e-mail to carefully selected members of the group.** You're on their turf, so be cautious. But if you select responders well, you can gather excellent, real-time information.

6. **Don't communicate by spamming.** This will only alienate recipients and blacken your virtual eye in future dealings with the group.

Establishing A Web Site: Your Virtual Business Address

An e-mail address gives you the absolute minimum Internet presence. But the pace of technology is advancing so quickly that many small companies are quickly concluding that an e-mail address isn't enough. Web sites are where it's at.

Your Web site represents your company's outpost on the virtual frontier. Every site has an exclusive address; visitors type the address into their browser software, press Enter and they're transported to your site. People still talk of Web pages, but more and more the Internet community speaks of Web sites. Originally, Web site addresses tended to be a single page, hence the phrase "Web page." But it's becoming increasingly rare to see a Web site with a single page, especially for a company. Many firms now have sites with scores of pages filled with product information, company news, electronic catalogs, contact people, pages for soliciting visitor feedback and much more amazing material.

Deciding whether you need a Web site, of course, depends on the type of business you have and who your customers are.

Seek And Ye Shall Find . . . Eventually

You type in a topic, and a search engine finds relevant sites on the Web. Some of the best-known search engines are Yahoo!, Lycos and WebCrawler. You access them quite simply through your browser window (the program you use to navigate the Web). Newbies often go bug-eyed on their first searches, when they get the message: "We have found 32,384,810 matches to your search criteria." Talk about information overload.

Much of what's initially found is not very helpful, but the various search engines have different ways to help you focus your search to yield better information. You can, for example, search just the matches to your first search with a second search term. If you're looking for plastic kites, for example, you might find a jillion hits on the word "plastic"; search just those matches for the word "kite" and you'll get what you're looking for. Search engines are rapidly growing more discriminating and useful. Most provide what is known as a "Boolean" search, where you can use pluses, minuses and other characters to limit your search. For example, you can type in plastic+kites and the search engine will only give you results that contain both words. Your best bet in using any search engine is to take a look at the "help" or "tips" that are offered to make sure you're entering your search criteria in a way the engine can understand.

Web Works?		
	Consider Web Site	**Don't Consider Web Site Now**
Geographic Market	Market extends beyond county.	Market is limited to city or county.
Demographic Market	Your customers or potential customers are online.	Your customers or potential customers aren't online in large numbers.
Staff Support	You can keep your site current.	You can't keep your site current.
Site Content	Your business can provide timely information of interest on your Web site.	Your business can't provide timely information of interest on your Web site.
	You can provide content that will improve on your printed materials.	You can't provide content that will improve on your printed materials.

Locating And Building Your Web Site

There are two opinions on whether small-business owners should design and create their own Web sites. Some people say it's too complicated and any time you spend learning how to do it just takes you away from your best work: running your business. In other words, stick to your knitting.

The other side maintains that with new Web site design software (like FrontPage Express), which is packed with attractive templates, it's relatively easy to get a simple site up and running in just a few hours. FrontPage Express is a highly respected piece of software.

Basically, if you want a simple site—a functional presence on the Web without the frills—then get the software and get to work. If you want your company's site to be a "full-featured" location, then have a designer do the work for you. Designers are not hard to find, as creating Web sites is now big business. Many small advertising agencies and creative boutiques have found Web site design to be a profitable market niche for themselves. After all, they've typically been using computer technology for years, and they have the design skills to make a site visually attractive and marketing-driven.

Look in the Yellow Pages for a list of the many, many companies that will help you build your Web site. Don't clinch any relationship without looking at sites the developer has completed and talking to those clients. Check that you both have the same understanding of what you're looking for. If you want plain vanilla, don't sign on with a developer with a reputation for building hazelnut Oreo crunch.

For locating your Web site, you have three options:

1. **Host it yourself on a computer with a dedicated phone line.** This will prove costly to set up and maintain, and if you're at all successful in using your site for business, you'll soon overwhelm your capacity. This is probably not a good option.

2. **Use an Internet service provider (ISP) with Web hosting services.** This is a good choice if you're somewhat comfortable dealing with Internet issues and won't need a lot of hand-holding. Some of the larger, more service-oriented ISPs provide considerable support.

3. **Use an online community like AOL or MSN, which offers a range of support services.** You're working in a very protected environment, with plenty of help if problems arise. A decision you'll have to make early on is the address of your Web site. In Web language, you'll need to decide on your domain name.

Cable station CNN has a strong Web presence with a Web site at cnn.com. CNN is the domain name; .com is the ending for "company." As you might imagine, every company with a Web site would like to use their company name as the site address. But there are too many businesses out there. And a few wily and farsighted entrepreneurs have already reserved Web addresses with the names of the largest com-

How To

You can find out what's being talked about where by using a search site called Deja News. Go to www.dejanews.com and enter the word or words you're looking for. It will give you a lengthy list of newsgroup messages with those terms.

Insight

Costs for Web site hosting are very fluid. For example, the ISP Earth-Link offers a range of different business Web site hosting services, running from $20 a month to several hundred dollars a month for very active sites. Generally, the pricing structure is based on the amount of space your site will take up on the ISP's server and sometimes on the number of visitors it receives.

panies. When those companies go to book the domain name for myempire.com, they find it's reserved by some little guy in Pittsburgh. Of course, he will let Myempire Corporation have the name . . . for the right price.

If you're looking into estalishing a Web presence, check on the availability of a few names you'd like to have for your address. They're going quickly, so check fast. If you can't get your company name, try for a common product or tool associated with your field (keypad.com, numbers.com, ohiofinance.com, and so on). Go to www.internic. net to check on name availability and then register your name. Two-year registration costs $100. You can also have your domain name registered by your ISP, but you'll be better off having your own. If you register it, you know what you've got. Some unscrupulous ISPs have been known to register a client's domain name under their own (the ISP's) name, and thus they grabbed ownership.

How To Build A Web Presence

When someone enters your Web site, he or she expects to see something. What do you want it to be? Some Web sites are a maze of different connections, leading to all points of the compass. Others show a disconcerting bareness . . . not much there. And what is there is proudly stamped as having been updated three months ago!

How can you make a stop at your Web site a positive experience? What can you give your visitor and potential customer? Here are some ideas:

1. **More important than anything else is organization.** Don't make traversing your Web site like hiking through Yellowstone on a moonless night without a map. Anticipate the visitor's

response to your page arrangement. Make it easy for the visitor to get the information he or she needs.

2. **At the beginning, place a clear statement of what your company does for a living in just a few words.** This will save everyone's time and hook the person who's truly looking for someone with your capabilities. Make your description benefit-oriented.

3. **Give a listing of your products, with visuals.** If your type of business allows you to list prices or price ranges, do it. If you have a large inventory, list the key products early on on the Web site. Let the visitor go deeper into your Web site as he or she is more interested. But show your basic products early in the visit. Don't be afraid to use the Web's excellent graphics capabilities . . . just avoid overdoing it.

4. **Show your real-world locations.** Make it clear where you're located and where you have distribution or sales offices. A map is nice, with phone numbers and fax numbers.

5. **If you can sell through your Web site, all the better.** You can list your 800 or fax order number, or your Web site or e-mail address. Many firms also include a built-in order form, which customers can cut and paste or download into their word processing software—where they can print it out and fill it in. For customers to place orders online, however, you need a sophisticated understanding of Web dynamics and technology. Because of security issues, a "click and order" system requires sophisticated password and identification safeguards. Contact your ISP or Web hosting service for information on how to get that done for you.

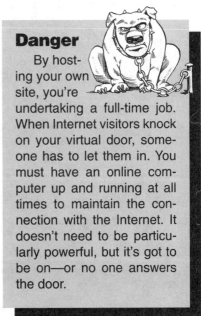

Danger

By hosting your own site, you're undertaking a full-time job. When Internet visitors knock on your virtual door, someone has to let them in. You must have an online computer up and running at all times to maintain the connection with the Internet. It doesn't need to be particularly powerful, but it's got to be on—or no one answers the door.

6. **Especially if you're a small company, use people pictures.** Give visitors a sense of the personality of your

company by showing your senior people and staff. Make them friendly . . . not "corporate."

7. **Offer a list of clients, completed projects or work samples.** This is your chance to trumpet your skills and successes, so make the most of it. If you have some killer case histories, applications stories or testimonials, don't hold back.

8. **Include e-mail capability and a guest book.** Don't create a site without e-mail. Otherwise, you're an online merchant who doesn't speak to the customers. Don't forget to keep absolutely current with e-mail. Everyone knows how easy it is to respond to e-mail. So if you neglect to do it promptly, the message you send is clear: "You're not that important to me."

9. **Keep the information on your Web site fresh.** You've got to change things often just to keep up visitor interest. Many Web sites carry a small indicator of when they were last revised. The better Web sites use this technique to prove that they're up to date. Web surfers have no patience for old information.

10. **Depending on your market, make your site fun to visit.** Use clever graphics. Write engaging page headings. Internet users enjoy an entertaining Web site.

As your Web site is nearing completion, make sure you register its name and address with the various search engines. Since most Web site visitors first find a site by searching for a keyword, you want to make sure you register your site under as many applicable keywords as possible. What words might a prospective customer of yours be looking for on the Web?

Danger

Web page designers like fancy graphics. Web site visitors hate fancy graphics—because they take so long to download (most Web users have modems that are much slower than the ones the designers use). Keep visuals to a minimum: Do you really need a graphic of your logo spinning majestically through the rings of Saturn?

A company named Submit It (www.submitit.com) will register your site with 20 search engines for no charge. They've already registered more than 250,000 sites and offer many other Web site-related services. Or you can register individually with the search engines of your choice. They're easy to find on the Web. The most popular ones are Yahoo!, Excite, Lycos, AltaVista and Infoseek.

Push Technology

A new, more intrusive technology is making the Web even more useful. Called "push technology," it enables you to use your Web presence as a "channel" to send information to "subscribers" or staffers at times when their computers aren't in use. It was initially developed by a company called PointCast, but its great promise has drawn more and more players into the act.

Some examples:

1. The regional sales force for a utility company receives a transmission every other evening at 2 a.m. It includes the latest sales figures, demand statistics, new application notes, answers to technical questions and so on. It's all sent from corporate headquarters automatically and received by the waiting desktops. The salespeople show up in the morning to scan the evening's harvest.

2. You manufacture a unique piece of software for the body shop industry. With push technology, you offer a channel giving shop owners current information on comparative prices region by region, insurance company reimbursement plans, equipment updates, tips on shop techniques and blurbs owners can use in developing communications with their customers.

Subscribers get pushed materials through special software built right into their browsers—this is starting to happen right now. The technology is evolving so quickly that it's gone through a new generation since you started this chapter.

New material can be broadcast on any line—if the computer is in active use, the push server buffers the data for later viewing. Contact PointCast for details (www.pointcast.com).

How To

Even if people don't leave you an e-mail or sign your guestbook, you can learn a few things about them . . . automatically. Your Web developer can include a visitor log in your site software. This will give you visitor counts, time they spent at your site, which parts of your site they visited and in what sequence, and from where they came to you. Use this valuable information to refine your site, to increase your visibility on those sites that send you the most visitors, and to track the results of each change.

Food For Thought

The ability to reach millions of people instantly has proven too seductive for some unscrupulous and short-sighted people. These are the advertisers who spread spam on the Internet. "Spam" is the Internet term for utterly undifferentiated advertising that's sent out to millions of people daily, offering instant riches, high-quality sex talk, lucrative investment opportunities and other suckers-only come-ons.

Spammers don't realize (or don't care about) the appalling contempt in which they're held and with which they affect the entire Internet marketing community. Be forewarned that many Web denizens have grown hypersensitive about spam, and they won't hesitate to "flame" you (send you a nasty, angry e-mail) if they feel you've spammed them.

You can avoid this practice by being sensitive. When doing a targeted, differentiated mailing, make clear you've selected them for the mailing for a particular reason—that you're not just blanketing the Web with your offer. You may still get blasted occasionally, but it will be the exception and not the rule.

Also, check with your ISP to make sure they won't block your e-mail because it has too many recipients. Many service providers have what are known as spam filters to keep spamming to a minimum. This can come as a big surprise if you're sending out a legitimate e-mail to a list of 54 people when your ISP's spam filter limits you to 50 recipients. The message won't get to anyone on the list and you might not find out for days.

The term "spam" appears to stem from a classic Monty Python skit dealing with a Viking restaurant in which every item was based on Spam, the processed meat product. Any cheap, cheesy, one-size-fits-all mass advertising on the Internet is spam, although the term is also loosely used for any assertive product or service offer.

Web Advertising

The commercialism of the Internet has spawned an advertising presence. It doesn't take more than 30 seconds on the Web before you feel like you're walking the midway at a county fair—everyone's trying to get your attention. The perimeter of your monitor pulsates with color, pattern, flashes of light, swimsuit models and the ever-present dancing dollar signs. Many mimic functional aspects of your browser—"Click me" they scream, and they look like you should click *here* to start your search. You click only to face the same experience U-boat captains did when they closed in on a lumbering freighter in the North Atlantic, which revealed itself at the last minute as a heavily armed sub killer. You've been had.

How To

Visit www. linkexchange. com to learn about how this cooperative ad swap shop serves more than 200,000 Web site owners. You'll see opportunities to link your site with thousands of others to promote visitors.

You can buy advertising—they're often called banner ads—on many Web sites. It provides you with a way to put messages in front of Web surfers who don't ever reach your actual Web site. The sites for the major search engines and news media are festooned with glitzy advertising graphics. Many of the more popular Web sites have a spot to click for advertising info. Such spots are reasonably affordable. If your market is one that's likely to visit particular Web sites, get the advertiser's kit and see how they fit into your marketing plan and marketing budget.

Linking Your Site

The Web contains a distinctive feature that makes it very easy to get around: links. A link is a navigational shortcut that can speed you from one place to another. Click on a link and you're there. In an article on nutrition, you might see the word "carbohydrate" underlined and in a different typeface. This is a link. Click on it and you'll see a new screen (or a new window) with more information on carbohydrates. Links also serve as gateways to other Web sites. If I want to give you a site to visit (like the sites I mention in this chapter), my Web page would have the site linked: clicking on the underlined text will transport you immediately to that site.

This is a great way to add value to your site; you compile links of interest to your audience. You're saving them the work of tracking down the sites on their own and then keying them in to their browser. Your Web site can include links to trade publications, suppliers, a

How To

What's a great way to promote your Web site? Make sure to put the address on all your printed marketing materials, including letter-head and business cards.

library of background materials on technical issues, a trade directory, show schedules, national or regional associations and more . . . all provided by you as a service to your visitors. You're limited only by your imagination and your resources.

You can also establish complementary link exchange programs with sites you uncover during your time on the Internet. Offer to put a good link on your Web site in exchange for being listed on another site.

Of course, you wouldn't want to link to your competitors—unless you're extraordinarily confident of your competitive position.

Chapter 12

Customer Service: The Soft Underbelly Of Marketing

It's easy, in the throes of business, to look at customer service as an afterthought . . . the mint on the pillow, the "inspected by #1442" slip of paper in our new slacks. We all like to assume that our "deliverable"—our physical product or service as listed on the invoice—is what will gain and keep our customers. People pay us for our product, after all, and whatever shortcomings might surface in how we provide it . . . well, we'll be forgiven, won't we?

Not for long, we won't.

An occasional lapse can be worked out, but the competition has raised the bar in customer service. Buyers of all sorts have risen from their comas of contentment to demand more, demand better and demand faster. The old ways don't cut the mustard anymore. Unless you market a unique product with an absolutely amazing customer benefit, you've got to please customers in every way you can. With the product, of course. But beyond the product as well.

Our society as a whole—not to mention the business-to-business marketplace—looks for more and more service. Naked products without the warm fuzzies of service just aren't enough. As a small-business person, this means five things to you:

1. **Pure service businesses represent a boom industry.** Our economy's health and society's wealth mean more of us can afford services. The money is there, and people are going to spend it on something. So we have gardeners and masseurs, private shoppers and housecleaners, personal trainers and private accountants, carryout gourmet foods and Fabergé by mail. These job slots have long existed for royalty, of course. But our culture's success has made them affordable for those of us not wearing crowns or bearing scepters. Our society has a service frame of mind. We expect more.

2. **Even product-based businesses have become more dependent on their service component.** The pace of business quickens each day. The rate of technological change raises the heart rates of customer and manufacturer alike. Competitive product advantages fade faster. Information can't be caged—it just flows through the bars—and what makes news in the morning is stale in the afternoon. Certainly making a buck has always been challenging, but technology and heightened service expectations sure make us sweat more for each greenback. People want more. Stuff is good; stuff with good service is even better. When it comes to burgers, you're told, you possess the birthright to "Have it *your* way."

3. **Well-delivered service—above and beyond the level expected—can provide you a competitive advantage.** Rather than

see service demands as just another business burden, look at them as one more chance to pack additional perceived value into your product. More perceived value means satisfied customers . . . and the opportunity to charge higher prices.

4. **A company that delivers good service to its customers generally has a happy, satisfied work force.** People like giving good service, especially if they can see that the company elders support their efforts and train them in how best to provide the service.

5. **Small businesses like yours have a built-in service edge.** As a small business, you're generally locally based, know your customers personally, know the local market conditions and preferences, and have a certain amount of "buy from someone you know" loyalty. For many products and services, these advantages are difficult for a large company to overcome. Don't underestimate the loyalty of hometown customers. But don't overestimate it either. Lackadaisical service will drive your customers right into the arms of the big boys. Ask the small store owners who felt small-town fidelity would let them beat big bad Sam Walton.

We've seen that marketing is all about focusing yourself on the mind of the customer as you establish and run your business: As you decide on products, set up product distribution and pricing, determine your advertising and so on. It's no different with customer service. The key to good customer service is keen customer orientation.

The fact is, you're delivering customer service whether you know it or not. You can't avoid delivering it. The question is, What kind of service are your customers now getting?

Sometimes it's easy to let the running of your business get in the way of how you take care of your customers. Every business needs procedures to operate on a

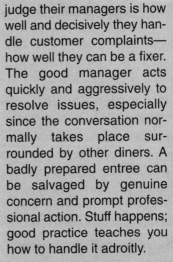

Insight

One of the ways restaurant owners judge their managers is how well and decisively they handle customer complaints—how well they can be a fixer. The good manager acts quickly and aggressively to resolve issues, especially since the conversation normally takes place surrounded by other diners. A badly prepared entree can be salvaged by genuine concern and prompt professional action. Stuff happens; good practice teaches you how to handle it adroitly.

The mail order industry thrives because of its service. Luxurious catalogs, a broad array of products, targeted mailing lists, rock-solid guarantees and inexpensive overnight shipping make for a customer's dream buying environment. You see the pretty picture this afternoon; you hold it in your hand tomorrow. Talk about instant gratification! Once the mail order business overcame the natural skepticism of people buying things through the mail, they had a multi-billion-dollar industry on their hands. But they never could have succeeded without die-hard, satisfaction-guaranteed customer service.

day-to-day basis. This is what gives your business continuity, helping new people get up to speed quickly. It's how any business learns from its past. But those procedures—the inherited company wisdom—can block customer service.

I've never seen a manufacturing operation, for example, without a healthy (or sometimes destructive) tension between production and sales. The sales staff make a living selling, and they'll go to any lengths to make the customer happy. Their compensation depends on it. So sometimes making the sale means stretching the production capability or canceling fundamental laws of space and time. "They gotta have it by the 14th!"

The production people, on the other hand, must make the stuff. They have raw materials and manufacturing equipment to worry about. Not to mention quality control. They want to slow things down a bit to make sure the product that ships is just right. No product before its time. "We can't deliver by the 14th!"

This tension can lead to time-line dishonesty. The salesperson surreptitiously builds a "fudge factor" into his commitment to the customer. No one at the plant knows about it. Of course, the production people have their *own* secret fudge factor, which gives them a little safety margin and allows them to look good by often delivering ahead of schedule. After a while, the whole function of schedule breaks down, and no one knows how long things take and when customers really need delivery.

Small businesses especially must put the customer ahead of procedures. Give your staff the discretion to make decisions to go outside procedures for customers. Work with your sales crew on being honest with dates—and to let you know when they really, really gotta get something quick.

All Customer Service Is Personal

There's an irony at the core of customer service. At its heart, service has nothing to do with business. It's about people and the way we feel about each other. When everything is said and done, we're all in this life together. Forget the commercial business side of things for a moment. Whatever we're doing, we feel genuinely appreciative when someone does a little something for us that they don't have to do: opening a door for us when our arms are full, helping guide us into a tight parking space, letting us into a long line of traffic.

Now bring it back to the business realm. Think of how warmly you appreciated it when someone went the extra mile for you when he or she didn't have to. Wouldn't it be nice if we did things for the customer that we didn't contract to do? Providing customer service is good for business and good for the soul.

I once had a printer working on Christmas Eve to finish up some desperately needed restaurant menus. He didn't have to do that. I wouldn't have blamed him if he'd said we'd have to wait until the 26th. But he gave me a few hours on Christmas Eve above and beyond the call of duty, which made me both personally grateful and a longtime future customer. I turned my sense of obligation into future business.

One good current example of the conflict between business efficiency and good customer service is the growing use of sophisticated voice-mail systems. Proponents of these systems maintain that they provide companies a way to guide customers directly to the information they need, not to mention the fact that they save payroll by automating the function.

Danger
You don't have to be in business very long to recognize there are countless ways to lose customers. Don't add your own insensitive service to the list. Customer service that isn't a top priority is bad customer service. The more competitive your marketplace, the more important your level of everyday service.

One More Time—With Feeling

You probably have some form letters you use in your business: brief notes that accompany standard requests for literature, cover sheets for standard proposals, responses to job applications, answers to requests for charitable funding. These are all customer service-related issues, broadly defined. We've all received form letters in response to questions we've asked of a company. You know how eerily impersonal they feel: filled with abstractions, passive voices, bureaucratic speak—totally bloodless.

Have your form letters and major public communications written by someone with a soul. If you have someone on staff who can do this, great. If not, draft the materials and have a real writer give them the once over. They should be human and conversational, fostering a face-to-face feel. Make it personal. Even the simplest of notes or letters gives you an opportunity to make an impression on your customer. Be certain it's the right impression. It should fit the personality of your company and leave your customer with a sense of the personal side of your business. The same applies to any equipment instructions and other product support literature. All customer service—even the written word—is personal.

But navigating these voice-mail systems makes for a bleak and annoying journey—endless prompts, long and unbroken instructions, layers upon layers of system architecture. Older customers often just hang up: They've learned to deal with answering machines, but these new systems just drive up their blood pressure. I think these automated voice-mail systems sometimes provide companies a way to economize on customer service, not to provide better service. Don't let your voice-mail system get between you and your customers. Limit the layers of messages and simplify the system for your customers. Remember, they want to talk to *you*.

Dealing With Hostile Customers

Complaints are an opportunity for fine-tuning your operation. Look at a complaint like an objection in a sales presentation. Or a brutal, one-person survey. It's bound to happen. Your best efforts at product delivery and customer service have come up short and you've got an angry customer on your hands. How do you handle it?

1. **Acknowledge your mistake.** Don't blame it on the computer, those slacker branch office people or the customer's lack of understanding of your requirements. If it's a genuine error on your part, just confess it and move on to the next step in the process.

2. **Admit the serious implications of your mistake for the customer.** You've got to empathize with your customer. For you, it's another business transaction. For the customer, your blunder can range from a minor inconvenience to a major trauma. Inquire gingerly about the implications of the problem. Try to get a feel for the actual impact.

3. **Ask how you can make things right for this particular transaction.** Do you give a new product? Do you redo the service? Do you discount your price? Do you perform your service *gratis?* Your response depends on a range of factors, including just what your product is. But make this decision as part of your effort to retain the relationship, not just to put out a fire.

4. **Learn how you can repair the relationship.** Once you've worked out the details of remedying the particular transaction, move directly to the next step. "How can we make things right with you overall?" you might ask, or "How can we restore our relationship to where it was before this problem surfaced?" Think big picture here: You should be willing to invest something in retaining the relationship, especially if it's a long-term customer for whom you've botched a transaction.

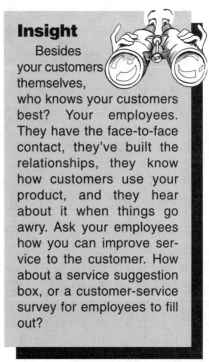

Insight

Besides your customers themselves, who knows your customers best? Your employees. They have the face-to-face contact, they've built the relationships, they know how customers use your product, and they hear about it when things go awry. Ask your employees how you can improve service to the customer. How about a service suggestion box, or a customer-service survey for employees to fill out?

Insight

Some industries thrive on customer service. Think of the salon business. Most of us, male or female, could probably go to the local Speedy Snip franchise for a simple, inexpensive hair trim. But instead we spend much more to go to salons, where—with a little extra atmosphere, special products with French names and more stylish stylists—we get fundamentally the same operation performed. Most of us are more than willing to pay for service. It just feels good. It provides value, even when it's largely psychological.

Although the customer is "always right," sometimes it doesn't matter. We've all run into customers for whom the "hassle per dollar" ratio proves just too high, the relationship just too painful—financially and emotionally. Sometimes you have to make the hard decision that a given customer must be let go. Several factors may lead to this:

- The dollar losses you take in meeting the customer's demands are too high.
- The person's requests throw your operations into internal scheduling turmoil.
- Your negative personal interactions have simply become too uncomfortable.
- You've changed the nature of your business and you're no longer servicing that type of customer.
- The customer has ongoing financial or credit problems.

Don't come to this decision brashly, but—once you decide—act immediately. Most experts suggest making the break in person rather than in writing or over the phone. This is a good time to "shade the truth": Couch your decision in the most general and nonconfrontational terms. Talk about how the goals of your two companies just don't seem to be compatible, no matter how hard you work at meeting their needs. You can mention that you've noticed that this customer just hasn't been happy with the type of work your company has provided, and that you've come to believe that only a different type of company will be able to meet his or her needs. You get the idea.

Just be sure to be politic and polite. Don't burn any bridges, and don't give in to the temptation to get all your feelings off your chest. It won't do you any good, and it may indeed cause you commercial harm—you don't know who your customer knows.

First-Class Service
Means Repeat Business

Let's look at five key reasons why you need to consider superior customer service as a "prime directive" for your business:

1. **Good service keeps customers.** We all know that it's easier to grow business from existing customers than to prospect and win new ones. Few businesses can stay afloat having to bring in a constant stream of new business to replace lost business.

2. **Good service builds word-of-mouth business.** You can't buy referral business—except by providing memorable customer service. You can be sure your customers talk about you with their friends and colleagues. What do they say?

3. **Good service can help you overcome competitive disadvantages.** This is especially true against larger companies. You may not have the same capital resources or research capabilities, but your smile is just as bright and you can work just as hard.

4. **Good service is easier than many parts of your business.** Developing innovative products, moving into new territories, prospecting new markets . . . this kind of hard work can be very demanding on a small business and its managers. Compared with this kind of heavy lifting, solid customer service—given the right point of view—is really quite simple. It's just a matter of making sure you and all your employees "get it."

Insight

Pay attention to the services you run across as you live your life. Can you translate them into similar services your business might provide? One piano tuner I know always books the next appointment—even though it may be four to six months away—before he leaves a tuning. He's locking in business rather than leaving it to chance. Can you use a "pre-booking technique"? The salesman who sold me my car knows exactly how old it is, and he sends me a "Hi, how are ya?" card every year or so. As the car ages, the frequency of the cards increases. Would this same timed approach work for your product?

5. Good service helps you work more efficiently. Make sure you extend your good service pledge to your internal customers as well. Any organization with more than one person has internal customers. You've got to ensure that your people inside the company treat one another with a service orientation. This will make your internal interactions proceed more smoothly, and it will lead to even better service for your external customers.

For many of the items we buy in our lives, we're willing to pay more for customer service. Take the differences in hotels. When we book a hotel, we're basically looking for a clean place to spend the night. Many hotels and motels provide just that for an economical price. But the range of hotel rates in any sizable city is enormous. Why? Because different people want different levels of service. Upscale hotel rates are notoriously inelastic (raising the price doesn't cut the demand) because, with enough wealthy people around, there's no upper limit for hotel rates—provided you deliver a thick and gooey layer of plush services.

Spot-Check Your Service: Be A Customer

Large retail businesses and franchise operations have long used outsiders to check on the level of service quality their customers are actually receiving. It's one thing to give employees a 20-minute presentation on how "the customer is the one who signs all our paychecks," but getting into the trenches and seeing the way customers are actually treated is something else.

Depending on your business, you can do this in several ways:

1. **Use secret shoppers.** Contract with a temporary agency to have outsiders "shop" your business and fill out reports on what they find. No single report will reveal any hidden secrets, but a number of reports over time will show you what your customer service is really like, no matter what managers and staff may tell you.

Insight
Every one of your employees has a direct or indirect impact on your customers. If they don't, why are you paying them?

Sample Service Plan For An Interior Designer

How do I get business?

- Initial contact

  1. They call:

     - responding to an ad.

     - responding to a referral.

     - responding to a mailing.

  2. I hear they're looking, and I call them.

- First meeting

  1. I come to understand their needs.

  2. I explain how we do business. *(I need to update my handout on business procedures to include business bio, customer list and so on. I should also do a frequently asked questions sheet to make customers feel more comfortable.)*

- Response with a proposal or pricing estimate:

  1. spells out pricing. *(Can I create a rough pricing sheet, with sample prices for typical projects?)*

  2. spells out scope of project.

- I get the go-ahead on the project. *(I should draft a general "Thanks for giving me the business" note to send to clients on project start-up.)*

- I produce a draft design plan for the project. *(Can I make a small ride-along sheet that explains how they can best give me their input on the first draft plan—maybe give some examples of helpful and not-so-helpful comments?)*

- I produce a second and third draft. *(Some clients have been surprised at how much billing can happen between first draft and final plan. Maybe I should give an interim billing report after the first draft and with each subsequent draft.)*

- I produce final plan.

Sample Service Plan, cont'd.

- We begin work on the project. (*How about a little flier that lets customers know what type of disruption they can expect as we do our work? I can fill in spots for how many days and how many hours a day.*)

- We finish the project, and I bill for the work. (*How much detail should I offer in my bills? I'll contact my last 12 clients and get their reaction to the format of my invoices.*)

- I send a thank-you note, expressing my appreciation for the business and asking them to refer me to friends and acquaintances.

---

2. **Establish a regular service evaluation with your customers.** Meet with the customers who interact regularly with your people. You're just taking the temperature of the relationship and looking for areas in which there remain unfulfilled, maybe even as yet unperceived, avenues for providing superior customer service. Ask customers to "blue sky" it: What dream services could you provide?

3. **Conduct a detailed study of the way you provide a product or service to your customer.** Put on your marketing cap. Create a flowchart highlighting each step in the sales and delivery process. How do you make the sales presentation? How do you establish pricing and terms? When does the customer make the buying decision? When are delivery options established and decisions made? Where in the process can you make customer-friendly alterations? (See the "Sample Service Plan For An Interior Designer," starting on page 233)

Setting Service Standards

We can characterize service by the old-fashioned American concept of "hustle." It means moving fast or thinking hard for your customers, even when they don't expect you to. In setting your company on the customer service tack, however, you'll need to be more specific when you talk to your people. They'll want to know specifics on what you expect them to do.

Service standards are measures against which we match our actual performance. They're like a salesperson's sales goal or the traffic cop's ticket quota. You want your people to understand what you want them to do and how often you want them to do it.

1. **Spell out your service policy.** Give a general statement of commitment, say how you want customers to be treated and why, and describe how employees will be evaluated regarding service.

2. **If your business allows you to establish measurable criteria (number of phone calls per hour, length of time spent with a client, number of orders through a station and so on), then set them.** These measures can help quality, but they can also hurt. Don't let efforts to "make the numbers" turn into customer-busting behavior.

3. **Specify actions you want employees to take in response to customers.** At the local Barnes and Noble superstore, if you ask a staff member where you might find a particular book, he or she is trained to actually take you there, not just point the way. Do you want your employees to greet customers with a specific phrase? Do you want your employees to wear a particular type of clothing? If someone calls accounting with a question about a bill, what steps do you want your employee to follow in zeroing in on the problem and then resolving it?

4. **Your service standards will get more notice if you reward employees who exceed them.** Is there a way customers can play a role in recognizing good service? Can they fill out an "I was well treated" card?

Danger

Don't make your service efforts too transparent. Kmart used to have stickers attached to its cash registers with the letters TYFSAK. This was to remind the cashiers to say to the customer: "Thank you for shopping at Kmart." There's nothing wrong with the sentiment, but why have the sticker in clear view of the customer? It takes away the genuineness of the words. How many times have you seen an Employee of the Month plaque that's more than six months out of date? It sends a message about customer service all right, but not the one the business intends!

If you have a business-to-business client or a distributor, remember that the purchasing agent isn't your customer. You have lots of other people who deal with your product. Is there a way you can improve the logistical details of your product: packaging, palletizing, shrink-wrapping, invoicing and so on?

In a business-to-business situation, do your employees know who your customers really are? Do they know how your products are used? Some manufacturers take key employees on tours of client factories to show them how the products they work to produce are actually used by their customers. It can be an eye-opening experience, since we're all prone to get locked into the worldview of our own workplace.

Chapter 13

Stay Strong
Through Training

How would you feel if one of your key customers asked you to share with him or her your thoughts on developing a well-trained work force?

How loud would that gulp be?

Train For Good Service

Training is a sore point for most small businesses, especially new ones, for obvious reasons:

- Training takes time.
- Training takes money.
- Training takes mental energy.

And we all know that owners and managers of small businesses, at the end of the day, have little left of time, money or mental energy.

Entrepreneurs often feel that training can wait until the company is more established, when it has a little extra time and money to spare. Many small-business owners resemble subsistence farmers—you make enough to feed the family and pay the farmhands, and maybe you earn enough extra to repair the tractor every few years, but you don't have much left for opera tickets.

If you've started your own business, chances are you feel you don't need a training program. After all, you make the rules and procedures. You or one of your trusted lieutenants may well have done most of the hiring. What's wrong with good, old-fashioned on-the-job training? What's all the hubbub, especially about formalized training? That might work in the state and federal government because those people don't work very hard anyway, right? It's also fine for large, successful, well-heeled companies—but we don't have that kind of luxury around here.

You must come to view training as an integral part of your marketing vision. If you've worked hard to align every part of your company with the needs and desires of the customer, you must follow through by communicating that to everyone in your company. Training will get all your people on the same page in dealing with marketing vision.

There's another reason, too. You can't market in a knowledge vacuum. You've got to keep up with what's happening in your industry. Your competitors certainly are. Training makes you more marketable.

For small businesses, training can be critical to survival. It's important for many compelling reasons:

- **Most vitally, it ensures the consistent delivery of quality service.** This is the lifeblood of your company. You can't deliver service if your people don't know what they're supposed to be doing.

- **It acclimates new hires to the company rules and guidelines.**

- **It provides customers with an added confidence in your viability as a long-term supplier who'll grow with them.** Without training, you're shooting from the hip, and you won't last long running your business like that.

- **It allows you to get the most out of your current staff.** In a small business, this assumes large importance. You can hire extra people, but you'll be ahead financially if you can cross-train a small staff to do several different jobs.

Stay Strong Through Training

- **It draws and retains better people.** High achievers recognize the value of workplace training and learning. They want to be in a place where they can better their abilities. When you invest in building your employees' skills, they're willing to invest themselves in building your company.

- **It lets your company and your people take advantage of changing conditions.** That's a lot better than reacting passively to changes in markets, production techniques, technology, regulatory issues and so on.

Jargon Alert

Cross-training is giving an employee the core skills to handle a position other than his or her regular job. This helps your company deal with unexpected departures, illnesses and employee leaves. It also keeps the cross-trained employees fresh: They're not likely to get stale in their regular jobs if they're exposed to the responsibilities of other positions.

- **It gives you the chance to inoculate everyone with your marketing vision.** No one in your organization can afford to be marketing-ignorant.

- **It aligns your operation with the trend toward business decentralization.** With flextime, independent contractor arrangements, virtual offices and job sharing, independent thinkers make businesses go. You want strong-minded people who have the confidence to use their good judgment to make wise decisions. You can't make all the decisions for your company.

Another way to look at training: If you could increase the production on a machine by 5 percent, you wouldn't hesitate to do it, right? But a good training course can boost individual efficiency by 15 percent to 25 percent. Don't think of your employees as flat-line producers who'll turn out work products at the same rate forever. You're selling them short. Give them some experience, some training and the right management support, and they'll surprise you. The productivity of workers can change dramatically with good training.

Training represents the wave of the future. It doesn't take a card-carrying futurist to predict that our economy will become increasingly more high-tech and knowledge-based. Germany's legendary manufacturing and engineering expertise relies on a long-established program of apprenticeships and training regimens.

Jobs that require little skill or training will offer little promise in our society. Many such jobs in manufacturing have already moved to the Far East or the Third World. Unless you want to position yourself as a low-cost supplier of a commodity product, you need to train your people to provide value and more service to your customer.

Two Kinds Of Training

There are really two types of training, both of which you'll need to harmonize with the lifestyle of your company:

- Training that integrates new hires into your current system: Each new employee needs to know what he or she is supposed to do for you.
- Training to expand or refresh the skills of your employees.

If you don't train your people carefully, how do you expect them to act any differently than they did at their previous job? Every business has its own procedures. You need to systematically show your new hires how to work smoothly in their new environment, with new processes and work rules and to help your long-term employees continue to develop their skills.

Training New Hires

You can smooth the arrival of new employees by developing a regular training process—with written documentation—that pairs a new hire with an existing worker in the same or similar slot. Small companies aren't typically able to field a "training department" or "training specialist." If you don't have detailed job descriptions, write them today. You can't run an organized company without job descriptions, no matter how inaccurate they may seem at the time. You need job descriptions to do the following:

- Create a salary structure
- Hire the right person
- Reward your staff for performing their jobs well
- Protect against lawsuits by employees you've fired
- Structure your overall training program
- Decide when training is done

You want to tie all your training efforts—both for new hires and for existing employees—to end results. The current terminology for

Stay Strong Through Training

this is CBT, competency-based training. People are finished with their training when they possess the skills you're out to teach them. You're not interested in whether someone has taken a high school or college course on a topic; you just want to know, Can they do it?

Because the development of training can be a controversial topic within a company, businesspeople tend to concentrate a lot of energy on describing what should go into training and relatively little effort on measuring what training is supposed to accomplish. What does successful training look like? What's the difference in a given worker before and after the training?

Think of a word-processing position. It would be reasonable for you to expect a graduate of word processing training to:

- Know basic computer skills: turning it on, saving and deleting files, organizing directories and so on

- Be fluent in English (or other necessary language)

- Be able to use a word processor skillfully, using basic editing commands, pagination, document merging, headers/footers and so on

- Be familiar with computer spelling checkers and know their weaknesses

- Possess good grammar skills to keep company correspondence on a literate business level

- Type at 75 words per minute

- Be organized enough to work with a number of documents at one time and merge them into a single report

- Be able to handle basic graphs, tables and figures

You don't care where your word-processor person learns these skills. You're not interested in whether he or she has ever taken a training course. You only want to know that he or she has the skills. Once the person has the skills, he or she has completed the training.

More Power?

Several years ago as I was upgrading my computer system, I was researching the best way to increase my efficiency at the computer. Should I go with a massive amount of RAM, faster chip, larger hard drive, more disk caching? Then I read an article that made an impression. It simply stated that, if you made your living as a writer (which I do), the single thing you can do to maximize your efficiency is learning to touch type well. I thought that made sense. And so I did, increasing my speed by 150 percent. And it's paid off in much greater productivity in both writing and editing. In this case, a little training gave me a skill that yielded much greater dividends than the slight increase available through a technofix. A solid training program often yields more than additional technology.

When you're establishing a training scheme, base it on job descriptions. What skills does a given job require? Which of those skills can you quantify or measure? Many job skills can be "counted" in some aspect: in manufacturing, phone sales, maintenance and equipment repair, to name just a few. The more you're able to attach numbers to jobs, the more clear-cut can be your performance expectations.

Develop Your Employees

Don't waste your time reinventing the wheel. Unless your business is unique (and no business is), owners of businesses like yours have wrestled with the identical problems you're facing. Many have solved them and moved on to a higher level of success. This is especially true of employee training. Look to your noncompetitive peers in business. How have they used training to move their companies ahead?

There are likely many different types of training courses that can benefit you and your employees:

- **Your national, regional and state trade associations most likely offer seminars or short courses at major trade shows.** This is a chance to learn at the hands of very experienced professionals in your field. There's no substitute for listening to someone who's been where you're trying to go. Such presentations by trade associations can be astonishing shortcuts to gaining business skills. Some also offer remarkably detailed correspondence courses in technical issues.

The Wisconsin Bankers Association, for example, brings bankers from across the state to Madison each year for an intense session with dozens of specialized courses.

The Credit Union National Association (to which almost all world credit unions belong) offers a wide range of courses at different sites in the United States for credit union managers and staff to become certified and increase their professionalism. They support this with extensive manuals, videotape training and home training opportunities as well. Over a hundred courses for all levels of tellers, supervisors and senior managers give standardized and highly professional training. It increases the professional image of the credit unions themselves, and the certification it brings provides a good personal and financial incentive for the individuals. It's win-win. Many industries have programs like this.

- **Your state government and the federal government offer courses on selling to the government, dealing with international sales and a host of similar issues.** You can find out about these courses through your state Department of Commerce.

- **Universities and university extensions offer more and more courses of great interest to the business community.** Many of these courses take place in the evenings to simplify life for employed registrants. They're an excellent way to enhance skills and knowledge. Consider reimbursing tuition when your employees take courses relevant to your workplace.

- **With corporate downsizing a fact of life in American businesses, there exist many small training businesses run by high-level professionals with big-company backgrounds.** Such companies or consulting groups offer many useful programs: team-building, quality improvement, internal communications, workgroup develop-

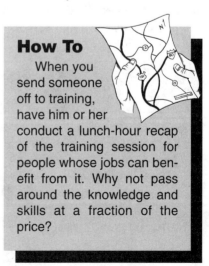

How To
When you send someone off to training, have him or her conduct a lunch-hour recap of the training session for people whose jobs can benefit from it. Why not pass around the knowledge and skills at a fraction of the price?

ment and so on. They'll come to your workplace and present seminars or act as facilitators for workgroups dealing with your company's particular issues. Look in your local Yellow Pages or talk to other businesspeople in your area for some recommendations. To be assured of a top-quality training experience, never hire such a company without speaking to references.

- **Your salespeople and key managers will likely benefit from a public-speaking course, such as those run by Dale Carnegie Training or Toastmasters.** Such skills boost self-esteem, increase presentation confidence and can yield you a dramatic return on your investment. Every company can benefit from a polished, forceful and eloquent presenter who is unafraid to talk about his or her company in front of a crowd.

How else can you encourage your employees to learn? Maintain a well-stocked library of relevant business books, and encourage employees to read them. In small businesses, many entrepreneurs leave their business reading to airports. But a look in any large bookstore will show you a wealth of solid thinking about all aspects of business and every industry. Make yourself and your top managers serious business readers, as well as sharers of the information and insights you uncover.

Not everyone can be a trainer. But some people are just born to be teachers. Latch on to one of these people and make him or her responsible for putting together and conducting training programs for your company. This person is probably a generalist and a warm people person. In small companies, human resources and training are often handled by the same person.

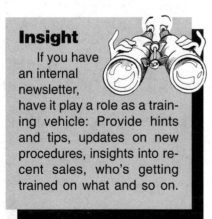

Insight

If you have an internal newsletter, have it play a role as a training vehicle: Provide hints and tips, updates on new procedures, insights into recent sales, who's getting trained on what and so on.

In addition to establishing a regular training program and staying on top of the latest techniques and technologies, your training chief must have the gift of instilling excitement in the learning experience. We can all remember school courses when we were bored witless as well as those courses that kept us engaged and high-spirited. It's the magical art of the teacher to make learning both thrilling and entertaining.

Stay Strong Through Training

Connect with your local training network. The American Society for Training and Development has about 70,000 members around the world and scores of active local chapters around the United States. It's a good organizational start through which to get in touch with the world of training. Visit its Web site at www.astd.org.

Chapter 14

Database Marketing Expands Your Horizons

Database marketing is the promotion of your company's products to your current and prospective target audiences by using computer-based, data-driven information.

The emergence of database marketing stems from the convergence of three separate strands of contemporary society:

1. **Computers now combine tremendous speed and power with a reasonable price.** The old 640K limit on memory produces a confused grin from the younger generation. New purchases of even moderately priced desktops arrive with gigabytes of disk space and a thousand times the RAM of the pioneer PCs. And processing speed seems to double every 12 months. Most small businesses will never use all the horsepower of a fully loaded desktop, or even of a notebook, for that matter. Programs have so much

power and so many features that it takes years to discover all they can do.

2. **The triumph of the marketing mind-set means most businesses recognize the importance of consumer focus in their marketing efforts.** If "cash is king" on Wall Street during harried times, then it's a safe bet that "the consumer is king" at all times in the retail or business-to-business marketplace.

3. **The information explosion has yielded a wonderful data glut of solid, practical information on the purchasers of our products.** Buyers are scrutinized more closely than ever before—both by the sellers themselves and by specialized research-oriented companies that peddle their information to manufacturers and retailers. Even the Census Bureau has piled its information into the market information avalanche.

What all this means for you is that you can understand the buying habits of your current customers—and build a pathway to new ones—with undreamed of precision.

In a sense, contemporary database marketing with the computer lets you return to the roots of modern commerce. Imagine the shopkeeper of Dickens' 19th-century London (he's given us great portraits of them in his novels). Because he sold only to the extremely local market, he knew most of his customers quite well—what they bought, who was in the family, what they didn't like and their income level. He maintained his database under his hat.

Based on this, the informed shopkeeper could hazard a solid guess that Mrs. Thomas, for example, might well be interested in the new lavender-scented candles that had just arrived from France. He knew she planted a lot of lavender along the streetfront near her house. She was always trying different scented candles to use in her dark home. He could suggest it to her, study her reaction and make a mental note to "refine the customer profile."

In one medium-sized Midwestern city, a specialty perfume shop sells upscale perfumes and sundries to its near west-side and mail order clientele. The shop is in an out-of-the-way specialty mall. In addition to a splendid memory for customers and a gentle but engaging personality, the Scandinavian proprietor possesses an extensive catalog of index cards. He can tell you everything any one of his thousands of customers has purchased for the last 15 years. He meticulously enters each new purchase along with date and price. He also asks how you liked that bottle of scent you purchased last

Database Marketing Expands Your Horizons

April . . . a little too much jasmine in the background, you say? As children grow up and into the perfume-wearing age, they get a card in this file. When husbands appear before birthdays, anniversaries or holidays, the proprietor provides an extremely accurate recommendation for a splendid gift. What an efficient database! Dickens would be proud.

Computers have replaced index cards for most businesses, but the principle remains the same. Your personal computer system allows you to gather information on your current customers so you can sell to them more efficiently. You can then put that data to work in various productive ways:

1. **You can identify your best customers.** Which customers spend the most with you? Which customers can you make the most money from? How often do they buy?

2. **Use repeated contacts to enhance customer loyalty.** You've got to protect your customers from inroads by your competitors. Use a mailing to tell them they're a special customer—and that they're invited to a "customer only" sale next month. Offer a special on a product related to one you know they often buy.

3. **Cross-sell products.** If you know a customer has purchased a barbecue grill, for example, make sure he or she receives a coupon for your barbecue serving tools or special barbecue sauces and spice blends. Maybe you can work out a cross-promotion with the butcher down the street to sell him the names of your recent grill purchasers in exchange for joining with you in creating a "Buy a grill and get 10 pounds of steaks free" promotion.

   Or, you're a furniture store owner. You've built your database over the last few years, and you're darned proud of it. You love fiddling with different comparisons and contrasts. You notice that the black leather couch with the golden trim has been a very good seller. You also notice that some 28 percent of the people who bought that couch also purchased the floor lamps that match up with it pretty well—gold trim on very dark mahogany. Well, how about a simple letter mailing (with color photocopies) to the other 72 percent of the black couch purchasers that offers the lamp at a 10 percent discount to families who've purchased the couch within the last year. But, of course, the offer is good only for 90 days from the date of your letter, just to add some urgency to the recipient's decision. You're cross-selling! Selling Y to a customer who's bought X.

4. **Build a profile.** You can collect customer names, addresses and phone numbers from their checks. What else can you learn about them? If you're selling through the mail, have them fill out an extended customer survey sheet for a 15 percent discount on their next purchase. If you're selling through the Internet, have their completion of an online survey earn them some computer-related premium. If you're just conducting a friendly conversation, take notes afterward and capture marketing content.

5. **Start with your first customer.** Build outward from what you know. Everything starts with your first customer. This is the known. You may have to guess at lots of things in targeting your market, but you know this customer purchased your product. An island of certainty in a sea of haze and obscurity.

   Where do your customers live? Sort by ZIP code. Do one or two ZIP codes stand out from the rest for a majority of your customers? What are the demographics of that ZIP code? The Census Bureau and other data suppliers can provide you with significant demographic data by ZIP code (and by nine-digit ZIP codes, at that). You can use this to get a more thorough understanding of the profile of your geographic market. Chances are you're selling much more in a few ZIP codes than in others, and it may have little to do with your physical location.

6. **Extrapolate from the known.** As you learn more about your customers, go the next step. If these people buy your product, then people like them will be likely to buy your product. At least they'll be more likely to buy your product than the public as a whole.

   One business sells desks, filing, shelving and storage units to the business market. They conducted surveys of their customers and found that a disproportionate percentage of sales were to what's come to be known as SOHOs: small office/home office. They purchased a mailing list of these companies (sole proprietorships with less than five people, sorted by the appropriate ZIP codes for their geographic market) and scored several successes in direct-mail programs. They supported their mailings with modest ads in several of the publications that target this growing market. They included tear sheets (color copies) of the ads along with their mailing to bolster their credibility in this market. Prospects can see they're sophisticated enough (and stable enough) to advertise in respected publications.

You can apply the same thought process to the business-to-business marketplace with SIC codes (see the section on "Segmenting For Business Customers" in Chapter 3).

7. **Step into a bold new frontier.** With your best customer profile in hand, go to professionals in the database/mailing list business and see what lists they have that match your current customer/prospect demographics. We'll get more into this in just a moment.

Getting New Customers From Existing Ones

Your customer and prospect database needs to be set up so that it's capable of dynamic interactions—you want to tell it things (new purchases, address updates, change in contact names) and you want it to tell you things (average time between purchases, average amount of purchase, types of products purchased and so on).

Sample Consumer Customer Database

Name, address, phone number _____

_____

E-mail address _____

Family members, with ages_____

_____

Home ownership _____

Car ownership _____

Educational level _____

Gross family income _____

Purchasing history _____

Publications read regularly _____

Radio station of choice_____

Newspaper subscriptions _____

Hobbies_____

Sample Business-To-Business Customer Database

Name, address, phone number _____

_____

E-mail/Web site address _____

SIC _____

Annual sales _____

Number of employees _____

Product lines _____

Purchasing history _____

Trade publications read regularly _____

Memberships in professional associations _____

You can't expect to get all this information on your customers when they first walk in the door. If you tried, you'd probably wind up with a former customer walking out the door because you asked too many questions. But you can build this information up over time on your key customers. Put together a contest that they can enter, and ask a question or two on the entry form. If the purchase price of your products is high enough, run a credit check on your client to determine creditworthiness and general financial overview. You can also add to this database by drawing on other databases available to you. You can also take the direct approach with good customers and simply send them a survey, explaining you need the information to refine your operations to serve them better.

If you make your database as adaptable as possible, you'll get the best use of it because you don't know how you'll need to use the information in the future. A good marketing database captures your past, records your present and helps chart your future. As you accumulate information on your existing customers, you'll be able to profile the typical customer within reasonably accurate ranges.

For a retail customer at your gourmet food takeout shop, your data might reveal your core customer profile as follows:

- Married couple without kids
- Gross family income of $55,000

- White collar occupations
- Own home in ZIP codes xxxxx and xxxyz
- Read *U.S. News & World Report* and subscribe to the local morning paper

You take that profile, with its gross numbers, and head to your local list broker or direct-mail consultant. You can start your search for a list broker by looking in your local Yellow Pages. Check out their references carefully before getting involved. "This is what I've got," you tell them. "Show me more of these." You're using your customers as templates for additional prospects. Depending on your product line, you might focus on ZIP codes, on subscribers to a particular magazine, sometimes on income or on the number of kids.

List brokers have access to many thousands of lists. You'll pay between $35 and $135 per thousand names on a list, depending on the size of the list and how much trouble it is to compile. Brokers typically have a very thorough understanding of their lists and can give you insights into the best list for your use. The more you know about your current customers, the better use you'll be able to make of your list broker's experience.

You don't buy lists; you rent them, usually for a single-time usage. If you want to send a second mailing later to the same list, that's another charge. If you know you'll be sending a series of four mailings to a given list, mention this upfront for a cumulative rate.

You can't simply fold these names into your database of customers. Not only would it be illegal and wrong, but you'd also get caught. Every list is "salted" with "ringers," names that aren't real but simply serve to give away any mailing done to the list. If the list broker's ringer gets a mailing from you for which you haven't paid the usage rights, you're busted. You do your mailing with the broker's list. Once people respond to your mailing, you're free to add them to your own database of customers. Your list grows and grows.

Direct Marketing: Precision Message Delivery

So far you've seen a number of possibilities for using your computer (and the computers of business allies) to extend the presence of your company, both to your current customers for other needs and to new customers.

Let's say you identify a new market, one that you think is going to be very receptive to your product. The cost of advertising to this market may be prohibitive: The best publications are frightfully expensive, and your ads couldn't appear for six months, anyway.

Direct marketing provides you with a way to conduct a test of this market relatively quickly, at a reasonable cost, and with convincing certitude. You'll know whether this is indeed the gold mine you hope it is.

Perhaps the most common use of a marketing database is to generate a target list for a direct-mail campaign. Of course, direct mail also works with purchased lists. Direct mail provides giant companies with the ability to target defined markets with specialized offers.

For smaller companies, using direct mail has a number of attractive advantages:

1. You can target recipients very precisely.

2. You can protect against overwhelming response. If you run an advertisement, you can't know whether you're going to get 10 responses or 10,000. For a small company, a powerful response to an ad can be even more disastrous than no response at all, since a poor reaction to a prospect's response will likely damage your relationship even before it's begun. With direct mail, you can start out with a modest-size mailing to study the response and make sure you can handle it expeditiously.

3. Costs can be modest. Or, more accurately, you can create a campaign to fit large or small budgets.

4. Direct mail can happen fast. With a modest campaign to a known target audience, you can acquire a mailing list, develop mailing materials (including direct-mail letter, flier, reply card), launch a mailing and start to receive results in just a few months. This is faster than the typical advertising campaign—and a lot faster than waiting for the phone to ring.

5. You can test different appeals, called "offers" in the trade, to reveal the most potent message. By making a different offer to randomly different portions of your mailing list, you can see which offer pulls best. Go with your best puller until you find a better draw. As you try different offers and different letters, you'll find one does better than another. Use the better one, and then try to beat that in your next mailing. Eventually, you should get better and better response rates.

6. You can mail to the same list again with a slightly different mailing and still garner worthwhile results. Most direct-mail experts say that companies don't get enough mileage out of their materials. Use them until they no longer pay their way.

7. You can never run out of prospects. Use your imagination to find new niche direct-mail markets for your products, whether retail or business-to-business. Your list broker or mailing consultant can suggest possible target markets worth trying.

With consumer products, you can often sell them right through the mail . . . or at least get customers to stop in. With business-to-business products, you usually face a two-step process. First, you get a response to your solicitation with an indication of inter-

Jargon Alert

"Direct marketing," "direct mail," "direct response": These terms are used confusingly in the trade. Direct marketing typically refers to marketing efforts by the manufacturer that are directed at the end-user when a retailer or distributor is in the middle. Direct-mail advertising uses the mail service to deliver your best sales effort directly to the mailbox of your prospect. Direct-response advertising is any advertising (print or broadcast ads, or direct-mail packages) that invites the recipient to contact you directly through an 800-number, a mailing address or a business reply card.

est (request for catalog, literature, report or sample). This is the lead-generation phase. Once you mail off the requested material, you then follow up with additional material or a phone call/fax/e-mail to use your skills at transforming the lead into a prospect.

Let's put you in charge of another business: a travel agency. It's been in business for nine years and has an established clientele of about 1,400 people. You've taken a close look at who books with you and why, and you've segmented several different submarkets that make up the bulk of your business: the elderly, school groups, and vacation and cruise bookings. You don't handle business travelers (they're always wanting you to make last-minute changes and cut back on your discount).

The senior market is the one that interests you. You'll define that as 60 and over. You know the demographics are working in your favor here: More and more people will be entering this age group as the baby boomers get older. Your community has an ample supply of potential clients, and you're not up to your eyeballs in cut-price competitors.

You notice that senior travelers are taking more and more "adventurous" vacations—to China, Australia, the Middle East, India, South Africa—not just to the traditional destinations of 10 years ago. There are lots of eco-tourists, too, in this age group. They have money to spend, they're not overly cheap on accommodations, and they're a trustworthy lot. You want more of them. How do you get them?

You talk to your buddy Glenn, who (after a career in advertising) does some consulting "just to keep his pulse steady." Glenn makes some suggestions on making more of the senior market:

1. Create a modest one-page newsletter and mail it out six times a year to your current senior customers. Material should address their travel needs in particular, and it should include lots of "idea starters" to get them thinking about exciting new destinations.

2. Send your best senior customers a "Reward Offered" special mailing. If they send you the names of some of their senior friends, you'll contact those friends about becoming their travel agency. If they book a trip with you, you'll reward your original customer with 10 percent off his or her next airline ticket.

3. Look to develop new senior customers by some thoughtful mailing-list shopping:

   - What magazines do the elderly read and can you get mailing labels for subscribers in your market area? A list broker can help you here, or you can contact the publication directly.

   - What local resources are there for mailing lists? Many cities have sophisticated "letter shops" with remarkably adept mailing-list departments.

Anatomy Of A Direct-Mail Campaign

	Consumer Direct Mail	Business-To-Business Direct Mail
Value of product or service	Low to medium price	Medium to high price
Potential target audience	Enormous, almost unlimited	Sometimes very small; can be several people at same company
Goal of mailing	Usually cash sale (via phone and credit card) sometimes store visit	Lead generation for personal follow-up
Mailing content	Short copy works best, except for expensive goods	Can be long, depending on complexity of product
Source of funds	Personal money	Company money
Buying process	Short and simple . . . one or two people make the decisions	Can be complicated for big-ticket items

4. Set up focus groups of senior citizens and establish a protocol for finding out how to put together tour packages that will appeal to them. Depending on the importance of this senior citizen demographic, you might want to set up an advisory board of senior citizens to advise you on proposed marketing ventures to the market.

Waging A Direct-Mail Campaign

Once you've outlined your target market, staging a direct-mail campaign has seven key steps:

1. **Develop a mailing list.** We've already covered many of the details of pulling together a list. Put your description of the targets on this list in writing, so you know exactly to whom you're mailing. If you're mailing to a larger-sized list (more than 20,000), you'll probably want to provide your letter shop with Cheshire labels: unglued labels that are affixed to your mailing piece with special glue. For smaller quantities, you might just provide pressure-sensitive (self-sticking) labels. When you have a small quantity of labels, you can put them on by hand with pressure-sensitive labels. Cheshire labels require machine application at the mailing house. Your list supplier will provide you the labels in whatever format you want.

2. **Create a mailing piece.** You don't just mail out a brochure to your list. That gets too expensive, and your brochures weren't designed for it. You need to create a direct-mail piece with a strong offer that will spur the recipient to action. All direct mail leads to the "call to action": What do you want the recipient to do next? Mail back the business reply card? Call the 800 number? Fill out the order form and fax it to your number?

   You can never be too pushy in direct-mail materials. You can also be clever, cute, whimsical, even overpowering, but only in connection with being pushy. Your goal is to get action. You don't create a direct-mail piece to inform. That's what your brochures are for. You want action!

   Designers of direct-mail pieces like to get creative with graphics. Your goal is to get the reader to respond to the offer. Any graphics that don't contribute to that are not worth the design and printing costs. According to most direct-mail gurus:

   - Forty percent of a piece's impact comes from sending it to the right list in the first place.

- Forty percent comes from the value of the offer.
- Twenty percent comes from the design or writing of the piece.

3. **Code your response vehicle.** Whatever way you ask recipients to respond, make sure you code your mailing. All you have to do is assign each mailing a batch number, such as 04992103: 0499 is the month/year of the mailing; 21 is the identifier for the particular list you mailed from; and 03 is the identifier for the particular offer. Coding provides a simple device for revealing just who has responded to which mailing and which offer. It makes individual responses much more valuable, since you can easily tabulate the different codes to see what's working the best for you.

4. **Test the campaign.** Even a modest campaign of a few thousand pieces can run up the budget with mailing and duplication costs. So you should always test mail a portion of your mailing list and check the results. No one can predict the response rate you'll get; there are just too many variables.

   What percentage of your mailing makes for a reliable test? Again, it varies, but most authorities would tell you to test 10 percent of your list and no fewer than 250 pieces. This will give you enough of a spread across the variables to make the results worth something. Before you do your test, you should decide what response rate will support your going ahead with the planned major mailing. This will depend on your budget. Writers on direct mail duck the issue of response rates because there are so many variables—and because no one really knows how to predict response. Experience suggests that if your rate is less than 2 percent, something is wrong. Either your list is wrong, or your offer is too weak. If you get a response rate above 7 percent for a mass mailing (without giving away the farm), you've done very, very well.

5. **Run the campaign.** Keep your mailing pace in line with your ability to handle the potential responses. Your test mailing will give you some sense of the rate of customer response. Use that as a gauge for how many pieces you should mail in a given week. Mail only those pieces you can support with your sales effort.

6. **Handle customer responses.** You can't handle the fulfillment end of a direct-mail campaign without considerable planning. If you're asking respondents to request additional information, what are you going to send them? How soon do you want to mail the information out? What else will you do with the responses? In other

words, how will you make maximum use of the names you've spent so much money to acquire?

If you're a company with distributors or sales offices, it's common to pass along the names of prospects so that follow-up can be handled on the local level. This can be handled easily with e-mail or faxes. The quicker the response the better, since your speed in dispatching information can quite justifiably be viewed as reflective of your commitment to customer service. Why should respondents have to wait for materials?

If you're mailing out product or samples, do you want that handled from your main offices? Many mail order campaigns depend on fulfillment houses, professional operations that handle the logistics of sending out materials to large quantities of customers. You provide the products and the prospects; they'll take care of the rest.

7. **Analyze the results of the campaign.** This is perhaps the most important, and underrated, aspect of the campaign. Did the final results match what you expected from the test? What parts of the demographic responded better than expected? Are there subsets of your target audience that you can focus on in future mailings?

Every direct-mail campaign you run should contribute not just to your sales figures but to enhancing your customer database. In very real terms, it represents the future of your business.

Creating Your Direct-Mail Materials

Direct mail is the weapon of choice for many small businesses because of its targetability and reasonable cost. It's also very versatile since you can include whatever you want in a mailing package to convince your prospect of the desirability of your product or service. All your company literature can become part of your direct-mail efforts, including company newsletters.

The Direct-Mail Package

The standard direct-mail package consists of four elements: an envelope, a sales letter, a flier and a reply card (see the sample direct-mail package, starting on page 262).

- **Envelope:** This carries your package to the recipient and bears the mailing label. There's no reason not to use the envelope to get the sales process started early. Use the outside of the envelope to carry an enticement to the prospect to open it:

1. "A new development in equipment rental reduces costs for your company."
2. "Important information for your financial future."
3. "Time-sensitive material enclosed."
4. "Spending too much on bank charges? Look inside."

- **Sales letter:** This is the workhorse of any direct-mail sales effort. It's been around for 100 years, and the experts have been working at fine-tuning its appeal for 50 years. Many direct-mail campaigns consist of nothing more than a sales letter. It's inexpensive to duplicate, easily reproducible and simple to test. No matter what your product or service, a well-written sales letter gives you the opportunity to "make your case" to the prospect.

All the thinking that's been done about the basic sales letter can be boiled down to just a few key principles:

1. **Write person-to-person.** That means it's an "I" writing to a "you." A sales letter is a one-on-one selling opportunity. The prospect has opened your envelope, which has appeared in the mailbox. For a few moments (and not much longer), you have his or her attention. Write as if you were explaining the benefits of your product to a friend. Use short sentences. Avoid formal language. Don't be afraid of contractions like "don't," "isn't" and "it's": This is the way we talk, and this is the way your letter should sound. You're not writing as a company; you're writing as a person.

2. **Make your first paragraph your best.** People are busy, and no matter how wonderfully crafted your letter is, you can't count on your prospect finishing it. So put your killer benefits to that prospect right in the first paragraph or two. Many sales letter experts suggest you also convey the problem to which your product is the solution. This highlights the benefit and emphasizes the importance of your product or service.

3. **Use boxes, subheads, bullets and bold type.** Don't make your sales letter look like an encyclopedia article. Break up any large chunks of copy with headings and indents. Your reader will scan the letter quickly in the first few seconds to decide whether it's worth reading. You want the message to get across even with a cursory review.

4. **Keep your letter short.** One page is best if you're including other material. You should never go over two pages.

Sample Direct-Mail Package

This is the classic direct-mail package, including outer envelope, sales letter, brochure, reply card and return envelope.

Outer Envelope

SYMANTEC.®
Symantec Peter Norton Group
10201 Torre Avenue
Cupertino, CA 95014-2132

SAVE UP TO 72% on The Norton Utilities Version 7.0 as a registered user of MS-DOS 6.

This headline on the outer envelope entices readers inside with a big savings opportunity.

The reply card's headline repeats the big benefit to the reader.

Reply Card

Save **44–72**% on *The Norton Utilities Version 7.0 as a registered user of MS-DOS 6:*

CHOOSE ONE:

A. You pay just $99 as a new user, an impressive $80.00 off the suggested retail price of $179.00 and a 44% savings!
– OR –
B. You pay only $49 if you're upgrading from an earlier version of Norton Utilities (no previous purchase required). That's $130 off the suggested retail price - a 72% savings!

Priority Code: AR85

Please make any necessary corrections in your name or address.

PLEASE HURRY! OFFER EXPIRES SEPTEMBER 15, 1993!

Quantity	Item	Please Indicate Disk Size	Suggested Retail Price	YOUR PRICE!	TOTAL
____	The Norton Utilities	☐ 3½" ☐ 5¼"	$179.00	$99.00	$____
____	Version 7.0*		(Upgrade)	$49.00†	$____
____	Loop Back Plugs**		$2.95	$ 9.95	$____

Add applicable state and local taxes (See back): $____
Shipping and handling ($8.00 for the first unit, $5 for each additional unit): $____
TOTAL: $____

*Quantity limited to three
*Available at this price only with your Norton Utilities 7.0 order.
†Please provide first page of any version NU manual. Limit one copy for each proof of ownership

PAYMENT METHOD
Check - Please make checks payable to Symantec Corporation in U.S. Dollars drawn on a U.S. bank.
Please charge my: ☐ VISA ☐ MasterCard ☐ American Express
Acct. Number _____ Exp. Date: _____
Signature: _____
Name as it appears on credit card: _____
Please provide daytime phone: (____) _____
See back for important ordering information.

The box highlights a limited-time offer, which helps motivate the reader to respond.

Return Envelope

PRIORITY ORDER PLEASE RUSH!

NO POSTAGE NECESSARY IF MAILED IN THE UNITED STATES

BUSINESS REPLY MAIL
FIRST CLASS MAIL   PERMIT NO. 501   DENVER, CO
POSTAGE WILL BE PAID BY ADDRESSEE

SYMANTEC.®
SYMANTEC FULFILLMENT CENTER
ATTN NU 7 SPECIAL OFFER
PO BOX 22335
DENVER CO 80222-9510

Make the return envelope postage-paid to improve response.

Sample Direct-Mail Package, cont'd.

This one-word headline grabs attention and forces the prospect to read further.

Underscoring directs the reader's attention to important points.

An indented paragraph offers visual relief, making the letter look easier to read.

Bullet points on front and back make it easier to find the benefits.

 SYMANTEC®
Symantec Peter Norton Group
10201 Torre Avenue
Cupertino, CA 95014-2132

Peter Norton

"Phew!"

Dear DOS 6.0 User,

That may sound like the relief you register on recovering a diamond from a sink drain.

But there's more frequent provocation for it in the world of computing. Recovery of <u>lost data</u>.

Accidental data loss can befall anyone, and if it hasn't happened to you, count yourself lucky. That's why all your input - the work you spent hours, even days keystroking - needs protection.

But how to achieve it? The easiest, most dependable, most economical way, as millions of people already know is The Norton Utilities, *the award-winning standard in data recovery and protection*. It's like having a bodyguard keeping your computer and your data out of harm's way.

And now with The Norton Utilities Version 7.0 available for the powerful MS-DOS 6 operating system (at incredible savings for registered users), you've got the protection that allows you to use dynamic MS-DOS 6 to its fullest.

<u>In fact, The Norton Utilities Version 7.0 is the only product available that can recover data from compressed drives such as MS-DOS 6-DoubleSpace, Stacker and SuperStor</u>. Is it any wonder *PC Week* recommends *"users of compression should have a copy of Symantec Corp's Norton Utilities 7.0"*?

That feature alone is worth the low price, but there's more, including...

- *Extraordinary Data Protection and Recovery* that includes a wide range of simple tools to keep your system flowing smoothly and trouble-free. And when you have sudden need for data recovery, The Norton Utilities comes to the rescue. All this plus support for standard and compressed drives up to two gigabytes.

There's more...

- *Hardware Diagnostics*, that examine your computer and peripherials from stem to stern, identifying any unstable or faulty components and locating potential problems before they occur.

- *Performance picker-uppers* like **Speed Disk** for defragmenting, **Norton Cache** for faster data access and **Calibrate** for hard disk tune-ups to give your minute-to-minute operations extra hustle.

- *DOS Enhancements like none you've seen* such as 200+ new command line options, color-enhanced directory listings, up to 40 characters for file name descriptions and more, all while reducing the amount of memory DOS requires.

I could go on and on about the virtues of The Norton Utilities Version 7.0. But let me stop here and urge you to read the accompanying brochure for more details on the utility I know you'll find indispensable - not to mention inexpensive!

If you're a registered user of MS-DOS 6 or Windows you get a tremendous price break. Pay just $99, a full $80 savings off the regular retail price of $179. If you have a previous version of The Norton Utilities and simply want to upgrade to Version 7.0 you pay only $49, a savings of no less than $130 off the suggested retail price.

<u>Keep in mind you only have until September 15, 1993</u> to take advantage of this offer. Why not do it now? Call 1-800-453-1072 for toll free ordering, or fax (303-727-4611) or mail the enclosed order form today.

Sincerely Yours,

Peter Norton

Peter Norton

P.S. Does everything still come to "he who waits"? Unfortunately, in this case, waiting can only mean a higher price. By responding now, you save up to 72% and you risk nothing with our 60-day money-back guarantee!

Sample Direct-Mail Package, cont'd.

Front Cover

Inside Flaps

Back Cover

This brochure's headline repeats the promise from the envelope and adds a little more information.

This is a good place for testimonials; use a heading on each quote.

Inside Spread

A whole panel of bullet points outlines the benefits for the scanning reader.

Show how easy it is to respond to this offer.

5. **Make an offer.** You're not providing information—you're actively selling. So you need to present the reason for sending your letter. There's something new about your product. You're writing to people who attended a particular show and are offering a discount. You're giving a second product free to people who order a first product. "Order five and get a sixth free." "Join for a year and get two months free." "For a limited time, respondents can take advantage of a one-time trial offer." "Book the service now and get a discount for summer delivery." These are all extra enticements designed to push the prospect over the edge and get him or her to respond.

6. **Repeat the offer.** State the offer at least twice in your letter, at the opening and at the close.

7. **Add a sense of urgency.** Give the prospect a reason to reply right away. If you can't persuade the person to act while he or she is holding your mailing package, chances are the person will never respond. So add a time deadline for a response. Or an offer on top of the offer for a quick response. Or maybe a limited amount of the offered product is available at this special price.

- **Flier:** You frequently support your direct-mail letter with a flier, a small brochure that provides additional information on the product or service you're offering. While the letter has to condense the benefits of the product, the flier gives you the opportunity to expand on them a bit. Here's where you can use photography, charts and graphs to make your case. Testimonials always work well in fliers to help convince the prospect of the truth of your claims. Stay focused on benefits.

  Don't make the flier depend on the direct-mail letter. It should be able to stand on its own in telling your complete product or service story. You'll undoubtedly have other uses for this flier than a particular direct-mail effort: as an invoice stuffer, as an item in a display rack and so on.

- **Reply card:** Reply cards can simply be inserted in the mailing package, or they can be attached to the brochure and torn off for return. You want the prospect to write his or her name, address and phone, and then generally to either place an order or ask for more information. Make sure your reply card has room and spaces for the respondent to include all the information you need. And have your business reply card checked by the post office so

Sample Sales Letter

Ms. Betty Smithers
XYZ Corp.
1234 Fifth St.
Irvine, CA 92614

Dear Ms. Smithers:

I know how hospital executives like you might react when it comes time to consider building an assisted-living facility:

Where's my Maalox? Where's my Excedrin?

For that reason, I think you'll be especially interested in the stress-free process we offer you at ABC Corp. We use our experience to take the uncertainty out of building assisted-living facilities.

You're comfortable every step of the way.

You will be fully educated in the process before we make one drawing or lift one spadeful of dirt. You'll understand exactly what we think it will take to help you build the finest facility for your purposes. If you're wondering about the feasibility of the facility in your market, we can provide a complete report. If you want to know whether you can build your dream facility within your budget, you'll get the answer.

ABC can also provide complete design and building services or work with local builders and other contractors of your choice.

In addition, you can learn:

- how to have an assisted-care facility connected to your hospital
- the various options for operating the facility successfully
- the range of financing and ownership options

Whether you're considering the development of an assisted-living facility soon or merely building a file of information for the future—get the facts from ABC. Nothing beats experience in building these facilities, and we've built scores of them. Take a look at the enclosed case materials; they show you how we work.

Get up to speed quickly on assisted-living facilities.

I know that a hospital executive like yourself will benefit greatly from the facts we provide on planning, building and running one of these facilities. And the information is yours for the asking. Give me a call or drop me a note.

Sincerely,

Bob Dibble
President, ABC Corp.

that it fits all their legal requirements for size, weight and color. You don't want the respondent to have to worry about postage, so your reply card has to carry your business reply permit information where the stamp normally appears (you can get such information from your post office).

The Self-Mailer

A scaled-down direct-mailing option is the self-mailer, which can incorporate virtually all the elements of a full direct-mail package on a single folded sheet of paper. And, of course, along with a decrease in elements is a reduction in cost (see the sample self-mailer, starting on page 268).

With a self-mailer, you eliminate the costs of producing additional elements, inserting them into an envelope and paying greater postage. The simplicity of a self-mailer also makes it easy to produce quickly, enabling you to introduce a new product, announce a sale or make contact with customers in short order.

The only challenge of self-mailers is overcoming the image of a flimsy fold-over that epitomizes so-called "junk mail." However, what the self-mailer lacks in format appeal, it can make up for in copy clout and design.

The "guts" of the self-mailer can be set up any number of ways. In a three-panel piece, one panel can have bullet points, another a personal sales letter and another the response device or order form. You can even make your self-mailer a four-panel affair, with the final panel for testimonials.

The Postcard

The postcard is perhaps the most elementary of mailing formats, offering many of the advantages of a folded self-mailer, as well as some exclusive to itself (see the sample postcard on page 271).

Since a huge percentage of direct-mail packages never get opened, it pays to consider a format that never has to overcome that obstacle. With a postcard, all the recipient needs is a flip of the wrist to read everything you have to say. This can be a big advantage in attracting the typically impatient reader.

Inexpensive postcards give you the opportunity to consider a mailing "campaign," enabling you to send out a number of such cards at regular intervals to remind the recipient of your product or service.

Sample Self-Mailer

This self-mailer uses a free-pass technique to motivate prospects to try the services.

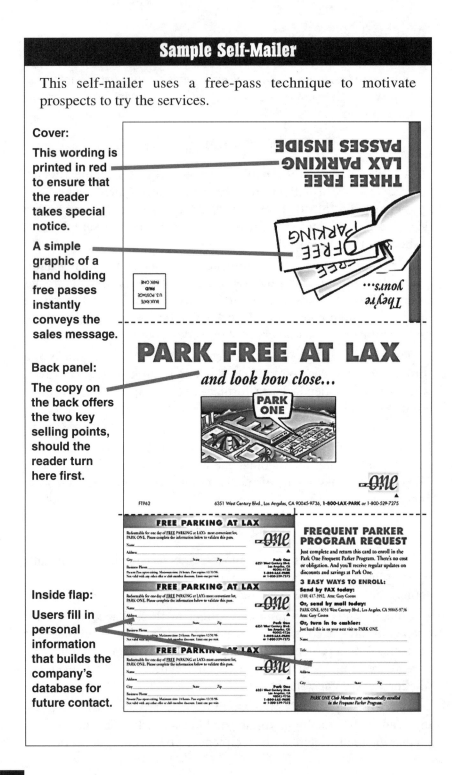

Cover:

This wording is printed in red to ensure that the reader takes special notice.

A simple graphic of a hand holding free passes instantly conveys the sales message.

Back panel:

The copy on the back offers the two key selling points, should the reader turn here first.

Inside flap:

Users fill in personal information that builds the company's database for future contact.

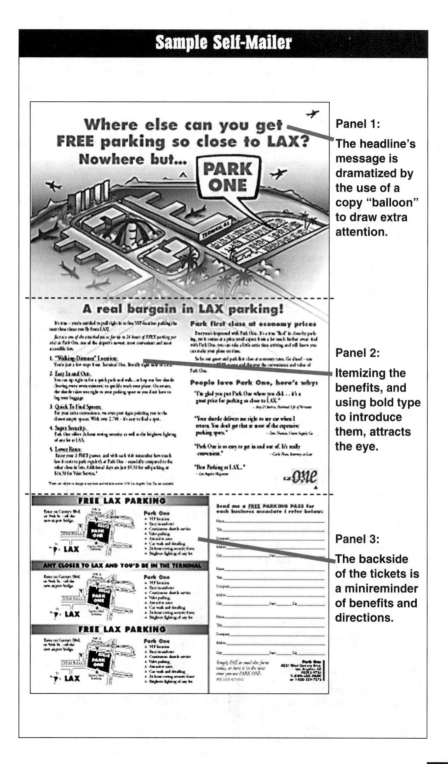

Sample Self-Mailer

Panel 1:

The headline's message is dramatized by the use of a copy "balloon" to draw extra attention.

Panel 2:

Itemizing the benefits, and using bold type to introduce them, attracts the eye.

Panel 3:

The backside of the tickets is a minireminder of benefits and directions.

You can also produce oversized postcards that give you more "canvas" on which to display your wares and make your sales argument. And while the larger size costs incrementally more in printing, paper and postage, its simplicity still makes it affordable.

Like the folded self-mailer, one possible downside of a postcard is that it won't get the respect of a sealed envelope. But if it's developed in a way that has originality and selling power, you could have yourself an inexpensive business builder.

Other Printed Materials And Catalogs

Every company needs "literature," printed pieces that do a careful and well-thought-out job of presenting its products and services: catalogs, newsletters, product sheets and brochures, letterhead, presentation folders, specification sheets, case histories or application sheets, special event brochures, annual reports, manuals, technical bulletins, posters, product insert sheets, labeling, recruitment materials and so on.

With the increased availability of powerful desktop publishing systems and software, many companies decide to meet these needs internally.

Resist this impulse. Your home-grown materials will betray their off-the-cuff origin to most of the people who read them. Appearance is reality in marketing, and you have to look as professional as you are.

Here are some tips in dealing with the literature needs you'll face as your company expands and grows:

1. **Get a logo and stationery package designed professionally.** Do this, and don't change it for at least 10 years. Either hire an advertising agency to create it or a design

Insight

Go to direct-mail school in your mailbox. If you're like most Americans, each day your mail brings you a handful of direct-mail solicitations that you can use as your hands-on education. Study the letters. Use design ideas from the fliers. Keep copies of different types of reply cards. Big-time direct-mail companies spend millions refining their mailing techniques. You can use that information for the price of tearing open the envelope. A real bargain.

Sample Postcard

An inexpensive postcard like this can be a powerful new business generator.

The "blackboard" effect makes this thought-provoking question leap out at the reader.

Repeat the message from the front side, in case the reader sees the address side first.

studio/graphic artist. Don't try this yourself, no matter how artistic you consider yourself. A professional artist will make sure your stationery materials reflect your corporate personality, while maintaining a clean and professional look. They'll look good in color and in black and white, they'll reproduce well in smaller sizes, they'll fax clearly, and they'll simply be more attractive than what you can expect to do yourself.

2. **Learn the principles of solid graphic design.** Understanding graphic design is a lifetime's work, of course, but some reading and a sensitive eye can teach you a lot. Get hold of some graphic design books at a local bookstore and educate yourself. All your printed materials should (just like your ads discussed in Chapter 7) follow fundamental design principles:

- **Keep the look clean and simple.** Don't overload the reader visually. Use a graphic grid to align the different elements in an orderly fashion.

- **Use heads and subheads to lead the reader.** When the reader turns the page, where will he or she look? Use heads and subheads to provide scanning points to keep the reader moving along.

- **Avoid too much type.** Pages filled with writing are not appealing to the reader. Break up the copy with photos, illustrations, cartoons, charts and so on.

- **Use white space.** Avoid a crowded look, despite the temptation to make use of every inch of paper you're paying for. White space serves as a visual frame for the rest of the content on the page.

- **Stay with standard formats unless you have a good reason not to.** All of us have grown accustomed to the standard $8\frac{1}{2}$ x 11 format for print materials. Even our filing systems are made for things that size. If you go with an unusual size, your pieces may not lend themselves to being filed easily for reference.

- **Put a caption with each photo.** We all want to know what we're looking at. And a caption gives you the chance not just to identify your product but to remind the reader of the benefit.

- **Use charts and graphs rather than tables.** A brochure is a visual document. Use graphics to boost visual interest and make numbers meaningful.

Sample Brochure

Without being fancy, this three-panel brochure looks classy and reads compellingly.

Inside Flap | Back Cover | Front Cover

Inside Flap

"It's a potent tool."

"I tell people 'you can stick with the old way of getting ahead, if you wish'. But with the Electronic Resume Network, a person can transform the plodding, laborious chore of career development into a simple, powerful technology that gets results. ERN puts one's accomplishments in front of literally thousands of companies–including the people they want to impress most. It's all done discreetly and no one ever has to know you're 'looking around'. There clearly is no smarter way to ensure that your experience, talent and education pay to the fullest in the job market."

William Kendall
President
Electronic Resume Network
A division of CareerPro

Back Cover

The Electronic Resume Network is the latest innovation from one of today's most respected career development specialists.

ERN is a division of CareerPro, itself a network of more than 400 career development centers nationwide.

CareerPro centers provide invaluable tools for individuals active in the job-search process, including: professionally written resumes, self-appraisal and interview preparation techniques, organization and time-maximization training, plus seminars and workshops on additional self-marketing skills useful in finding new employment.

The Electronic Resume Network is CareerPro's innovative new approach to effortlessly maintaining year-round career development and job search activities.

ELECTRONIC RESUME NETWORK
775 Sunrise Avenue, Suite 260
Roseville, CA 95661

Front Cover

How to confidentially find out which companies are willing to pay you more.

This inside flap is a great place for a testimonial or a personal note from the sender.

Here you can lay out your company's credentials, after a show of sales-manship inside.

Using a provocative "how to," the headline spurs the reader to open the brochure.

Inside Spread

Introducing THE ELECTRONIC RESUME NETWORK

A dynamic new way to keep top companies in your field aware of your qualifications. And help you get the money you're worth.

You don't have to be lucky any more to find terrific jobs in your field. Because when you plug into the Electronic Resume Network, such jobs can find you.

Through this powerful new network, thousands of top companies nationwide are continuously notified via computer disk of your qualifications. So the moment a position opens up in your field the ERN disk is scanned and your abilities flash across the screen. This assistance gives you the single

greatest edge you have in advancing your career: being in the right place at the right time.

You can specify the industry you want, as many as ten positions–or job titles–for which you'd like to be considered and the salary you require. You can also indicate specific geographic areas where you prefer to work. This enables potential employers to know if, and where, you might be willing to relocate.

Here's how the Network works for you, step-by-step:

1 SIGNING UP IS EASY. When you return the enclosed acceptance form, we will send you an ERN Registration Kit. It will ask you to complete a resume form and other information and return it to us (Should you wish free consultation on your resume, it's available.) After that, we do all the work.

2 ENJOY COMPLETE ANONYMITY. Once we receive your information, it is loaded into a computer data base and segmented according to your profession, qualifications, industry and geographic preference. *Your name is replaced with a code number for complete anonymity.*

3 REACH ALL THE RIGHT PEOPLE. The data is then dispatched monthly by computer disk to hiring decision makers at thousands of top firms of every size.

4 YOU "STAR" ON COMPUTER SCREENS. Each day, managers in search of top talent scan their ERN disks for the right people. They punch in the job requirements and up pop the resumes of the most qualified candidates–perhaps you among them.

5 YOU'RE CONTACTED WHEN THERE'S A NIBBLE. If a company is interested in you and wishes to make contact, it calls ERN headquarters and gives us your code number. We then contact you and you can decide if you wish to pursue it.

Even if you're not actively looking, don't miss out on a better job.

Like many, you may be reasonably content in your current position and not officially in the job market. But that doesn't mean if a higher-paying opportunity came along you wouldn't want to know about it.

Even if you decide to stay where you are, listening to another job offer lets you know how valuable your "stock" is elsewhere. And that can be a useful bargaining chip in renegotiating your present salary.

That's why the Electronic Resume Network should be considered a valuable year-round resource. For about the cost of a movie ticket or two each month, you can stay plugged into the most powerful career advancement service ever developed.

ENJOY CONTINUOUS, ON-GOING CAREER DEVELOPMENT, *WITHOUT ANY EFFORT ON YOUR PART.*

THE ELECTRONIC RESUME NETWORK DOES THE WORK FOR YOU, YEAR-ROUND!

The headline and subhead pay off the curiosity aroused on the cover.

Subheads and generous spacing keep an all-type treatment from being boring.

These big numbers draw the eye to this important section.

Talking About Your Business (Stage 4)

Here's the final work sheet about your business; this time it's specifically related to your printed materials. List each piece of print materials you currently have on hand for your company and describe its purpose.

1. How long do you think each of those pieces of literature will last without revision?

2. Which new printed pieces will you produce in the coming year?

3. Do you anticipate using any outside help to produce these pieces?

4. Have you considered having your literature reviewed by someone in the industry (but outside your company)?

5. Who is the "lit boss" for your company?

3. **Be sure your materials have a "family look."** Every piece of literature doesn't have to look identical, but they should all look planned as a compatible unit. Imagine your literature laid out in front of you on a conference table. Does it all look like it comes from the same company? It should.

4. **Invest in good photography.** Small companies sometimes scrimp on getting good photos of their equipment, their job sites, their equipment in use or their accessories and supplies. Strong, professionally done photography will set you apart from other small companies. Your customers want to be reassured of the quality of your product. Amateur snapshots give a very damaging impression of your professionalism. Good photography is an investment in your future.

5. **Appoint one person as lit boss.** Your literature needs will be ever-changing, with trade shows, with new products and markets and with normal growth. You must have one person responsible for anticipating future needs, handling literature production and maintaining inventory. Untended literature grows increasingly less useful and more frustrating. Every new piece should have a written rationale, audience description and content outline, not unlike the rationale you develop for a piece of advertising copy.

Your Company Newsletter

One popular technique for staying in touch with customers and establishing yourself as a source of valuable information is a company newsletter. For small businesses, they offer a lot of advantages:

1. **They're easy to produce in-house.** While they're labor-intensive, they don't demand special skills. Any personal computer with a word processing program or page layout program can turn out an attractive newsletter. Many programs include newsletter templates to make your job even easier. Be sure to use a two- or three-column format for easy scanning. Employ photos or illustrations to clarify your articles. Keep your typeface large enough for all your customers to read the articles without straining.

2. **They let you inform and sell.** You can provide your customers and prospects news on your company, information on your products, case histories of how your products perform, background on key employees, market overviews and so on. You dictate the content. Your only requirement is to keep it interesting for the customer . . . and to keep the sales content from overwhelming the information content.

3. **Their size can deliver more complex information.** Ads and brochures always restrict what we can say. Newsletters provide you with an endless brochure. You can put together multipart articles, conduct lengthy interviews, show new ways to use your products—all within a comfortable space allotment.

4. **They let you offer lots of different types of information.** Don't be misled by the previous point. Although newsletters give you room for lengthier articles, keep the bulk of your newsletter as short pieces, so they are very scannable. You want lots of different items in the hope of providing something interesting to every reader.

5. **You create credibility.** Your newsletter lets you show off your knowledge and product savvy. Your customers get to see you, your products and your company directly, outside the typical selling framework.

6. **You can think long-term.** Good newsletters don't just happen. Editors have editorial calendars that link newsletter themes with conferences, new product introductions and other company events. You should plan your newsletter at least six months in advance.

7. **You can get your customers involved.** Establish a newsletter advisory board to give you ideas on content. Profile some of your largest customers in your newsletter to show other customers the quality of your product. Have customers write articles for your newsletter on industry trends, new applications, reports on trade shows and so on.

8. **You can use your newsletter to prospect for new customers.** Send out extra copies of your newsletter with a cover letter to prospects. It's a softer sales approach that can be very effective with some potential customers who may resist more direct sales efforts. You can win them over with your knowledge, not your sales persistence.

9. **You control frequency.** Newsletters can be a lot of work to maintain. Plan on four a year to start, and add more if you're getting interest and your company can handle the workload. You can always put out special issues for extraordinary reasons—new product introduction, large contract, special trade show exhibition, story in national press and so on.

Chapter 15

Keeping On Top

By now, you should be at the top of your game. You've earned your title of Marketing Guru, and your colleagues are all amazed at your savvy and acumen. You need a rest because look at all you've done:

- You've done your customer homework: You know who they are, where they live and what they're looking for from you.

- You've compiled a full benefit inventory, so you know what each niche market wants from each of your products.

- You've figured out how to work the Four P's (product, place, price and promotion) to your advantage. You've put them into the marketing mixer to come up with diverse variations on your core marketing themes.

- You've looked at each of your audiences using the Four Utilities (form/function, place, time and ease of possession) and learned how to keep all your sales literature and advertisements focused on your customers' point of view, not your own.
- You've learned to think like a marketer.
- You've avoided the traps that come from an entrepreneur's confidence and drive, and you've dodged the Four Fatal Marketing Assumptions.
- You've studied how to segment your key markets and tailor your appeals to the most important benefits to those markets.
- You've captured the unique charm of your company in a memorable positioning statement.
- You've put in the work to pull together a good marketing plan, one that sets high goals while keeping in reasonable contact with reality.
- You've clearly distinguished features from benefits in all your literature, and you've made sure that distinction has become a part of your company's fabric.
- You've learned how to inspire your people to make face-to-face presentations—and to overcome any objections and close the sale. They know how to determine the real buying process.
- You've determined how best to price your product, and you've begun to use the full range of distribution channels to move your product to the buyer's hand.
- You're nuts about testimonials and case histories, and you've got your whole organization developing them.
- You've evaluated the best advertising choices for your company, include advertising content and the best media for your budget.
- You've been able to support your advertising with a pro-

Insight

With marketing plans, it's tempting to look back at last year's plan and note with regret all the things you didn't accomplish, or at which you tried and failed. Make a point of starting out each year's plan with a recap of your marketing accomplishments from the previous year. When you set ambitious goals, you're bound to fall short now and again. But keep your eye on the successes.

motional budget that adds some spice to your marketing mix.

- You've worked your distribution channels with incentives to get yourself some prime exposure in your market. And you've pressed your advantage with appearances at prime trades shows.

- You've utilized the tools of public relations to create a good image for your company in the popular and trade press.

- You've made your company a force for good in the community.

- You've examined the Internet and decided how your company can best make use of it, whether as a communications tool or as a full-fledged sales arena. You know this decision will need to be reviewed often.

- You're sold on the value of customer service, and you've made it a priority in the mind of each of your employees.

- You've recognized that only training can keep you in front of the pack. You've committed to ongoing training for all managers and key employees.

- You've harnessed the power of your computer system: You've used your database capability to refine your marketing and to target markets through direct mail and other venues.

Quite a day's work, wouldn't you say?

Regular Marketing Plan Review

The work you've done, much of it framed in your marketing plan, is part of an ongoing process. Some of tomorrow's challenges you can predict today; others you'll never anticipate. Market conditions change. Technology spurts forward. Your can't-miss advertising campaign may bomb. An important distributor may switch over to a competitor. A key manager may leave to start her own competing company.

A changed business needs a changed marketing plan. You've got to look at it at least every three months, and on a formal basis every six months. At one point, it represented your very best thinking about where you thought your company should travel. If you're not on track, why not? Has your thinking changed . . . or has the market thrown you a curve?

Keeping your marketing plan current just means being realistic. Share your updating of the plan with all recipients of the original plan. Make sure all copies reflect the changes. And be sure to keep a copy of *all* plan versions; they might be interesting a few years down the road.

Your newly developed marketing vision will serve you well in the years to come. Soon you'll be developing new products to meet the real needs of new markets or the new needs of some of your familiar customers. If you stay in touch with your market through regular research and steady informal contact, you'll know when the market's going to shift before the competition does. And that advantage is priceless.

Glossary

Account executive: the individual at an ad agency who handles the client and coordinates the efforts of the advertising team

Added value: the extra benefit you're able to add to an item in the customer's mind, generally through marketing and advertising; added value means you can charge more, while branding adds value

Advertising campaign: a coordinated effort, often using several media, to achieve particular marketing goals through the use of planned paid advertisements; lasts a limited amount of time and has a single theme or a group of related themes

Advertising specialty: physical items used to support a marketing effort, typically carrying the product name and meant to be given away

Arbitron: the major rating service for local radio; also provides some TV rating information

Audience: viewers or listeners of a TV or radio advertisement; same as circulation in the print media

Benefit: a product's customer-oriented strength; a statement of a valuable product feature, with an emphasis on what the customer gets from the product

Brand equity: a brand's long-term value in the consumer's mind after it has built equity by being in the marketplace for some time

Business-to-business: advertising from one business to another, either in products or services; more specialized than mass-market or consumer advertising

Closing: that part of the selling process when you actively move to get the prospect to agree to the sale

Clutter: the mass of advertising impressions that the consumer faces each day; your ad must break through this clutter to be recognized and have an impact

Collateral materials: typically, printed support pieces that tell the story of your company and its products; includes sales sheets, case histories, product brochures and so on

Comparison advertising: a style of advertisement in which you directly compare some aspect of your product with competitive products

Consumer: generally used in the marketing business as the undifferentiated retail general public, as opposed to the business-to-business market

Co-op advertising: advertising by retailers that includes the specific mention of manufacturers, who—in turn—repay the retailers for all or part of the cost of the advertisement

Copy: the written portion of any advertisement, print or broadcast

CPM (cost per thousand): the typical way to compare costs of different advertising venues

Customers: the people who buy your product and whom you've made it your life's goal to understand; your customer determines your product

Database marketing: using computer technology to categorize your existing customers and to introduce your product to new customers through profiling, building mailing lists and so on

Demographics: a statistical view of a population, generally including age, gender, income, schooling, occupation and so on

Direct-mail advertising: a marketing effort that uses the mail service to deliver a promotional printed piece to the target audience

Direct marketing: a sales effort that goes directly from the manufacturer to the consumer, without the use of a retailer or distributor

Direct-response advertising: a marketing effort that, regardless of the media used, encourages the target audience to respond directly to the advertiser: through the telephone, a business reply card, a coupon and so on

Distribution channel: the manner in which goods move from the manufacturer to the outlet where the consumer purchases them; in some marketplaces, it's a very complex channel, including distributors, wholesalers, jobbers and brokers

Drive time: prime radio advertising time: 6-10 a.m. and 3-7 p.m., when audience members are driving to or from work

Focus group: a controlled group interview of a target audience demographic, often led by a facilitator; a set series of questions or topics are covered, and the results are used to guide marketing efforts

Four P's: product, place, price and promotion; the four elements of the marketing mix; the raw materials with which a marketer must work

Four Utilities: form/function, place, time and ease of possession; the four elements representing the client's perception of the marketing exchange; as you increase the value of the Four Utilities in the consumer's mind, the exchange becomes increasingly beneficial

Frequency: the number of times a given radio spot appears over a time period; with reach, determines the number of impressions made on the target audience

FSI (free-standing insert): a colorful stand-alone sheet or sheets that ride along with newspapers and carry coupons

Full-service agency: an advertising agency that offers a complete range of creative, media and marketing services; as opposed to a boutique or studio, which focuses on creative services

GRP (gross rating point): TV and radio system in which each GRP represents a portion of the listening/viewing audience; in television, one GRP is 1 percent of the area households with televisions

Institutional advertising: advertising that promotes a company rather than a product; generally produced for larger companies

Internet: virtual electronic landscape of connected computers, rapidly becoming colonized by commercial interests; you access the Internet with a computer, modem and browser software

Letter shop: a printing and mailing company that specializes in handling the production and dispatch of direct-mail campaigns; often includes mailing list capabilities

Line extension: adding a similar product to an existing product line to gain additional shelf space or to draw a slightly different demographic

List broker: a company that gets mailing lists from various sources and rents them to direct mailers

List manager: the in-house person who maintains a company's internal customer mailing list

Loss leader: a product that a retailer might sell at a loss to stir interest and to lead to sales of other items

Marketing goal: goals you set to enable you to reach the marketing objective; they're the rungs on the ladder; achieve the goals and you've reached your objective

Marketing objective: the marketing task you want to accomplish; should be relatively independent, clearly graspable and measurable

Marketing plan: the written document that describes your advertising and marketing efforts for the coming year; it includes a statement of the marketing situation, a discussion of target markets and company positioning and a description of the marketing mix you intend to use to reach your marketing goals

Marketing tactics: you develop these basic action steps to enable you to reach your marketing goal

Market segmentation: taking a market and analyzing its members; allows you to speak more specifically to members of a particular segment (the market of males, for example, can be divided into many segments: by age, education, wealth, activities, interests and so on)

Media plan: the portion of a marketing plan that deals with print and broadcast media; aims to get the most reach and frequency in your target demographic for your advertising dollar

Media schedule: the details of your media plan: stations, publications, spot lengths, flight duration and ad size

Niche: a portion of a market that you have identified as having some special characteristic and that is worth marketing to

Perceived value: the value the target customer sees in your product, regardless of its actual value; the higher the perceived value, the greater the price you can attach to your product; perceived value is the key to branding

Point-of-purchase advertising: colorful, intrusive materials that are set up where customers do their shopping; typically used in in-store advertising at grocery stores

Positioning statement: a brief description of the claim you want to stake for your product in the consumer's mind

Product life cycle: products go through a distinct cycle: introduction, midlife and decline; of course, advertisers try to accelerate the introduction, prolong the midlife and delay the decline

Psychographics: mental or lifestyle profiles of potential customers used by advertisers in the creation of advertising

Public relations: using the news or business press to carry positive stories about your company or your products; cultivating a good relationship with local press representatives

Publicity: promoting a positive image of yourself, your company or your products in the media without paying for space

Reach: the number of consumers in your target audience who see your ad; generally, applied more strictly to broadcast media

Response rate: the percentage of people who actually respond to a mailing; you calculate a response rate to determine the relative effectiveness of a mailing program

RFP (request for proposal): a solicitation to submit a proposal to perform work; generally, issued by government agencies

Sales promotion: efforts to gain extra sales on a product through short-term, usually price-related activities: couponing, special mailings, sales and so on

TAP (total audience plans): a type of radio ad purchase plan that gives you access to a range of dayparts at a reasonable rate.

Trade show: a commercial gathering at which vendors meet, conduct workshops and seminars, demonstrate products and gather information on each other

Web site: a location on the World Wide Web; can be used as a sales tool or merely a marketing and informational site about your company; each site can contain hundreds of pages of information or just a basic, simple layout

Marketing Resources

Associations

- American Marketing Association, 250 S. Wacker Dr., #200, Chicago, IL 60606-5819, (800) AMA-1150, (312) 648-0536, fax: (312) 993-7542, e-mail: info@ama.org, www.ama.org
- Direct Marketing Association, 1120 Ave. of the Americas, New York, NY 10036-6700, (212) 768-7277, fax: (212) 302-6714, e-mail: membership@the-dma.org, www.the-dma.org
- Business Marketing Association, 150 N. Wacker Dr., #1760, Chicago, IL 60606, (800) 664-4BMA, (312) 409-4262, fax: (312) 409-4266, e-mail: bma@marketing.org, www.marketing.org

Books

Browse the aisles and shelves of any large bookstore to find scores of books on how to develop your marketing and sales skills. You can learn something from any book. Entrepreneur publishes a quality line of books helpful for the individual running a small business.

The best single book is *Advertising Procedures* (Prentice Hall) by J. Thomas Russell and W. Ronald Lane. Although it's written for a university audience, you'll benefit from its very thorough coverage of all marketing topics. It includes hundreds of examples to illustrate its points. I highly recommend it.

Magazines And Publications

For the small business, business magazines and newsletters contain lots of interesting material—and it's usually more up-to-date than what you'll find in books. I've listed here a number of the best journals on marketing- and advertising-related issues. You should also be very familiar with the best journals in your particular industry.

There are two kinds of journals in the marketing, advertising and sales industry: academic journals and trade journals. Avoid the academic journals. They're written by professors for professors and have little to do with day-to-day life in the world of commerce.

There is no replacement for deep and extensive reading to increase your marketing and sales judgment. While it's true that you can't learn everything from books, expanding your knowledge by reading will save you from the horror of experiencing every business mistake yourself. Experience, as they say, is the best teacher . . . and the cruelest.

Set aside a few hours every couple of weeks to catch up on your journal reading. Besides the marketing-oriented magazines listed below, you should be a regular browser or reader of *Fortune, Forbes, U.S. News & World Report* and *Entrepreneur.*

- *Advertising Age,* 740 N. Rush St., Chicago, IL 60611-2590, (888) 288-5900, (312) 649-5200, e-mail: subs@adage.com, www.adage.com

  The bible of the advertising business. More news than practical information but some good case histories. Also publishes *Advertising Age's Business Marketing.*

- *Adweek,* 1515 Broadway, 12th Fl., New York, NY 10036, (212) 536-6527, fax: (212) 536-5353, e-mail: awsubs@adweek.com, www.adweek.com

  Also an industry magazine, with a bit more how-to content.

- *American Demographics,* 127 W. State St., Ithaca, NY 14850, (607) 273-6343, fax: (607) 273-3196, e-mail: subs@demographics.com, www.demographics.com

  More indirectly interesting than useful. It will help you understand the potential impact of demographics on your business.

- *Direct,* Primedia Intertec, 11 Riverbend Dr. S., P.O. Box 4294, Stamford, CT 06907-0225, (800) 775-3777, (203) 358-4160, fax: (203) 358-5812, www.mediacentral.com/direct

  A good basic magazine on the world of direct marketing.

- *Direct Marketing*, Hoke Communications, 224 Seventh St., Garden City, NY 11530-5371, (516) 746-6700, fax: (516) 294-8141, www.hokecomm.com

  Very hands-on with lots of good ideas.

- *Guerrilla Marketing Newsletter,* Guerilla Marketing International, P.O. Box 1336, Mill Valley, CA 94942, (800) 748-6444, fax: (415) 381-8361, www.gmarketing.com

This newsletter is put out by the enormously prolific Jay Conrad Levinson organization, which originated the concept of "guerilla marketing." Take a look at any of his many books at any large bookstore.

- *Promo,* Primedia Intertec, 11 Riverbend Dr. S., P.O. Box 4225, Stamford, CT 06907-0225, (800) 775-3777, (203) 358-4160, fax: (203) 358-5812, www.mediacentral.com/promo

  The best magazine on promotion. Much industry news but filled with ideas you can use.

- *Sales & Marketing Management,* Bill Communications, 355 Park Ave. S., New York, NY 10010, (800) 821-6897, fax: (212) 592-6309, e-mail: service@salesandmarketing.com, www.salesandmarketing.com

  As the title indicates, this magazine focuses on managing sales and marketing.

- *Target Marketing*, North American Publishing, 401 N. Broad St., Philadelphia, PA 19108, (215) 238-5000, fax: (215) 238-5457, e-mail: editor.tm@napco.com, www.napco.com/tm/tmcover.html

  A how-to magazine for direct marketers.

Reference Sources

- The *Small Business Sourcebook* is a wonderful resource. Published by Gale Publishing, this hefty two-volume work gives you great industry-by-industry background, including start-up information, associations, licensing information, reference books, trade periodicals, statistical sources, special libraries, computerized databases and relevant education programs. It covers 326 industries, with general articles on 79 business topics.

  Gale Publishing, 27500 Drake Rd., Farmington Hills, MI 48331-3535, (800) 877-GALE, (248) 699-8061, fax: (800) 414-5043, (248) 699-8061, e-mail: galeord@gale.com, www.gale.com

- The Standard Rate and Data Services (SRDS) publishes a bookshelf full of invaluable and unique monthly books that you should be familiar with. Everyone in marketing and advertising uses these volumes; they give the demographic and rate information for each of the media below.

  Standard Rate and Data Services, 1700 Higgins Rd., Des

Plaines, IL 60018-5605, (800) 851-SRDS, (847) 375-5000, fax: (847) 375-5001, www.srds.com

1. *Television And Cable:* lists all TV and cable stations in the country
2. *Radio:* lists major radio stations
3. *Consumer Magazines:* lists all consumer magazines
4. *Newspapers:* lists all daily and weekly newspapers
5. *Business Publications:* lists all business publications by industry category
6. *Radio Small Markets:* lists small-market radio stations
7. *Direct-Mail Lists:* gives more than 40,000 mailing list choices

With the Polk Company, SRDS also publishes an annual *Lifestyle Market Analyst,* which analyzes geographical markets by assorted lifestyle interests and market segments. It then matches these elements with broadcast and print media.

- *Thomas Register of American Manufacturers* has been a standby for years. It lists some 155,000 companies with core information. A good place to go to get the basics or to find particular types of manufacturers in your area. You can find these at your local library. Also check their Web site at www.thomasregister.com.

- *Market Share Reporter* is an "Annual Compilation of Reported Market Share Data on Companies, Products and Services" published by Gale Publishing, www.gale.com.

- *Standard and Poor's Industry Surveys* are issued twice annually on 52 different industries.

- *The Almanac of Business and Financial Ratios* by Leo Troy, published annually by Prentice Hall, gives you some financial rules of thumb for what others in your line of work are spending on marketing, advertising and many other facets of their business. If your ratios are wildly different, get curious.

Market Research

- Published by CACI Marketing Systems (www.demographics. caci.com), *Spending Potential Indices* covers home, entertainment and personal financial services, cross-tabulated by income, age and U.S. ZIP code.

- Mediamark Research Inc. (www.mediamark.com) publishes a 20-volume ongoing survey of consumer buying habits for the advertising agency. You can find this in a good library. It correlates demographics of buyers with the products they buy. What consumer magazine will deliver you a higher percentage of sweater buyers? This will tell you *Golf Digest* is a good buy.

- *ACORN Lifestyles,* from CACI Marketing Systems (www. demographics.caci.com/databases/acorn.html) is a useful mass-market analysis tool. ACORN stands for "A Classification of Residential Neighborhoods." All ZIP codes are broken down into neighborhoods (226,000 of them), in 43 clusters categorized into nine groups, with useful demographic information presented. For example:

Affluent Families:

- Top 1 Percent
- Wealthy Seaboard Suburbs
- Upper Income Empty Nesters
- Successful Suburbanites
- Prosperous Baby Boomers
- Semirural Lifestyle

Upscale:

- Urban Professional Couples
- Baby Boomers With Children
- Thriving Immigrants
- Pacific Heights
- Older Settled Married Couples

Up-And-Coming Singles:

- High Rise Renters
- Enterprising Young Singles

- Simmons Market Research Bureau (SMRB) publishes its *Study of Media and Markets.* This multivolume set contains demographic and lifestyle information for users of specific products, and it relates product usage to users' media habits (magazine, radio and television). It shows which media do the best job of reaching particular market groups. The data may also be used to learn the demographic characteristics of the users of specific types of products. Provides enormously useful information on the consumer marketplace. Simmons also puts out useful summaries on all large urban markets.

Simmons Market Research Bureau, 309 W. 49th St., New York, NY 10019, (212) 373-8900, fax: (212) 373-8918, e-mail: simmonsres@aol.com.

Web Sites

Here's a grab bag of interesting sites on the web. Things are changing all the time, so don't be afraid to do a keyword search to catch new arrivals.

- The Census Bureau's "Official Statistics" (www.census.gov): Tremendous amount of information. Easily searchable by topic. You'll need Adobe Acrobat or another PDF file reader to get the best look at the data.

- The Silicon Valley World Internet Center (www.swic.com): If you want to feel the future, pay this ambitious and high-minded site a visit. Information on e-commerce, samples of selling on the Internet.

- Database America Companies (www.databaseamerica.com): Some useful marketing and resource links.

- Claritas (www.claritas.com): Extensive marketing capabilities in this world-class company. Lots of big-league techniques for segmenting consumer markets.

- infoUSA Inc. (www.salesleadsusa.com): A prime source for business and consumer mailing lists. Has good lists of 11 million business and 110 million households.

- Direct Marketing World (www.dmworld.com): Links to mailing lists and databases. A directory of direct-marketing professionals, and a library of articles and other resources.

Index

Index

Index

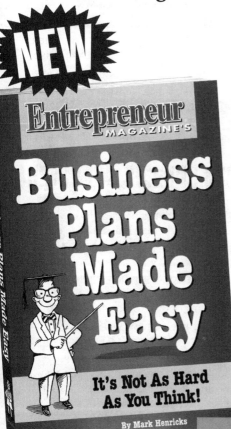

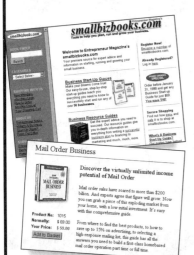

FREE ADVICE

When was the last time you got **free** advice that was worth something?

Entrepreneur Magazine, the leading small business authority, is loaded with <u>free advice</u>—advice that could be worth millions to you. Every issue gives you detailed, practical knowledge on how <u>to start a business</u> and run it successfully. Entrepreneur is the perfect resource to keep small business owners up-to-date, on track, and growing their business.

BREAK OUT

Business Start-Ups helps you **break** out of the 9–5 life!

<u>Do you want</u> to get out of the 9–5 routine and take control of your life? <u>Business Start-Ups</u> shows you the franchise and business opportunities that will give you the future you dream of. Every issue answers your questions, <u>highlights hot trends</u>, spotlights new ideas, and provides the inspiration and real-life information you need to succeed.

MILLION DOLLAR SECRETS

free issue!

Exercise your right to make it **big.**
Get into the small business authority—
now at **80% off** the newsstand price!

Yes! Start my one year subscription and bill me for just $9.99. I get a full year of Entrepreneur and save 80% off the newsstand rate. If I choose no to subscribe, the free issue is mine to keep.

Name ☐ Mr. ☐ Mrs. _____
(please print)

Address _____

City_____ State _____ Zip _____

☐ BILL ME   ☐ PAYMENT ENCLOSED

Guaranteed. Or your money back. Every subscription to Entrepreneur comes with a 100% satisfaction guarantee: your money back whenever you like, for whatever reason, on all unmailed issues! Offer good in U.S. and possessions only. Please allow 4–6 weeks for mailing first issue. Canadian and foreign: $39.97. U.S. funds only.

5G

Mail this coupon to **Entrepreneur. MAGAZINE** P.O. Box 50368, Boulder, CO 80321-0368

OPPORTUNITY KNOCKS!!!

save 72%!

free issue!

Please enter my subscription to Business Start-Ups for one year. I will receive 12 issues for only $9.99. That's a savings of 72% off the newsstand price. The free issue is mine to keep, even if I choose not to subscribe.

Name ☐ Mr. ☐ Mrs. _____
(please print)

Address _____

City_____ State _____ Zip _____

☐ BILL ME

☐ PAYMENT ENCLOSED

Mail this coupon to

Entrepreneur's Business Start-Ups.
P.O. Box 50347
Boulder, CO 80321-0347

Guaranteed. Or your money back. Every subscription to Business Start-Ups comes with a 100% satisfaction guarantee: your money back whenever you like, for whatever reason, on all unmailed issues! Offer good in U.S. and possessions only. Please allow 4–6 weeks for mailing of first issue. Canadian and foreign: $34.97. U.S. funds only.

5HBK